WILD VENTURE

A Bird-Watcher
in Scotland

The Buzzard and I

WILD VENTURE

A Bird-Watcher in Scotland

by

KENNETH RICHMOND

LONDON
GEOFFREY BLES

© KENNETH RICHMOND, 1958

Printed in Great Britain by
Wyman & Sons Ltd Fakenham
for the publishers
Geoffrey Bles Ltd
52 Doughty Street London W C 1

Contents

CONTENTS

Illustrations

ILLUSTRATIONS

Except where otherwise acknowledged, all photographs were taken by the author.

Acknowledgment

I have to thank the B.B.C. and the Editors of "Country Life", "The Field", "Scotland's Magazine" and "The Countryman" for permission to reproduce material originally presented in another form in broadcast talks or in periodicals.

I. Introduction

A BIRD-WATCHER IN SCOTLAND

NATURE AS WELL as history, it seems, took a hand in drawing the line between England and Scotland. Crossing the Border at Coldstream or Gretna Green, the newcomer from the south is confronted with something more than an unfamiliar style of architecture, a shrewder speech or a change in the colour of banknotes. No need of sprigs of white heather or the sound of bagpipes to tell him that here is a culture pattern very different from the one to which he has been accustomed. There is a tang in the air, a new spice. He has arrived at a frontier.

The further north he goes the stronger is this feeling likely to become. Oddly enough, the sense of having arrived at a frontier is borne in on one much more strongly in Glasgow than it is in Kansas City, though it is only a hundred years since the latter stood at the edge of virgin territory; so that for those of us who go in search of the last wilderness the drive along Loch Lomondside can be more of an adventure than crossing the Missouri. This is no fanciful, far-fetched impression, either, for the truth is that whereas the American frontier, physically speaking, has ceased to exist, in Scotland it remains more or less where it was in the days of Antonine Wall. From Balloch, where the last of the suburbias is left behind, all the way to Cape Wrath lies a land so barren and intractable that it has resisted every attempt to rough-hew it to human convenience. Its appearance has been changed, if at all, only superficially. True, it can be argued that the Highland landscape is just as much man-made as England's is —between them, the destruction of the Caledonian Forest, the clearances, the introduction of sheep and the conversion of vast areas into deer and game preserves brought about changes which are not to be minimised—but there is little force in the argument. The Highland scene does not *look* man-made. Again it is undeniable that the hydro-electric schemes now going forward in some of the remoter glens and the extensive reafforestation which is taking place in many counties are changing the face of Scotland more rapidly, and more drastically, than ever before. All too starkly, the pylons stalking across the hills mark the advances of an age of technology. As yet, however, the blastings of the engineer and the plantings of the forestry worker have done no more than scratch the surface. Viewed from sea-level, the pipe lines on Ben Nevis may be an eye-sore and the cabbage patch of conifers on the flanks of the Cobbler above Loch Long an unpleasant reminder of the shape of things to come—but climb a couple of thousand feet or so and monstrosities such as these are quickly reduced to insignificance.

The great hills stand where they stood when the Ice Age finally relinquished its grip upon them, their scars still fresh, as if it were only yesterday that the glaciers had retreated. From the summit of any one of them you look out over the emptiness of Scotland, a rolling waste in which a man may at last be alone with his thoughts: yet never quite alone, for gathered around are its guardian spirits—Ben Lui, Cruachan, Starav, Heasgarnich, Lawers, Shiehallion and a hundred others, each a silent presence. Here, you may say, is a country where a man can stretch his legs and freely set his face against all the winds that blow: a country where the naturalist really enters into his own.

And here, breaking off for the moment, it is necessary to ask a question. Why this passion for the desolate places? Beyond question, the extraordinary growth of interest in bird-watching during the past fifty years is a social phenomenon of no small significance. The cult may be explained as being due to a variety of causes, among others the provision of education for all, the five-day week and the internal combustion engine, but the underlying motive, surely, is the desire for release from the frustrations of a too-urbanised way of life. For most of us, it seems, bird-watching is a form of escapism. The question is whether it represents an *escape from*, or an *escape into*, reality. If the urge is compulsive, born of a secret dread of facing up to things as they are, then it is to be pitied. Only if the interest is truly wonder-waking can it be justified.

One of the great advantages of bird-watching, it goes without saying, is that it is the sort of pursuit which can be engaged in anywhere at any time; and no one need be such a purist as to think any the worse of a Temminck's Stint, say, if it turns up on Perry Oaks sewage-farm instead of on Speyside. Nevertheless, the supreme moments in a bird-watcher's experience, the ones that touch off his wonder, are the ones that occur in the lonely places. The trouble is that in England these places are few and far between. Here and there the illusions of being "away from it all" may still be preserved—on Dartmoor, in parts of Broadland (outside the holiday season) or the northern Pennines—but too often the illusion is at best fleeting. Those parts of the English countryside which remain unsmutched by industrial develop-ment have been gardened and tilled for centuries. They have their own peculiar charm—and let no one try to depreciate it—but for anyone who hankers after untamed country the feeling of being hedged in is at times inescapable.

Not so in Scotland where the number of square miles of open country per head of the population is so much higher and where trespassing is a virtually unknown offence, "Loch" and "ben", "corrie" and "bealach", "merse" and "moss",—the names themselves indicate that these are habitats which have no exact English equivalents. Each stands for a physical feature which in some way or other is distinctly and definably Scottish; and yet each exhibits an infinite variety. What a world of difference there is, for instance, between Loch Ken (reed-fringed and pastoral) and Loch Coruisk (rock-rimmed, with the sea waves lapping against its outlet) or Loch Etchachan (set austerely among the screes of the Cairngorms)—but try to picture any one of them in an English setting and immediately it becomes clear that the differences between them are less important than the features they share in common. Sgurr nan Gillean is no more like Braeriach than the Taj Mahal is like St. Peter's, yet both are recognisably Scottish—they are not "dead" mountains like the Lakeland fells or Snowdonia, which lost their eagles long before the days of the youth-hosteler and the week-end climber. No wonder, then, if this book is inspired as much by an enthusiasm for places—for the Caledonian sternness and wildness, if you will —as for the birds that are to be found in them.

But if the atmosphere of Scotland is distinctive, capable of bringing new zest to jaded minds, so too is its fauna. At first, perhaps, the newcomer will be more conscious of the losses than the gains, for many of the species whose presence can be taken for granted farther south are missing. While it would be foolish to pretend that the Border acts as a sort of invisible barrier, it seems clear that it coincides with the limits of distribution of quite a number of British birds, though naturally there is an overlap on either side. The Green Woodpecker, for example, stops short in Dumfriesshire and Berwickshire, with an odd pair or two infiltrating as far as East Lothian. The Marsh Tit and Willow Tit are both quite common in Northumberland, but for reasons best known to titmice they become rarities in Scotland. Even the Tree Sparrow is apt to be local. The Woodlark and the Lesser Spotted Woodpecker are to all intents and purposes unknown, and that indefatigable coloniser, the Little Owl, has so far failed to establish itself. Another sad miss is the Pied Flycatcher, common enough in Cumberland but petering out rapidly thereafter though it occurs sporadically in the West of Scotland and seems to be extending its range. As for the other summer visitors there is a longish list of absentees: Red-backed Shrike, Lesser Whitethroat, Wryneck, Hobby, Turtle Dove (apart from an isolated pocket in Berwickshire), and Nightingale. Once in a blue moon the latter may turn up, as it did a year or two ago on the ramparts of Stirling Castle, but when it does so it looks (and sounds) as out of place as it would in Berkeley Square. Sometimes, too, a whole summer may go by without the watcher hearing a single Blackcap. The Kingfisher is another bird that does not take kindly to conditions north of the Border: the salmon pool and the Highland burn, "its roll-rock bedrock roaring down", do not suit its requirements as well as do the chalk-streams of the south country or the slow-moving rivers of East Anglia.

For all that, when the final balance sheet is drawn up it will be found that the gains more than compensate for the losses. At the head of the list, of course, is the Golden Eagle, by any reckoning the grandest and most impressive of all British birds. Next in the popular estimation, perhaps, come the Ptarmigan, and that giant among game-birds the Capercaillie. Then there are the Divers, red-throated and black-throated, known to bird-watchers in England only as pale ghosts of their true selves as they fish the inshore waters and the estuaries in autumn and winter but startlingly transformed when seen on their breeding lochs—and several of the waders which occur only as passage migrants further south, among them the Dotterel, Greenshank, Whimbrel and Red-necked Phalarope. Add to these the various species of wild fowl which are normally classed as winter visitors in other parts of the country but which are regular breeders in Scotland—Whooper Swan, Grey-lag Goose, Goosander, Red-breasted Merganser, Common Scoter and Wigeon. For good measure, throw in a number of sea-birds which, if not exactly confined to Scottish waters, can safely be included in the list— Great Skua, Arctic Skua, Black Guillemot and Leach's Petrel, for example—and the issue is fairly clinched. If there is any doubt about it, one can always keep a trump card or two in reserve— the Slavonian Grebe, say, or, better still (a genuine ace, this one), the Hen Harrier. Last but not least, except in point of size, there is the Crested Tit.

Still, Scotland's advantages as a happy hunting ground for the bird-watchers are not to be estimated simply by totting up the names of species which are mainly or exclusively confined, as breeders, to North Britain. There are others which can claim to be distinctively Scottish, even though they are to be found south of the border. The Black Grouse, for one. No matter if the bird can be seen on Exmoor, in Wales and in many places in Northern England, the fact that it has come to be recognised as a sort of national emblem (for who has not seen the Black-cock's curly tail feathers stuck in the war bonnets of our Highland

15

regiments?) is a sufficient guarantee of its claim. The same can be said of many other species—Gannet, Eider Duck, Common Gull, Twite, Rock Dove, Hooded Crow, Buzzard, and without stretching things too far, even the Woodcock and the Oystercatcher—which cannot, strictly speaking, claim to be added to the profit side of the balance-sheet, but which are certainly much commoner and more widely distributed in Scotland than they are elsewhere on the mainland. To pretend that the Oystercatcher and the Woodcock are "Scottish" birds is to invite controversy, if not instant refutation, seeing that both are well known throughout the length and breadth of the land, but anyone who has walked in Galloway in springtime and heard Oystercatchers piping in every field or has stood in the twilight of a Perthshire wood and watched half a dozen Woodcock roding together, will concede that the pretence is not altogether hollow. Nor will anyone who has seen the chevrons of Pink-feet passing over Dundee on a winter's day or a gaggle of Grey-lags in full cry over Glasgow's Great Western Road be inclined to doubt that the Scot is luckier than the Englishman so far as seeing wild Geese is concerned.

The London bird-watcher may well count it a red-letter day if a Whooper Swan is recorded, whereas for six or seven months in the year his opposite number in Edinburgh can see Whoopers galore whenever he pleases. As for the rarer winter visitors, fabulous species from the higher latitudes like the Snowy Owl or the Iceland Falcon, the chances of seeing one are obviously much greater. Granted a lifetime may go by without a stroke of luck of this kind coming one's way, but the very fact that the possibility exists keeps the edge of hope sharper than it might otherwise be, for, when all is said and done, there is something of Mr. Micawber in the make-up of every bird-watcher. In Scotland, such optimism is easily justified. If some of the passage migrants from the Continent seem to be less numerous than they are south of the Border—fewer Waxwings in Fife than along the Yorkshire coast, perhaps, and nothing like the numbers of Black Terns that drift over East Anglia—one has only to point to the astonishing records of the observatories on

INTRODUCTION

Fair Isle and the Isle of May to realise that Scotland is as strategically well placed as any country in Western Europe.

With this brief review in mind, the rationale of *Wild Venture*
should become tolerably clear. While the book adheres to no
strict plan and may be thought to suffer from a certain lack of
continuity in that each chapter is intended to be self-contained,
it has its own logic, albeit the logic of the heart rather than the
head. Not being a textbook, it makes no systematic attempt to
describe *every* Scottish bird, only some of those with which the
author may claim to have some degree of familiarity. Its primary
aim is to evoke some of the personal pleasures and excitements
that bird-watching has to offer, and to do this by highlighting
actual occasions as graphically as possible.

THE PREDATORS

GOLDEN EAGLE

HEN HARRIER (1)

HEN HARRIER (2)

BUZZARD

GOSHAWK

ICELAND FALCON

SHORT-EARED OWL

II. Evening at the Eyrie

GOLDEN EAGLE

NOT LEAST AMONG the compensations of living in Glasgow is the thought that an hour's journey from the centre of that much-maligned city will take you to the fringe, if not into the heart, of the country of the Golden Eagle. Having got that far you must, of course, be prepared for some rough going in trackless country, otherwise the chances are that you will spend days and weeks in the field without once catching sight of Britain's grandest bird and return feeling that you are as far away as ever from realising your schoolboy ambition. The truth is that although the Eagle is now safely re-established throughout the length and breadth of the Highlands it is nothing like so easy to see as might be expected. Its fastnesses are usually well away from the beaten track, and though rarely so high above sea-level as is commonly supposed, they are remote enough to call for a deal of effort in reaching them. Enormous as the eagle's wing-span may appear when viewed in a museum case (or, more impressively still, through the peep-hole of a hide), size counts for nothing against the scale of mountainous surroundings. Unlike the Buzzard, which spends half its days wheeling and puling above the lochside woods, the Eagle is not given to making itself conspicuous. When not hunting, it will remain at its plucking-post or stand blockishly on some boulder for hours at a time, so that the chances of spotting it are virtually nil, even with a high-powered telescope. Its soaring is of the empyreal kind, adrift in the blue and as effectively lost to sight there as the star Venus in a clear sky. To make things more difficult, the Eagle is a singularly silent bird. Maybe there *are* places where the sybarite can drive up and watch one through the sun-roof of his car, a dark speck leaning into the wind above the rim of the corrie or beating heavily along the upper slopes, but such places cannot be called typical. Outside the breeding season the only way of meeting the king of birds on anything like level terms is to climb; for while the mere sight of an Eagle is always an event —the hundredth as heart-stirring as the first—there is nothing to equal the excitement of watching it in the high places. Besides, only the hill-walker can appreciate the difference which two or three thousand feet make to a man's point of view and the new horizons which open up as the summit is neared. From below the watcher can only hope to learn part of the story: from above he may be able to take it all in at a glance.

Even where Eagles are known to be frequenting a district where they have not bred before the precise whereabouts of the new eyrie is apt to remain a secret and weeks of hard work may elapse before it is located. A territory of as much as seventy-five square miles of hill-country is difficult to "cover" on foot, particularly when it includes any number of apparently suitable sites. Fortunately, however, the Eagle is conservative by nature. It has its own traditional—even ancestral—sites (often the Craig na Iolhaire of the map), to which it is remarkably faithful. Here and there a pair will be found occupying the same eyrie year in and year out, but the more usual practice is to ring the changes between two or three sites. If there are eggs in nest "A" this spring it is tolerably certain that next year the birds will be found either at "B" or "C"—which sounds delightfully simple and labour-saving on paper, until it is known that "B" is over in the next glen and "C" on the other side of the mountain, involving a thirty-mile detour by road before you can get within comfortable striking distance of either. The behaviour of the birds, too, can be quite baffling: as often as not they will play around all three sites in March, carrying new material to each of the nests as if unable to make up their minds which one to use. After spending a whole morning watching them do this you may be satisfied that they are definitely settled in at "B", only to return a few days later and find no sign of them there. A visit to "C" shows that the alternative nest has hardly been built up at all this year, and here again there is no sign of the birds. Can it be that they have decided to use "A" two years running after all? At this point you begin to be haunted by nasty suspicions. A week ago, you tell yourself, "B" eyrie was lined with fresh woodrush, ready for occupation. Someone must have taken the eggs as soon as they were laid . . . or something has happened to one of the birds. (Never *did* like the look of that shepherd fellow.) On the whole it seems highly improbable that the pair will be at "A" again but the only thing to do is to find out. Another roundabout journey and another wearisome trudge in the rain reveals what you have expected all along—the eyrie is clearly derelict. A branch or two and a few sprays of heather have been added in a haphazard sort of way, but the general appearance of the nest is much the same as it has been all through the winter and there are no tell-tale traces of down blowing in the wind. Having now drawn a blank at all three sites, you may come to the conclusion that the game is not worth the candle : as it is, you have wasted more time and effort than you care to think of, and all to no purpose. Were it not that the lure of the Eagle is so strong you would have given up before this.

Discouraged, but determined not to be beaten, you resolve to have a last look at "B", though by now it is the end of April, getting on for a month since your previous visit. The long green glen is no longer quite so deserted as it was then : there are Sandpipers flitting and trilling along the burnside and Cuckoos calling from the slopes. A Curlew yelps distractedly but you have no eyes for him today, only for the line of crags which walls in the head of the valley. If the eyrie *is* occupied the cock Eagle should put in an appearance any time now, cruising over the skyline to keep an eye on things—but, no, he is not to be seen. Doubt increases the further you go. Anxiously you scan the hillside and the empty skyline. Is it worth going any farther, you ask, remembering the miseries of the last, long, strenuous mile? More heartbreaks ahead? Another hour of steady plodding brings you to the ledge itself. Without hope, you lean out and peer round the edge of the buttress which protects the eyrie on this side—and five yards away the hen Eagle stretches her wings and goes off without a sound! At this distance she looks colossal. Her departure is unhurried and supremely dignified—you can see the basilisk look in her eye (the colour of a blood-orange) as she flaunts out—and in a moment she is sailing easily along the line of the cliff. At the far end she banks gently, gaining height all the time and returns to take another look at you before leaving: then, seeing that there is nothing to be done about it, she swings away and lets the wind carry her over the far side of the glen. There, at last, the cock rises to meet her and the pair try a tumble in mid-air, playfully linking their talons as they roll over, after which they cruise off over the crest of the hill, lost to view for the rest of the day.

So brief, so abrupt is the encounter that you are left with a sense of anti-climax when it is over. It is the kind of incident which only the cine-camera can record successfully—only who would be fiddling around with a cine-camera, all thumbs at the critical moment and so missing the whole thing? Still, it has to be admitted that human eyes are a shade too slow to make the most of their chances on such high occasions. As with all triumphs that are hard come by, whether it is winning the Derby or setting foot on the summit of Everest, the big moment is here and gone before you can seize hold of it. And yet, looking back, there is a once-and-for-all quality about it which stamps it into your very being: for the rest of your days will never forget this scene and all its details—the blue shadows of the clouds trailing up the farther slopes, the pincushions of moss campion, pinks on the rock-face, the clump of rose-root sprouting below the nest, the hollow voice of the Cuckoo below in the glen. . . . And to think that all the time you were plodding up here—for two long hours—you were being kept under observation by both cock and hen Eagle, and that neither gave the game away until the very last moment. No wonder some eyries are hard to find.

True, it is not every pair which displays such a high degree of aquiline intelligence as this. In the ordinary way the cock Eagle leaves his look-out post as soon as the human intruder comes in sight, either because he is anxious or in order to warn his mate of the approach of danger. For her part, she may sit tight—so tight that at times she will refuse to budge even when a man claps his hands within a few feet of the eyrie—or she may slip off unobtrusively while he is still a long way off, even if it means leaving a hard-set clutch or newly-hatched chicks. Individual temperaments vary a great deal. So, for that matter, do the size and plumage of the birds. In some pairs there is a very con-

Golden Eagle

"Her departure is unhurried and supremely dignified—you can see the basilisk look in her eye (the colour of a blood-orange) as she flaunts out"

Buzzard

siderable difference in the size of two sexes: in others it is often difficult to be certain which is which unless they are seen at close quarters. Normally the hen Eagle is much the more massive and thickset of the two, tawnier on the back, and the older she is the more massive and the tawnier she becomes. By contrast, a young cock is darker and altogether more trimly built, but with age he, too, may take on a somewhat faded appearance and grow in stature. Since Eagles are so long-lived it is only natural that they should differ in their behavioural as well as in their physical characteristics.

For all that there is a family likeness about all Eagle eyries. After seeing a dozen or so, it becomes evident that each of them has been chosen because its situation satisfies a number of special requirements. In the first place, the rock (a craggy outcrop rather than a full-scale precipice) must be high enough to be out of harm's way but not so high as to be exposed to the full rigours of mountain weather. March is never a gentle month in Scotland and early April, when the eggs are laid, often sees the hills snow-bound. Most eyries, accordingly, are located somewhere between the 1,300 and 1,500 feet contours. Like the Raven's, the nest is almost invariably sheltered by an overhang which serves a double purpose in keeping it dry, not to mention protecting it from damage caused by minor avalanches or stone-falls, and also making it inaccessible from above. Very often a lee slope is chosen, one with a southerly or easterly aspect, though there are so many exceptions—eyries on north faces where the sun hardly ever gets at them—that it cannot be stated that this is the general rule. If necessary, the nest may be built on the ground, always providing that the slope beneath it is steep enough to allow of an easy take-off, for Eagles lose quite a bit of height in becoming air-borne. Ideally, no doubt, the eyrie should possess the combined advantages of impregnability, comfort and an uninterrupted view of its approaches. It seems, however, that these are not such important considerations as the need for finding a recess big enough not only to hold the huge nest but also to accommodate both eaglets and parents. The foundation platform need not be perfectly level—as often as not the outer edge is shored up to a height of several feet—but it must provide adequate elbow-room for at least three, and possibly four, occupants.

Occasionally, it is possible to scramble straight up to the nest or to look into it by traversing along some convenient ledge where hand-holds are two a penny, but in nine cases out of ten it turns out that the site is so cunningly chosen that it cannot be reached without taking neck-or-nothing risks. The first eyrie I was shown was so absurdly vulnerable that an old lady with a parasol might have strolled up and sat down inside it without turning a hair—but that was beginner's luck: most of the others have been in situations which could only be reached with the aid of a rope or by a short climb of the "Very Severe" class. At first sight it looks deceptively easy to get at the nest, but in nearly every case there is some snag or other which makes it impracticable, if not actually impossible. So near and yet so far! Sometimes it almost seems as if the birds had knowingly picked the one spot which is almost but never quite within reach.

Nest "C" was just such an eyrie. It was early June on the occasion of my next visit, one of those rare days which win golden opinions of holiday-makers in the Highlands. For the past week the weather had been utterly atrocious, lashed with rain and wind, but now the clouds had rolled away, leaving the mountains pin-sharp against a clear sky. This time, instead of keeping to the glen where I was sure to be seen—(to say nothing of being midge-bitten all the way)—I tried an outflanking movement, and crossed over the spur of the hill a mile or more before the nest came into view. Not that I had any real hopes of escaping detection in this way: no one can set foot in Eagle territory without its owners being very soon informed of the fact. Even if the cock was not in a position to spy on me from his eminence he could hardly fail to notice the Greyhen that bustled out from the birches or to hear the accusations of those busy-bodies the Hooded Crows.

I had not gone far when, to my surprise, both cock and hen Eagles hove into view above the heathery rise ahead of me. They were quite near as Eagles go, less than a quarter of a mile away and apparently quite unaware of my presence. Keeping low, the pair circled and counter-circled in an aimless sort of way, their shadows skimming the slope beside them. Suddenly the hen alighted, shambled a few steps forward and tore up a great beakful of dead woodrush. Without waiting, she took off again,

flapping slowly over the rise with the cock still in close attendance. I waited, expecting them to reappear any moment higher
up the hill, for though they had made off in the direction of the
eyrie it seemed unlikely that they would return to it with me
standing there in full view. Surely they had not missed seeing me?
Or had they simply chosen to ignore me? The latter seemed the
likelier explanation.

Filled with surmise, I put my best foot forward, stumbling
through the last of the accursed bracken. At the top of the rise,
where the cragside came into view, the silence was broken by the
squealing of a Common Gull. *Keer keer*, it cried, *keer keer*. . . .
and at that things began to happen thick and fast. Like the
proverbial bolt from the blue, the cock Eagle appeared from
nowhere, hurtling down on the white Gull. Almost at once
the hen Eagle threw herself into the fray, coming in with a rush
and a whoosh that could be heard a hundred yards away. No
sooner had the Gull somersaulted under the first onslaught than
it was forced to dodge the second. Now the three of them were
right overhead, the wretched Gull squealing in terror as the
Eagles manoeuvred for yet another strike. Watching them
through binoculars, the illusion of being singled out as the target
for their attack was quite unnerving: as they folded their wings
for a nosedive, I cringed inwardly.

Such striking power, such concentrated venom!

If this was play there was more than a hint of exasperation
in it. Yet the sheep which were grazing nearby, some of them
with lambs at their sides, seemed to take it all philosophically.
Not one of them so much as raised its head.

As it happened, the Gull got away unscathed. Even at the
time I had the impression that the aerobatics were somehow
lacking in lethal purpose, though they were certainly impressive,
not to say daunting, while they lasted. The curious thing was
that although they could not help seeing me—and did any bird-
watcher ever feel more like a dead duck than I did at that moment?—both Eagles once again appeared to ignore me. Throwing caution to the wind, they came sweeping down until they
were less than fifty feet from the ground, only spreading their
wings and lifting clear when it seemed that their fell swoop must
carry them irresistibly on to my defenceless head. Certainly it

looked as if they were in earnest. Open-mouthed, I waited for the next move. Each of them as it dived half-dropped its bony legs and unclenched its talons. With their shoulders hunched and their heads thrust out they looked like solid wedges of bronze falling out of the sky and when they flattened out, throwing up at full spread, the effect was quite overwhelming. The Angel of Death could not have been more terrifying.

This exhibition of derring-do was so completely unexpected that it left me rather at a loss. Hitherto I had not seen anything to suggest that Eagles were prone to any sort of distraction-display when the eyrie was threatened: normally they sheered off whenever a human being was around and kept out of sight until the coast was clear again. Possibly my presence had caught them in two minds and the Gull, chancing to pass over at the same time, had been picked on as a scapegoat. It is common knowledge, of course, that birds are liable to be caught between conflicting impulses—fear and aggression—when their nest is in danger; and in this instance it seemed that any sense of fear had been displaced (overmastered, rather), by hostility towards the lesser of the two evils. For Eagles, apparently, attack is the best form of defence against an acute emotional crisis! What I had yet to learn was that in no circumstances would this pair allow any bird above the size of a Ring Ouzel to cross their territory without having to make a dash for it. The cock, as I soon found, was particularly intolerant in this respect. Throughout the season any ne'er-do-well Hoodie or prowling Gull that ventured too near was invariably singled out for the same rough-handling.

When it was all over, I picked my way up the bed of the ravine leading up to the eyrie which as yet remained hidden. Half way up, the way was blocked by the debris of a landslide which had recently carried away tons of loose earth and freshly splintered boulders from the cliff-face. Surmounting this obstacle I turned a corner, and there it was . . . a great cart-load of brushwood dumped in a corner of the crag. A small rowan tree growing from a crevice beneath it served to hold the bulky structure in place. Immediately above rose a wall of silvery mica-schist, holdless and sheer, with the most villainous-looking overhang jutting out at the top. From this angle the nest looked decidedly top heavy, as if the first strong gust that caught it would topple it from its place. As it was, the foot of the rock was littered with fallen branches, roots of heather, bones and other remnants.

There never was such a nest. Five feet high and broad in proportion, the huge pannier of sticks must have been used for several years. It was so big that a man might have curled up and made himself comfortable inside it, so old that the lower half was green with mildew. The right-hand retaining wall prevented any sort of view into the cup of the nest and the ledge on the left side petered out abruptly leaving the observer at eye-level, with a nasty drop in front, but by scrabbling about and jamming one's fist into a crack it was possible to gain a few extra feet.

There squatted the solitary eaglet, a month old to the day, still covered in white fluff with a few black feathers beginning to sprout on its shoulders and along the stumps of its wings. An expression of intense dislike came over its face the moment it saw me. For a time it relapsed and lay inert, but whenever I moved it reared its scawny head, baring its gape in horrid defiance. Stretched beside it with its hind legs hanging over the edge was a freshly killed Blue Hare, untouched as yet, also a spray of larch which one or other of the old birds must have brought in earlier in the day. So far as I could make out, the clump of woodrush which I had seen the hen Eagle carry off a little while ago had not been deposited. ("False-building" perhaps?)

The situation was at once uplifting and faintly intimidating. Among its other natural advantages, the eyrie commanded the most wonderful view not only of the whole length of the glen but of an extensive stretch of country beyond. Looking out from it, the eye travelled over miles of brown moorland to the end of Loch Awe, backed by the whole range of Cruachan, now bluer than ever in the evening sun. Beside me the buttress leaned out crazily, dripping all the time like a leaky roof, and every drop that fell splashed on the screes fifty feet below. Across the gap, the eaglet continued to stare me out.

There was no answer to that glassy stare. Absurd as it seems to say it, now that I was eye to eye with the little demon I could not help feeling just a little apprehensive. Maybe an insecure stance and the grimness of the place had something to do with it, maybe not. Perhaps "apprehensive" is not the word for the feeling I wish to convey. "Awed" might do better, only it seems old-womanish to pretend that anyone can be awed by a chick in down, even if it does happen to be an eaglet. Nowadays, when objectivism is the only acceptable philosophy among naturalists, the bird-watcher does well to keep his sensibility under the strictest restraint. Nevertheless, there are moments when he finds himself subjected to strange fits of fancy, and this was one of them. The Athenian who was conducted into the shrine of Delphos and heard the oracle's voice of doom must have had much the same feeling. *Procul o procul este, profanes.* .... The sullen walls of rock that guarded it on either hand, the slow drip-dripping of waterdrops from its eaves, the hush, the shadowi-ness—everything proclaimed that the eyrie was a sanctuary and that anyone who presumed to violate it did so at his peril. Per-haps, then, "conscious-stricken" is the word that should have been used. If this was not the king of birds at least it was a princeling, and who was I to invade its privacy? What else was there to do but acknowledge the blunder and withdraw as discreetly as possible?

Meantime neither of the old birds had put in an appearance.

Further up the hill, however, at the head of a shallow gully above the eyrie I came upon their roosting tree—another rowan, and so liberally splashed with ordure that anyone with half an eye could hardly have passed by without noticing it. By the look of things it had been used for some considerable time. The ground beneath it was littered with pellets (solid chunks of rabbit fur, mostly) and feathers, one of which, a great scimitar of a primary, I was glad to accept as a keepsake. It was not much of a tree, hardly above the size of a bush in fact, so stunted that the thought of its being tenanted by two such regal birds seemed not a little ludicrous.

By this time the sun was going down behind Mull yet the light continued to be as brilliant as ever and now that the whole lay-out of their territory was mine to command it seemed a pity to turn back without seeing more of the Eagles in action. Nor had I long to wait. After scouring one rock-terrace after another without seeing anything I had a look at the bony ridge of the mountain's eastern shoulder—the spot where, more than once before, I had seen the cock go up to join his mate when she was put off the nest, and there, sure enough, he was. He was too far off to make much of him with binoculars but through the telescope he looked as large as life. And what a majestic figure he cut, idly preening his mantle and occasionally cocking his head on one side to look at something in the grass. Killing time, evidently. His crown and neck were honey-coloured, as if dusted with buttercup pollen. In that westering light the auburns and umbers of his plumage seemed to blaze with a new, incomparable lustre. Standing with his legs wide apart and the load of his wings piled loosely on his back, his whole attitude was indicative of sinewy strength, sculpturesque.

Away over on the far side of the hill a Cuckoo called. At that the cock Eagle stiffened. Stooping forward, he cast off. A few casual strokes and he spread his sails, and as he careened I saw the Cuckoo flying low beneath him. Easing back his shoulders, the Eagle slid after it down the slope, gently, so very gently at first, yet gathering momentum with every yard, then working up to racing speed with a few determined strokes—like an oarsman "giving her ten"—as he closed in, hot pursuit. Power, purpose and a dash of devilry were joined in that flight. Had the fugitive been a hare or a rabbit it would certainly have been rolled over and nailed to the ground at the first attempt. Slow as it was, though, the Cuckoo jinked aside as its assailant tore in from behind. But the Eagle was in no mood to let it go at that. Obviously he had taken a violent dislike to this fool of a bird and meant to chase it off its ground or put an end to it there and then. Overshooting his mark by twenty yards and more, he recovered instantly, wheeling around and going after his quarry again with all the resolve—and not a little of the nippiness—of a Merlin chasing a Linnet. Again his onrush was mistimed and again he recovered in full career. It was like trying to kill a butterfly with hand grenades. Then when it seemed that there could be only one end to the affair, the Eagle lost interest and called off the attack. Full-sail, he allowed the Cuckoo to go on its way unmolested. In half a minute the great bird was a thousand feet up, rising fast, without so much as raising a finger to help himself, and as he swung over I saw him tilt his sickled head to look down at me. And as he did, he scratched the back of his head with his left foot—a nonchalant gesture if ever there was one. For a time he hung around, getting higher and higher until at last he looked no bigger than a lark, after which he drifted slowly away into the distance. When he was almost out of sight he began his descent, falling headlong a hundred feet at a time in a series of steep dives until he disappeared behind one of the rocky bluffs. Half an hour later he was back on the outcrop where I had first seen him.

Once again, his behaviour struck me as decidedly puzzling. Clearly, there was no trace of fear in his make-up—how could one think of such a thing when the bird treated one with such superb indifference?—yet rather than go anywhere near the eyrie when a human being was about he would stay there on that pinnacle until doomsday if necessary, impassive as the rock itself. On the other hand, it only needed some dithering Cuckoo or wandering Gull to enter the territory for it to be chased off with the utmost vigour, even if it meant flying straight into the face of danger. Supposing that I had been standing beside the nest and that the Cuckoo had sought refuge there, would the Eagle have pressed home his attack? Probably he would. When provoked by some harmless creature that asked to be struck down, the most headstrong action was possible: failing which, it was inhibited and discretion got the better of valour. Why, a Blue Tit would have shown more spirit in defending its young than these birds did!

Maybe, though, it was just as well: imagination boggles at the thought of what might happen if Eagles lived up to their story-book reputations—and the casualties which would be caused if they had half the pluck of an irate Hen Harrier are not to be thought of.

It was nearly two hours now since I had last seen the hen Eagle. No doubt she had made a virtue of necessity and gone off hunting over the moor. Either that or she was perched on a rock somewhere in the background waiting for her mate to give the all-clear. Now that the eaglet was well on the way to fledging it could be left more or less to itself; and for the time being, at any rate, it was well provided for. Still, with the light fading and a chill wind beginning to blow up from the loch it seemed only fair to give her the chance of brooding the youngster if she wished. In fact, no sooner had I set off downhill than she cleared the summit ridge behind me and circled, hanging on the air to see me off the premises. So, she had been watching me all the time! In the dusk she looked bigger and more vulturine than ever. Evidently she was satisfied that all was well for after a few moments she turned away and flapped off slowly over the sky-line.

And at that, without once looking back, I jogged on down to the forest gate, weary but rejoicing, down through the sweet-smelling larch plantations (where a pricket roe shied at my coming), down at last to the lights of the lochside where the Sandpipers were tinkling in the darkness.

III. A Pair of Harriers

HEN HARRIER (1)

FOR THE MOMENT I took it for the sub-song of a Redwing. The soft, chortling notes were somehow familiar—vaguely thrush-like—and yet for the life of me I could not place them. It was a raw, cheerless day, as grey as they come in November, past four in the afternoon and the light failing. Still the notes continued, quietly reflective rather than subdued, a lively ditty full of starts and stops. The only birds in sight were some Redwings and Fieldfares which had crowded into the top of a rowan bush beside the burn; and they, so far as I could see, were all busy, snatching and gulping the berries as if their lives depended upon it. Not a songster among them.

How easily the ear is deceived! The ventriloquist turned out to be a Dipper which had ensconced itself in the bankside and which flew out, almost under my feet, zit-zitting to itself as it shot off upstream. At this the Fieldfares chattered a warning and took off in a body, only to settle again in the field a furlong or so away. The last of them was hardly down when a dove-grey hawk came breasting low over the rise, light as a puff of air. A cock Hen Harrier, indolent-looking as ever. It was over and on them before they could move. In a trice it sideslipped and pinned the nearest Fieldfare to the ground.

The incident was over in a twinkling, as neat as a slip catch taken on the half turn. There was no chance, no twisting and turning of pursuer and pursued, hardly a pounce even. The trick was done at the drop of a hat, with the consummate ease of a master of legerdemain; and though, for once in a lifetime, I was lucky enough to be at the right spot at the right time it was hard to say just what happened. How easily the eye is taken unawares! The thrust was quicker than thought.

34

With its wings held loose and its tail spread, the Harrier shrouded its victim and was about to pluck it when the cry of a passing Crow caused it to look up.

Kra-ark! shouted the Crow accusingly, circling overhead.

No peace for the wicked! Rather than have its meal disturbed the Harrier rose at once, yikkering in annoyance, and continued on its line of flight as if nothing had happened. Like all hawks, it carried its prey slung beneath its tail. But for some reason (either because it was not hungry or because the kill was too heavy, or maybe because in its nervous haste it had failed to clutch it securely), the Harrier had not flown twenty yards before it let the bundle fall. I saw where it pitched in the grass, rolling over, its wings still flapping. Graceful and buoyant now, alternately flapping and sailing as if it had all the time in the world, the Harrier made off across the heather and was soon lost in the haze.

To cross the burn and run to the stricken Fieldfare was the work of a moment, but the bird was already dead by the time I reached it. All but one of its tail feathers had been torn off and blood was oozing from its bill. There were claw marks on the head, and the lower half of the body had been well and truly transfixed. Warm and limp, the little corpse lay in my hand, its eyes still bright, its richly coloured breast feathers unruffled. Its crop was as firm as a well-fed pigeon's, stuffed full, no doubt, of rowan berries.

What is the appropriate emotion for such occasions, I wonder? Pity for a wasted life? Hardly that, seeing that it made so clean an ending. Anger at a cold-blooded killing? Not that, either, seeing that the execution was so swift and carried out with such adroitness. Standing there in the gloom I was filled with admiration and, yes, with a fierce joy: for this was no ordinary act of violence that I had been privileged to witness but a feat of incomparable skill performed by an aristocrat. For a bird-watcher it was, you might say, the moment of truth.

This particular cock Hen Harrier was by way of being an old acquaintance of mine. Though this was the first time I had caught him in the act of killing I had seen him on three or four occasions near this same spot and about the same time of day. He had his regular beat which carried him over many miles of peat moss and moorland, and he kept to it. How far he ranged afield during the autumn and winter months there was no saying, but invariably towards evening he returned to roost in the vicinity of his breeding territory.

Of all the predators, none is more immaculate than the Hen Harrier—and this fellow was an Adonis even among Hen Harriers. At rest he looked as slender as any Montagu's, the palest of powder blues. His face was small and owlish, and there was restlessness in those yellow eyes which gave him a rather shifty look. True, he had little or none of the dash of the blue-blooded falcon but what he lacked in verve he more than made up for in stylishness. Merely to see him, let alone watch him at work, was a sufficient reward for a long day's bog-trotting. In the air, and nine times out of ten I saw him flying, his every movement was instinct with grace and elegance. Unlike the Short-eared Owls which meandered over the waste, quartering the same stretch over and over again, wheeling aside every few moments and inspecting every minor hollow and unevenness in the ground, he followed a straight course. Unlike them, too, he rarely stooped to try his luck unless there was a good chance of succeeding, but when he did he showed an astonishing turn of speed. Usually, though, he fairly floated along with a gentle rise and fall of the wings, which seemed to bespeak of certain negligence of purpose. Never in a hurry, he kept his head well down, eyeing the ground immediately in front as it unrolled its carpet beneath him.

Throughout the autumn and winter the cock Harrier hunted alone. For a time it appeared that his mate had left the district, but towards Christmas she turned up again and was occasionally seen quartering the moors. Like the cock, she had her own regular beat, and it was about the middle of March that the pair joined forces again. A fortnight before this, however, the cock's way of life had undergone a marked change.

Leaving his hunting grounds on the moss (where now the Lapwings were tumbling and the first Curlews rippling), he took to the hill country. Day by day he sailed the brown moors, at first aimlessly, or so it seemed, though time and again he drifted back to the same place, the head of a secluded valley sheltered from the winds by the hulk of Beinn Bhreac. This was his rendezvous. Here he spent hours patrolling the heathery slopes, a furlong this way and then back, almost as if he were tethered to some invisible stake. Here, too, at times, he would indulge in soaring flights, urging himself up and up in a series of steep climbs, muttering to himself as he did: *Chukkerukeruk . . . chukkerukeruk . . .*

With the return of the female, this aerial sporting was stepped up to a new pitch of intensity. Together, the two of them would ascend to a height of up to a thousand feet, first one, then the other taking the lead, stunting and stooging this way and that, often touching talons as they rolled over, whinnying aloud in their excitement. His spotless white underpants (set off with jet black pinions) and her soberer brown made a fine contrast as they wheeled and careered in the April sunshine. She was bigger and more powerful than he, with an ampler stretch of sail, and from now on it was she who was to be the dominant partner.

The first egg was laid on April 19th, an early date for Scottish Harriers, and the others on alternate days. After the 26th it seemed only wise to leave the nest very severely alone. The previous year this pair had had their entire clutch destroyed by an unknown hand and the possibility of the same thing happening again was not to be ignored. Unfortunately the whereabouts of any Harrier's nest is apt to be an open secret and the ceremonial behaviour of the birds themselves, delightful as it is to watch, has precious little survival-value in a Grouse preserve. At irregular intervals, the cock calls off his sitting mate for the delicate rite of handing over the food he has brought here—and anyone who sees the "pass" has not far to look for the nest.

Of the four eggs one was addled and another was accidentally broken, at least so I was told. The first chick hatched out on May 19th, the second nine days later, on May 28th. For the best part of two months, that is from the laying of the first egg until the time the fledglings flew, the female hardly left the nest at all, except for the occasions when she was disturbed and, of course, when she was called off for the "pass". For his part, the cock seemed to prefer to remain in the background. His visits to the nest were few and far between, tip and run affairs at the best of times. It was as though he realised that his presence there was an unwanted intrusion and that so long as the female was in full possession the expedient thing was to keep out of her way. Most of the time, to be sure, he was kept more than busy fetching and carrying and towards the end of June he had his work cut out to keep the growing family supplied. His return was always unobtrusive, through a gap in the side of the hill where his entry was least likely to be observed. *Quee-uk* she would whistle as he slid down the slope towards her and without more ado the bloody offering would change hands in mid-air. That done, off he would go again, not to be seen for another three or four hours. Never once did he need to call her twice, never once did she fumble the catch. The transfer was carried out with clockwork precision, he gliding into position like a bomb-aimer looking for his target, she rolling over and taking the fistful of red meat with outstretched legs.

As with all symbolic behaviour, there is more in the "pass" than meets the eye. Outwardly it appears to be simply a device for handing food over without having to touch down at the nest. It seems improbable, however, that the habit ever served any useful purpose in keeping the site secret. This aerial manœuvring, with all its niceties, is so highly formalised that it might almost be compared with etiquette in human affairs. No doubt it affords the female a welcome, if momentary, relief from the tedium of her ground duties and gives her partner a sense of triumph and recognition after his long spells of hunting. The division of labour between the two sexes being absolute, it provides the means of harmonious adjustment between them and ensures that their mutual excitement is kept at a high level. The love-life of Harriers must always be a touchy business. Neither party is capable of any feeling that might be called affection. The female in particular is so quick to fly off the handle that any relationship is apt to be explosive. Only in the air can they feel entirely at ease in each other's presence. There, at least, the cock bird retains a token ascendancy. At the nest he can hardly move without putting a foot wrong in the eyes of his mistress.

Be this as it may, as the season wore on the "pass" tended to become more and more perfunctory. The female, it seemed, was in no mood for idle careerings: once she had risen to his call she expected him to hand over without any nonsense, and scolded him if there was any delay. But, then, she had always been the hectoring kind. The longer she brooded the more wicked her tantrums grew.

Hen Harrier attacking the author. Normally the male is less aggressive than
the female, but this one never pulled its punches

Duncan, the laird of Drumore, is a great ox of a man. Sixteen stones of muscle and bone, in his tartan trews he looks the very picture of the wild Highlander—as if he had stepped straight out of the pages of a Scott novel or a film of the '45—and yet, on the one and only occasion when I took him to see her, this virago knocked his bonnet flying, caught him on the wrong foot and left him sprawling in the heather. Thereafter we nicknamed her Lady Macbeth. From the start she had shown herself to be no respecter of persons, and now that the youngsters were on the point of flying she became more reckless than ever.

On the 27th June she left the nest while I was still wading through bracken a quarter of a mile away. Motionless and relaxed, she sailed above the hollow for all the world like a paper glider: round, round and round, with the sun showing auburn and coffee-coloured through the trailing edges of her wings and the barrings of her tail. *Coo ikikikikik* she whinnied fretfully. Then, as I drew steadily nearer, her mood changed. The cries became accentuated, the circlings narrower, and at last, screwing her courage to the sticking point, she half closed her wings and came at me with a rush. There was really no need to duck— the first swoop was intended as a shot over the bows, as it were. The second, which followed hard upon it, was pressed home with much more venom, out of the sun, and while I was looking over my shoulder to see what had become of her, she drove in un-expectedly from behind, almost brushing my shoulder. *Coo-ikikikik* . . . without waiting she twisted about and dived straight in my face, only throwing up at the last instant to hurtle over my head with an impressive flurry of quills.

In the nest the two young Harriers were jigging up and down like puppets on a string, waving their wings in a frenzied attempt to fly. In its terror one of them managed to flop off and become air-borne for a few yards, only to collapse in a tangled heap. The other stood at bay, hackles up, its mouth gaping wide in horrid revulsion and its talons clutching convulsively. There were no traces of down on its Kestrel-red plumage. The pupil of its eye was dark grey. A silent fury, it lay back, ready to lash out with its yellow fist the moment I raised a hand towards it.

Meantime the female had worked herself up to a fine pitch of spite, swooping and counter-swooping so viciously that there was nothing for it but to duck—and to keep on ducking. The longer I stayed the more exasperated and the more venturesome she grew, dropping her shanks and loosening her talons to show that she was in earnest. If this was bluff, it was certainly effective; and once or twice her near-misses were a shade too near to be comfortable.

She had two favourite modes of attack. The first, and by far the more intimidating, was to stoop out of the sun, mounting again almost vertically and immediately repeating the move from a new and, if anything, steeper angle. Usually she gave fair warning of her approach with that nattering cry of hers, but she was so incredibly agile, looping and switching about in an instant, that one needed eyes in the back of one's head to know the direction of her next thrust. When these tactics failed to produce the desired result, she sheered off for a time, disappearing over the hill. After a prolonged bout of mobbing her nerve seemed to fail her, but not for long: within the minute she would rally to the attack again, beating low over the tips of the heather like some outsize Sparrow-Hawk, and then come in with a last-second rush to spurt over the top of my head. I could see her measuring the distance as she accelerated, her buff face set in a ring of darker feathers, the mask of a demon, and the glint of hate in her orange eyes.

For bravura and sheer recklessness in defence of its young this performance of the female Hen Harrier has no equal among British birds. The Bonxie may fetch you an occasional clout over the ear, but, then, he is a buccaneer by profession—the gesture comes naturally to him. By contrast, the Harrier's whole instinct prompts it to avoid the human presence at all costs; it is more timid by nature, and this displacement of fear in a crisis is therefore the more remarkable. For the ornithologist to think in terms of moral attributes may be inexcusable but in this instance it seems that there is no alternative.

This bird's "morale", certainly, was nothing short of magnificent. To be singled out for her truculent attentions was at once a heartening and a humbling experience. Several times I could have knocked her down with a stick had I wished to try. Time and again she renewed her onslaught with complete abandon, never leaving off flaying the air about my ears until she had driven me (shamed me, rather), off the territory, and afterwards keeping me in view all the way down to the road.

A week later I returned to find the nest empty. The two young ones had flown and there was no sign of the old birds. Somewhere away up on the hill a Merlin was calling sadly, *airk airk airk*, and when I looked I saw the little tiercel cutting across the base of the crags. A Meadow Pipit danced up in front of me, spilling its song in the stillness as it dipped back into the heather. The air was sweet with the fragrance of bog-myrtle, the ground bright with the flowery spikes of blue butterwort and yellow asphodel. At long last summer had come to the Highlands, but for me there was only a feeling of anti-climax. The *genius loci* had departed.

Then, when I had resigned myself to the thought that the Harriers had gone for good, I heard the shrill whickering of the female again, and there she was, hurrying over the slope to warn me off as usual. The fact that the nest was no longer in any danger made not the slightest difference: she just could not endure the sight of a human being trespassing on her ground. Now that she was free to go off hunting on her own account this latest show of resentment was, to say the least of it, unexpected. How long would it be, I wondered, before discretion got the upper-hand again and her behaviour returned to normal? After a time she withdrew and for the next hour I did not see her again.

But if she had not finished with me yet, neither had the midges. To stand still for a moment was to have them swarming and whining about one's ears. There was only one way of escape, to get up on to the ridge as fast as possible and hope for a breeze that would make life bearable again, so off I went, putting my best foot forward and switching a frond of bracken in the air like a punka-wallah, only a good deal more vigorously.

Half way up to the ridge, at a height of little over a thousand feet, an extensive panorama suddenly opened up to the south and east, brown moors rolling away to the lowlands with here and there a little lochan winking its eye at the sun. That way, I knew, lay the main hunting grounds of the cock Harrier. If the family had followed him the chances of finding any of them in that desolation of peat-hags were less than bright. Behind me was the green trough of the glen which until a day or two ago had been their headquarters. From this bird's-eye position, I could see it for what it was, a hanging valley enclosed on three sides, with the dip there below me through which the cock used to make his furtive exits and entrances to the territory: a perfect hide-out. On the opposite slope a herd of deer, fifty strong, was quietly grazing. Further down, where the road came into view, I could see the rows of Forestry Commission workers cutting the bracken. A lark shrilled in the silence and then was quiet. A peaceful, pastoral scene, only now it lacked drama. The Buzzard, yonder, wheeling out from the skyline was a dull fellow . . .

And then I saw him, the cock Harrier cruising over the breast of the hill and (wonder of wonders!) coming towards me. I sat tight, squatting behind a turf baulk, but he had seen me all right. *Chukkerukkeruk* . . . His chatter was always less shrill than the females. A matter-of-fact mutter. Still he came on, with purposeful rhythmic strokes until he was near enough to see the yellow of his eyes. *Chukkeruk* . . . and then, when he seemed on the point of mounting an attack, he broke off, swerving away at a tangent to hang, like a kite, above the glen. Above the glen, but still at eye-level. I saw him turn to look at me anxiously, his pinions fingering the updraught from the corrie. Laconically he lifted one foot and scratched his head. Then lifting his tail and raising his wings, he planed softly down and perched on a clump of heather. There he pretended to preen but could not give his mind to it. Facing about he stood bolt upright, looking in my direction and yikkering in a half-hearted sort of way.

Now this was puzzling. Hitherto it had always been the hen who had seen fit to make herself objectionable. All through the critical period of incubation and fledging the cock had kept in the background, so much so as to give the impression of being a pusillanimous individual, yet here he was, going out of his way to chivvy me, as cool as you please—and all, so far as could be seen, to no purpose. Here he came again, casting off and heading up the slope, his mouth wide open as he cackled. Nearer, nearer . . . and again he thought better of it, canting over with a scream of execration when he was thirty yards off.

What had got into him?

I might have known it. All the time I had been watching him one of the young birds (a "Ringtail" if ever there was one), had been sitting in the heather a furlong or so away. It was only when it planed a few yards and settled again that the movement caught my eye.

The cock crouched, hitched his shoulders and took off. As he swung round in a wide arc he heckled me again but, for once, refrained from trying anything and, instead, allowed himself to be borne aloft at full spread until he was soaring five hundred feet and more above me. At this level he eased forward into the stiffish breeze, drifting, and as he drifted he kept up his anxious rattle at intervals. By contrast with the languid motion of the utterer, riding the heavens with feather-bed ease, the cries sounded curiously expressionless, almost mechanical. Were they intended as a warning to the young Ringtail below or to summon his absent mate or were they merely an expression of his helplessness in a conflicting situation? Something of all three, no doubt.

After havering and hovering around in this way for another five minutes the mood of uncertainty seemed to leave him and he swept overhead at speed, heading towards the moor. Sure enough, there, coming up the slope to meet him was her satanic majesty. *Quee-uk* she whistled. In her talons she dangled a grisly relic, some skinned and skinny thing that was mangled beyond recognition.

In a flash she had sized up the situation. In the ordinary way she would have known what to do, but evidently that handful of hers was a hindrance to action and she hesitated. *Kikikikikiki* she muttered half peremptorily, half nervously, in two minds whether to charge me in her usual bull-at-a-gate fashion or to hold back for the sake of the young ones. Fortunately for her the situation was saved by the Ringtail itself which suddenly took wing and flapped off owlishly over the rise and out of sight. Now for it, I thought, knowing her only too well, but for once she disappointed me. Disappointed? The moment I took my eyes off her she came up from behind with a chatter of defiance, vengeful as ever. Big as a Buzzard, still trailing the torn carcase, she gave me one of her most killing looks as she whirled headlong past.

That, so far as I was concerned, was her last fling. Not that she had shot her bolt by any means but rather because there was no longer any call for heroics now that the youngsters were safely on the wing. Letting the breeze take her, she rose effortlessly and joined the cock who was now sailing idly above the territory. It was as though some tension inside had been broken, the midsummer madness gone: she was herself again. Together the pair sailed higher and higher, in the dreamiest of spirals, a white speck and a dark speck winding against the landscape until at last they were lost in the grey-blue Highland air. They would be back, of course—for another week and more they would hang around the territory—but it seemed fitting to take my leave of them like this. Southwards the sky had a swollen, heavy look, grumbling with thunder as I made my way down the hill. It was the end of a chapter.

It only remains to add a postscript. Months afterwards on a wild autumnal day when the woods were heaving and the army of Grey-lags out on the moss was more than usually clamorous, I came upon a keeper's gibbet. A row of tattered fragments, they swung in the wind. Nailed to the fence post was the dried husk of a Hedgehog and beside it, suspended on strings, a maggotty Jay, a Crow and a sodden bundle of feathers that was too far gone to be recognisable. With a sudden feeling of misgiving I picked up the skull which lay beneath it. It was the skull of a female Hen Harrier.

That, too, for a bird-watcher was the moment of truth, only this time the truth was bitter.

IV.   Lady Macbeth's Daughter

HEN HARRIER (2)

"SHE SHOULD HAVE died hereafter. . . ." In this instance
the impossible wish was granted for it turned out that, far from
having been put to silence her ladyship was still very much alive.
As often happens when one's affections are deeply involved I
had been overhasty in jumping to conclusions: that sorry bundle
of feathers which I had seen dangling from the fence post must
have been the remains of some other Hen Harrier, not hers as I
had at first imagined. Before Christmas I saw her again, scattering the grouse to left and right beneath her as she breasted over
the high moor, her old beat; no case of mistaken identity this
time, either—I would have recognised that bird anywhere by
her markings (those ash-grey wing coverts, the pattern of her
facial disc, the distinctive patch of white on the rump), to say
nothing of the killing look she gave me as she swept past. It
was rather like meeting a friend after writing his obituary notice,
only without the embarrassment. Regret gave way to relief and
delight in an instant, and as I watched her flaunting up the shaggy
hillside, swinging into the wind to hang for a moment before she
disappeared across the skyline, I could have cheered.

As in previous winters the pair did not migrate but remained
in the district. Since the cock and the hen hunted separately, it
seemed unlikely that they ever met, at any rate during the day.
His ways lay east and west across a twelve-mile stretch of level
bogland, hers north and south over rough hill-country; and so
regularly did they keep to them that it was possible to hazard a
fair guess as to the whereabouts of either one or the other at any
hour of the day. Hard as I tried, I was never able to confirm the
suspicion that they were in the habit of returning to the breeding
territory to roost together as some Golden Eagles are said to do.

The days were too short and the distances too great. Several times, however, the cock Harrier was to be seen making for the head of the valley in the late afternoon, and though the movements of the hen were never easy to follow (imagine the difficulty of plotting the course of a brown hawk travelling uphill and down dale over brown moors!) she was twice seen heading in the same direction an hour or so before nightfall.

By the beginning of March it was clear that the pair intended to return and nest in the same spot as before. Each morning they played around the slopes, urging themselves up in a series of steep climbs, the hen whistling between-whiles (*tsee uk*, that peevish begging-note of hers), as they soared and spiralled together. Then, after promising fair, the Spring turned freakish with heavy falls of snow on the hills. To complicate matters, two new Hen Harriers had appeared in the district—complete strangers and, by the look of them, both immature birds. These newcomers were more than welcome, of course, though it seemed improbable that they would remain to breed: still, their presence on the same ground meant that it was never easy to be sure about the movements of the original pair. In all probability these new arrivals were Lady Macbeth's own offspring—young Harriers returning to their birthplace. At the time I thought no more about them. I was too much taken up with the affairs of the others.

Whether or not the cold weather was to blame for the setback, it seemed that their affairs were not going too well, either. For his part, the cock was in no mood for aerial sporting: despite all her solicitings he kept drifting off over the ridge, leaving her to sail above the valley on her own. Most mornings she hung around the old territory, occasionally pitching in the heather as if prospecting, but never settling in the same place for more than five minutes at a time. She, too, apparently, was undecided. Then, for a whole fortnight, the pair seemed to disappear off the face of the earth and it began to look as if they had gone elsewhere. At the end of this period the hen showed up again. By now it was well into the third week of April—and still she was in two minds. Hour after hour she wavered around, dilly-dallying with the breeze, as full of fits and starts as the breeze itself, but as the days went by it was noticeable that she spent more and more of her time hidden on a stretch of heather high up on the northern slope. A new site this year? It began to look like it. Occasionally she would call in at the old familiar place lower down on the opposite slope, as if reluctant to leave it. At long last, however, she made her choice and on April 20th she laid her first egg.

The new nest was a sketchy affair, a handful of dried grass with a few birch twigs strewn round the edges as an afterthought. For some reason, either because the site was too exposed for his liking, or because the heather did not provide adequate cover— or maybe because he was conservative by nature—the cock let it be seen that he could not approve of her choice. Rather than go near he insisted on patrolling the same strip of ground as he had done in previous years.* Instead of passing his prey to her over the nest he hung back, forcing her to come and fetch it and generally behaving in a thoroughly offhand manner. If that was the way she wanted it, well and good, but until she came over to his way of thinking, she would find him an unwilling partner. In the end, too, he carried his point, for after laying a second egg and begining to brood, the hen suddenly deserted. The date was April 28th.

Without wasting any time at all, she immediately installed herself at the original site. The second nest, which had evidently been got ready for occupation before she moved in, was within a yard or two of the spot where I had expected to find it all along. So strong is the hold of a *place* on the mind of a bird. It was the same with the Merlins and the Short-eared Owls which were nesting nearby. All three predators had returned to the territories which they had occupied in previous years.

From now on the hen was all set. Before the month was out she had laid again. By May 3rd she had two eggs, three on the 5th, four on the 7th, five on the 9th—the full clutch. Knowing her as I did and confident that there was no risk of her deserting a second time, I visited the nest on alternate days in order to

* This strip about two hundred yards from end to end and more than thirty yards wide, constitutes the Hen Harrier's territory. For the cock bird, at any rate, its boundaries are clearly delineated. Its peculiarly elongated shape accounts for some apparent discrepancies in the birds' reactions when the nest is threatened. Thus anyone approaching from the far end of the strip is liable to be attacked while he still is a considerable distance away. On the other hand anyone walking just outside the boundary and parallel with it can often pass close by the nest without being molested.

check the incubation period and the dates of the various layings. Needless to say, my interference was hotly resented and on more than one occasion I came in for some really savage treatment. The difference between her behaviour at the two nests was quite astonishing. At the first, no doubt because she lacked the moral support of the cock, she had never put up much of a fight. At the second, right from the start, she became a creature possessed.

Yet curiously unpredictable. Usually the cock was at his look-out in the heather and gave warning of my approach the moment I came in sight. *Chukkerukkerukker.* . . . That dry, matter-of-fact chatter of his. Flying slowly towards the nest he would dip over it, then turn and come wafting back to head me off, chattering off and on as he came. Sometimes the hen would take the hint and leave her eggs immediately, in which case her tactics were always the same: without any preliminaries she would turn and bear straight down on me, becoming more and more malignant with every step I took. This year, after taking a few sound thumps on the skull, I took the precautions of wearing a hat—and whenever I was safely off her ground I took it off as a mark of respect to her indomitable spirit. Yet on other occasions she would show herself to be strangely irresolute. Instead of heeding the cock's warning, she would sit tight until I was almost on top of her and then fly off to perch on a tree and heckle me at a distance. One day she would stop at nothing, while the next she would fly around impotently without making any attempt to drive off intruders. There was never any accounting for her reactions. Weather conditions, certainly, had little or nothing to do with this changeableness: it was simply that, being broody, she was more temperamental than ever. If the cock happened to be away hunting and if there were two humans to deal with, she usually funked it, but not always—on one occasion she excelled herself, knocking my cap askew and then in the same breath (swerving in full career), whacking my companion over the ears. Her adroitness in the air beggared description, and when she was out for blood it was a case of every man for himself. You could see the hate in her eyes as she drove in, hunching her shoulders like a giant bat, threshing her pinions as she power-dived—and then look out for trouble! The dash, the sheer acceleration of those headlong thrusts was quite electric. There was never any-

Hen Harrier

Female driving in to attack, male *(above)* waiting his turn

Pouncing

"Cry havoc!"

Lady Macbeth's daughter chattering at an intruder

thing accidental about her strikes, either: once she had taken aim she was not given to pulling her punches. Believe it or not, to be slapped on the pate by a surly Great Skua is child's-play by comparison. Sometimes, too, she varied her terror-tactics in a way which was truly alarming. When all else failed she would hover overhead, low down, almost within arm's reach, like some enormous Kestrel in the act of pouncing on a mouse. More than once this pipit's-eye view of a Hen Harrier was so completely unnerving that rather than try conclusions with her I made off *ventre à terre*.

This year, too, the hen was aided and abetted by the cock who was much more to the fore than he had ever been formerly: Though never half so mettlesome as she (who could have been?) he showed his spirit by swooping at my head time and again; always careful, however, to pull out in good time rather than risk a collision. Hell hath no fury like a woman's scorn they say, and often it appeared that he had no choice but to put on at least a show of hostility, for the moment he settled in the heather she was on him in a flash, goading him into action again. No rest for the wicked. More than once she showed her exasperation by flipping him with the tips of her pinion as she whirled past, as much as to say, "Lend a hand there, useless!" At other times she would leave him to do most of the fighting—and it was always the cock who escorted trespassers off the premises. In an ineffectual sort of way he did his best, but somehow the performance lacked fire. There was never any danger of being struck by him as there was when she was in one of her berserker moods. His stoops were gentler, nothing like so breath-taking, and it was easy to see that for all his coming in so close he was holding something in reserve.

I had expected that the longer the hen brooded the more fearless she would become. Nothing of the kind. If anything, she showed herself to be more implacable in the early days of May (that is, before the clutch was complete), than she did later on when the eggs were due to hatch. But, then, she was a creature of moods. On a cold, blustery day she might leave the nest while I was still a furlong or more away, yet on a warm, airless afternoon (when she might safely have left them uncovered), she often sat tight and refused to budge until the last moment.

On May 30th, exactly thirty days from the time it was laid, the first egg chipped. At regular intervals, every twenty seconds, it heaved. Inside, a tiny voice kept lisping *kittikeeuk . . . kittikeeuk . . .* By evening the shell had burst open and the chick was born: a flesh-coloured mite with dark rings round its eyes.

On my way down from the nest that night there occurred one of those lucky accidents which bird-watchers often dream about but hardly expect to witness. I could see the car below there, at its usual parking-place by the road-end. Just then an Eagle hove into view—one of the Tarsuinn Eagles, a ragged-looking specimen long past her best. (She often stooged around the glen of an evening. At a loose end, I suppose.) Now, as she cruised in a clear sky, I heard the familiar chatter of a cock Harrier somewhere in front of me. It *sounded* as if it came from the hillside just above the car. Next moment I caught a glimpse of grey and white against the fresh green of the bracken: a cock Harrier and no mistake. But this was impossible: impossible! Why, it was less than five minutes since I had turned my back on the other cock. Where on earth had this one come from, then? Sooner than it takes to tell came the answer. There, skimming low across the heather and blending so closely with it as to be well nigh invisible was the second hen—the young Ringtail which I had seen earlier on in the season.

Lady Macbeth's daughter!

Round and round she flew in narrowing circles, nattering all the while in her shrill falsetto—and suddenly pitched in the heather less than a furlong away from the roadside. Incredulity now began to yield to growing conviction as I made my way over to the spot. Even now I half-expected to see her rise and make off but no, she waited until my shadow fell upon her—and there, sure enough, was the nest. The five bluish-white eggs were shiny-smooth, proof positive that they had been brooded for at least a fortnight.

Open-mouthed, I stood and stared. For the past three months I had been coming here two or three times a week. How many hours I must have spent watching the original pair from this very hillside I should not like to say, hundreds, probably, yet never once had I seen anything to suggest that there might be a second nest hereabouts. As the Harrier flies, the two territories were little more than a quarter of a mile apart, close enough for anyone standing beside either of the nests to pick out the cock bird at his look-out near the other. Once one knew where to look, that is ! For weeks this second pair must have been soaring aloft and beating up and down the slopes, but until that moment when the cock chattered I had missed seeing them: so extraordinarily well had the newly-weds kept their secret. To this day I cannot understand how they contrived to get away with it for so long without being seen.

This second nest was very different from the first, carefully constructed of fine sprigs of heather which had evidently been plucked from the growing plant. Very different, too, was the behaviour of the hen. At first it appeared that, far from being a chip off the old block, she was a complete faint-heart. Whenever she was disturbed she flew straight off the nest and made her getaway across the valley, leaving the cock to take charge of the situation. Sometimes she was in such a hurry that she would sneak off without a sound: and more than once she stayed away so long that the cock had to turn-to and brood the eggs himself—an unheard of procedure among Hen Harriers. In the air, too, she was so clumsy, missing her catches time after time, that rather than let it go a-begging he took to presenting the prey to her on the ground. Obviously she was young and inexperienced. Considering how shiftless she was, the cock looked after her extremely well. So long as she was tied to her eggs he remained on guard, ready to sally forth and challenge anyone who came near: and when he went off hunting he was rarely away for any length of time, no doubt because he was anxious about leaving her on her own. His record time, out and "home", was under five minutes—not bad considering that he never killed anywhere within sight of the nest—and it was not often that it took him more than a quarter of an hour to find and fetch his fledgling Pipit or Skylark. In his haste, of course, he never bothered to pluck them. All credit to him, too, for holding the fort the way he did: if he never pitched into me with quite the same abandon as that virago further up the hill at least he showed himself to be no respecter of the human person.

In short, so far as this second pair were concerned, it appeared that the rôles normally assumed by the two sexes had been reversed. No doubt, in any pair there must always be a dominant partner; and if either is lacking in initiative the other makes good the defect. No doubt, too, size has something to do with the possession of a masterful nature—the second cock was noticeably bigger than the first. But the point which emerged most forcibly was that individual differences are no less important in determining bird-behaviour than they are in human affairs. To write about a pair of Hen Harriers is one thing: to generalise about *the* Hen Harrier is quite another. As Eliot Howard once remarked, "Conformity of action is in direct proportion to paucity of observation"—and how true a saying it is! The longer I watched these four birds the more I realised how unsafe it was to predict what any one of then would do next.

And then it happened! When I visited the second nest on June 13th (a Friday at that) I was somewhat taken aback to see the hen rise from the heather and fly straight towards me, heckling me as she came. Overnight—literally overnight— her whole personality had changed; and all because the last of her chicks had hatched out since my previous visit. For once I had left my hat behind, never for a moment expecting the assault and battery which she had in store for me. Even Lady Macbeth had never been quite so murderous as this. Faint-heart did I say? In the next few moments she made me eat my words. As I neared the nest she caught me looking the wrong way, such a buffet as made my eyes dance in their sockets, and then, while I was still wondering what had happened, she whipped in from behind and slit me across the scalp. A direct-hit if ever there was one— and when I clapped my hand to the place there was blood in my hair.

How I loved her for it, though! Now at last there could be no doubt about her parentage. Lady Macbeth's daughter is the only bird who has ever made me feel afraid, the only one who has put me in my place and left me chidden. We bird-watchers, I fear, can make dreadful nuisances of ourselves, prying and poking into the private lives of the wild creatures the way we do. For once in a while it was heartening to find one that showed its resentment by hitting back, and hitting back to good effect.

The rest of the story is soon told. Unfortunately for the

hopes I had placed in her, the part played in it by the second hen proved to be somewhat inglorious after all. Unlike her dam, who went from strength to strength as the summer wore on, she ended as she had begun, the most indifferent of mothers.

On June 14th, the day after she had sent me scurrying home in search of sticking-plaster, it was raining hard and blowing half a gale. In this weather, of course, there could be no question of disturbing her. Towards evening, however, the sky cleared like a charm and when the cock came in for the "pass" the hen remained aloft with him, no doubt for the sake of an airing. After weeks of squatting on the ground she was looking not a little bedraggled, especially the ends of her tail feathers, so perhaps there *was* some excuse for her taking a short respite after the downpour. In view of this there seemed to be no harm in paying the nest a quick visit. The five chicks were huddled together, wet and miserable. At the bottom of the pile lay the youngest, lifeless and cold. Apparently it had been smothered. While I was examining it, the cock never once left swooping at my head, but after a few dramatic gestures the hen retired and took no further interest in the proceedings, swinging up and away on the wind. Next morning there was no sign of the dead chick. As like as not it had been served to the others—if she did not eat it herself!

The wonder was that the chicks continued to thrive as they did, seeing how neglectful she was in attending to their needs. Days before the youngest had lost its egg-tooth she gave up brooding them during the daytime (and the fact that the fifth egg took nearly five weeks to hatch suggested that she had begun to lose interest earlier than this). Long before they were able to feed themselves she left them to their own devices, too bored, apparently, to portion out the food among them. As for the cock, he was quite tireless in his hunting. All day and every day he worked like a slave, bringing in Pipit after Pipit, but she was such a good-for-nothing, that very often, after relieving him of his bundles, she would sit by herself on a rock and pick at the best of the meat until he brought her another tit-bit, while the fledglings were left to go hungry. In fairness to her, however, it must be said that she was highly-strung, so touchy and suspicious that the mere sight of a human being, even at a distance, was enough to make her withdraw into her shell.

On June 24th, for example, I watched her continuously for two hours, during which time the cock brought in four small birds, none of which found its way to the nest. The fact that it was raining heavily made no difference. Though I was well concealed, three hundred yards and more away from the rock on which she was sitting, she made no attempt to feed the young ones. *Koikekekek . . . kikkakekkikekek . . . wikkikikekek.* Every few minutes she chattered to herself, half-angrily, half-fretfully. She had seen me the moment I left the car and that, so far as she was concerned, was that: she would never be herself again until she was satisfied that I had gone. Meantime she gorged herself. Let the fledglings twitter away there in the heather, let them scuffle about and shake the raindrops out of their rabbit-grey down—she had no thought for them. *Tsee-uk!*, she squealed, pleading for the cock to bring her yet another bird. No matter if the larder remained empty—it never occured to her to deposit the prey in the nest as he did sometimes when she was not there to receive it. In the end she stared me out. For the sake of my own peace of mind as well as hers, to say nothing of the young Harriers', I was left with no option but to withdraw.

Not that my departure did much good, I fancy: the plain truth was that she was not much of a hand at raising a family, and had it not been that the cock was such a good provider things would certainly have gone hard with them. Nevertheless, for all her being so remiss, it seemed likely that all four youngsters would succeed in leaving the nest before the middle of July. So far, despite the casual treatment they had received their development had been perfectly normal. Oddly enough the first-born, and therefore the most advanced, was also the smallest of the four. When he was three weeks old this starveling (a cock bird judging by his spindly legs), was well on the way to being fully feathered, nippy on his pins, too, always the first to scuttle off through the heather while the others lay on their sides with their tongues hanging out hardly able to raise themselves upright, yet he was no bigger than a Sparrow-hawk. By this time, naturally, the nest was no longer big enough to hold them all in comfort: it now served them as a kind of table, and how they crowded round it at meal-times, chittering aloud the moment they saw the hen rise for the "pass". Leading away from the nest in different directions were four tunnels or creepways at the ends of which each of the four young ones had its own sheltered corner. Here it concealed itself throughout the day, only hastening back to the centre at the promise of food. The floor of the nest was a shambles, littered with feathers and bones, spattered round the edges with excrement, and swarming with flies.

By rights the oldest and most active of the four should have been the first to fly. Not only had he lost his initial advantage, however—he was no longer able to hold his own in the free-for-all squabbles that were continually taking place, with the result that he was not getting his fair share of the food. A clear case of arrested development. Yet to look at he was a trim little fellow and as active as any of them: quick-tempered, too, rearing up and flashing his talons whenever a hand was stretched towards him. For all that it was easy to see that the others were growing much faster than he. Daily they became more and more aggressive: and to make things worse, his two sisters had taken to persecuting him unmercifully.

At the original nest (Lady Macbeth's), all the young had got off safely by the end of the first week in July. At this point, unfortunately, I was called away for ten days—the first break in continuity since March—with the result that I cannot vouch for what happened during my absence. When I visited the second nest on the 16th, I fully expected to find it abandoned. Instead, the hen was there waiting for me as usual at her plucking-post on the rock. Seeing me coming, she took off, cackling, and flung herself into the attack with something of her old *élan*, but as I drew near three young Harriers rose from the heather and flew off, a little uncertainly at first but gathering confidence as they gained height. At this, she left off cackling and let the updraught carry her away across the valley. The nest was empty, littered with the remains of their latest meal, but the starveling was still there, gaping with the heat as he crouched in his corner—and a shocking sight he was. All his flight feathers had been wrenched out, leaving the quill sockets bleeding. Not only that, but most of the down had been plucked from the undersides of his body, exposing the raw yellow flesh. Tailless, he flourished the stumps of his wings in a vigorous effort to leave the ground, but it was clear that, short of a miracle, this pitiful little scarecrow was so badly maimed that he would never fly. Given proper treatment there was just a chance that he might recover from his injuries, but it would take weeks and weeks for a new crop of feathers to grow and as it was the season was very nearly at an end. Obviously the hen was having nothing more to do with him. If it was left to her, the poor little devil's fate was already decided—and what could the cock do by himself? He could hardly be expected to carry on indefinitely. Even if he continued to bring food in to the nest, the chances were that it would immediately be filched by the others. While I was still pondering what to do, the cock came in with a Grouse cheeper tucked beneath his tail. At once he drove straight in to the attack, dropping his free foot in readiness while he hung on to the prey with the other. Then, finding it too much of an encumbrance, he dropped his bundle in the heather and came for me double-fisted, throwing up a yard in front of my face with the utmost savagery. (Incidentally, I was always sorry to be the cause of his jettisoning a "kill" like this and made a point of finding and placing it in the nest whenever possible, for if for any reason a Harrier releases its hold on its prey in flight, the rule is that no attempt is made to retrieve it afterwards.) Never before had I seen him quite so valiant in the defence of the nest as he was now. No matter if his mate had left him, no matter if three of the brood had flown, he was going to see this thing through to the end. So, after stuffing a sliver or two of red meat into the young bird, just enough to keep body and soul together for another twenty-four hours, I left him to it. A wrong decision as it turned out—the best course would have been to take the little wretch home and look after it myself—but seeing that at least one of the parents was prepared to stand by, it seemed only right to give him the chance to do what he could.

The end came two days later. That morning as I made my way uphill the cock took off from his look-out and flew to meet me, chattering anxiously and swooping low over my head again and again. There was no sign of the hen. So far as she was concerned, evidently, it was all over. Two of the young Harriers rose from the ground beside the nest, looking very dusky in their chocolate-coloured juvenile plumage. Though they were now strong on the wing, they still spent a good deal of their time at the family hearth, attracted thither by the food which the cock continued to bring in at regular intervals.

It was as I had expected. A few feet away from the edge of the nest, its brown eyes as bright as ever, the starveling lay dead. It had fallen forward on its breast bone, too weak to stand upright as the last remaining strength ebbed from its scraggy body. Too late now for regrets and misgivings. Even so, it was a sad moment. Rather than leave the carcass for the blow-flies, I decided to keep it as a *memento mori*, and stowing the handful of skin and bone in my pocket, I set off to climb further up the hill in the hopes of seeing something of the rest of the family. All the way up the hill, the cock Harrier followed me, nattering angrily and making passes at me long after the nest had been left behind— a thing he had never done before. Was it possible that he could see the yellow shank of the dead youngster sticking out of my pocket and was protesting against the abduction?—or was it simply that he was concerned about the safety of the others, concealed in the bracken somewhere in front of me? A little of both motives, perhaps. Sure enough, when I came to the top of the ridge one of the young birds that I had seen before flustered out from its hiding-place, tittering excitedly—*wit-wit-weeky* . . . *wit-wit-weeky*, it shrilled as it climbed into the breeze, and then (incredible as it sounds), this tyro wheeled round, half-closed its wings and made as if to attack me. The precocity, the effrontery of it! Barely out of the nest, yet already this babe in arms was acting true to type. In a flash the cock came hurrying in to save the situation, chattering to the young fool to leave off and be gone. Even then the other seemed reluctant to leave it at that, like a wilful child that cannot understand the danger of playing with fire; but then it felt the pull of the mountain air in its pinions and tilted away, soaring out above the valley. From lower down the slope came the answering call of its companion and soon the two of them were safely out of harm's way, weaving circles together high overhead (almost as if they were courting).

Turning, I made my way downhill again for the last time, passing the nest on my way. Meanwhile the cock Harrier kept an eye on me from a distance, only now there was nothing to keep him there or hold him to his purpose any longer. The territory had lost its meaning. Now that there was nothing for him to defend, the devil had gone out of him and left him "in calm of mind, all passion spent". The frenzies and crises were over. For once he did not trouble to watch me down to the roadside—no need for it now. Long before I was out of sight he had given himself to the breeze and made his leisurely exit round the far end of the hill.

The last scene of the last act had reached its quiet close. And as if to anounce the fact, three Hoodies put their heads together and raised their raucous voices in unison. Shoulder to shoulder, the grey-backed crows perched on the rock above the deserted nest—the first crows that had dared to set foot anywhere near it for four months. One by one they hitched their wings on their backs and cocked their heads inquiringly, weighing the chances of one or other of the late occupiers returning and catching them red-handed. Down there where the bluebottles buzzed there was scavenging work to be done and as soon as they were satisfied that the coast was clear they meant to begin.

V. The Buzzard and I

COMMON BUZZARD

THERE IS A lot to be said for the bird in the hand. Make no mistake about it, the medieval falconer *knew* his birds a good deal more intimately than most ornithologists can claim to do nowadays—this despite the fact that the modern student of animal behaviour has at his disposal vastly greater sources of information. There is, after all, a vital difference between "knowing" and "knowing *about*" a creature or a person.

In the same way, and for the same reason, I have always felt that anyone who has kept a tame Owl or looked after a "pricked" Goose gains an insight into the workings of the bird's mind which tends to be denied to the watcher in the field, no matter how patient and painstaking the latter may be. To be sure, there can be no substitute for observation of the bird in its wild setting: any creature that is kept in confinement is inevitably seen as it were in a distorting mirror. Its style of life being cramped, it becomes at best a simulacrum of its true self. Only one side of its nature is revealed. What makes it so intriguing, however, is the fact that this is the side which in the ordinary way is as effectively hidden from us as the other face of the moon: so that if our aim is to see the bird in the round—to *know* it, that is, as distinct from "*knowing about*" it—there may be no alternative to studying it in captivity. Ninety-nine times out of a hundred admittedly, there is no justification for such a course. Reverence for life does not stop short at the mere refusal to kill: and one does not have to be a Schweitzer or a St. Francis to respect the unique identity of each and every creature, or to recognise that it is entitled to lead its own life. Still, casualties of one sort or another occasionally come to hand, and when this happens the bird-watcher can satisfy his curiosity while keeping a clear conscience.

Not long ago, then, I became the proud possessor of a Buzzard: no ordinary Buzzard, either, but as grand a hawk as ever graced the wooded glens of the west of Scotland. The story of how she came into my keeping was quite a chapter of accidents in itself. In the first place she had been caught in a rabbit trap (and the less said about that the better, perhaps, in view of what the Protection of Birds Act has to say), a mishap which had left her with the middle talon of the right foot missing. Apart from this, the bird was more or less unharmed. For several weeks after this she had been kept cooped up on a farm (no point in asking why), at the end of which period she turned droopy and refused to feed. Because of this the bird was sent off to the Kelvingrove Museum in Glasgow and it was here that I first saw her. Unfortunately, a museum is not a dispensary for sick animals as some people seem to think and it was clear that the new arrival had placed the authorities in a bit of a quandary, so that when the suggestion was made that I should take charge of her I can only say that I jumped at the chance.

Somehow I canot bring myself to use the impersonal pronoun in writing of this fine bird. From the start, she revealed herself as a personality, with moods and idiosyncracies which were all her own. Her markings, too, were singularly beautiful, showing almost as much white on the underside of the wings and the body as a Rough-legged Buzzard. Her size alone was a sufficient indication of her sex—and her hooked bill was almost aquiline in its proportions.

She had lost nothing of her wildness when I first made her acquaintance, dashing madly from side to side in the makeshift cage which had been used to transport her to the museum. By rights, I suppose, she should have been released forthwith, for she was perfectly able-bodied. But when I saw how her pinions were twisted and bent and how the yellow skin of her cere was red-raw with beating at the wire-netting, I decided against it. Besides, she had not taken a scrap of food for nearly a week. At the time, moreover, the countryside was snowbound and there was no sign of a break in the hard weather. Before giving her the chance to fend for herself she needed building up a little, I told myself. Better hang on to her just for a day or two until she was in rather better shape: in her present state she would almost certainly starve to death if I let her go. . . .

Just for a day or two! I can see now that it would have been less dissembling to have confessed that I coveted her from the start, as a horseman covets an unbroken stallion. Yes, I coveted her all right, though I still like to think that I did so from motives which were not entirely selfish. There was no question of my wanting to tame her or train her to the fist: even if I had had the necessary skill I do not think I could have brought myself to try it. No kindness of mine, and Heaven knows it was little enough I had to offer, could ever soften the harsh look in those imperious eyes of hers. In any case, it was understood from the beginning that my part of the bargain was simply to provide temporary board and lodging.

Those eyes! Pale brown, their irises glittered like precious stones, contracting and expanding all the time as they adjusted their focus of attention. At the first hint of a movement—say the raising of a little finger—they were wide open in an instant, glaring with fear and hostility. At times it almost seemed as if the size of the pupils was regulated by the bird's heart-beats. Naturally she could not bear to be touched. Whenever I tried she drew herself back in a frenzy of apprehension, taut, and ready to lash out with one foot—and she had a kick so powerful that sometimes the clutch of her talons drove clean through the thickest leather gloves. At the same time she would set up a rapid, clicketty-click note, quite unlike any sound I had ever heard from a Buzzard before: and sometimes in the hysteria of her panic she even clucked like an old hen. If only I could add that she also uttered the familiar, mewing cry of the free-flying Buzzard, but the sorry truth is that all the time she was with me I never once heard it.

Left to herself, she quickly recovered her composure and would sit for hours without stirring. When there was nothing to attract her attention she remained utterly sphinx-like. No stimulus, no response. In the dead-calm air of the shed in which she was housed she seemed to be reduced to a state of complete inertia. For the first time I began to realise the extent to which a soaring bird is dependent on strong air-currents.

Once, and once only—it was the second day I had her—she condescended to drink from a bowl of water, raising her head time and again and sipping it down with the relish of a wine-taster sampling some rare vintage. Thereafter the water was persistently ignored. Occasionally she preened, plucking away at her wing-coverts quite savagely, but without much interest or method. For the most part she was content to ruffle out her "pinafore", give herself a vigorous shake, and leave it at that. This done, she would raise her damaged foot, stretch it in front of her like a pianist exercising his fingers and then draw it in beneath her breast plumes. In this position she made herself comfortable for the night. Unlike the smaller hawks, which tuck their heads in when they go to roost, she invariably dozed off in an upright position as Eagles are said to do.

For the first three days there was nothing for it but to feed her forcibly, an operation which caused no end of bad blood on both sides but for all her struggles and tantrums, I was not prepared to stand aside and watch her die of hunger. For her part, she would have nothing whatever to do with the cold scraps which were left for her—not until she was presented with the carcass of a freshly killed rabbit, fur and all. At this she immediately perked up and found a new interest in life, and from then on she fed whenever she felt like it. Even then it transpired that she took food only on alternate days, though perhaps this was explained by the sedentary life she was leading. Only when she had fetched up a wet pellet of solid fur the size of a pigeon's egg did she display any signs of genuine appetite, clamping the meat down firmly with both feet while she stooped to tear it into slivers. Between each pull she raised her head glancing to left and right, wild-eyed for fear of being surprised: and, needless to say, she would never touch a thing if there was the least suggestion of her being spied on.

Before long I had her sitting on my fist. She protested, of course, clicking away at the top of her voice, quick to take offence or throw a temperament; but once she had got a grip on the glove and felt herself secure she soon calmed down and accepted the situation. After the first convulsive clutch, her talons relaxed (only to tighten again the moment she panicked—the vice of fear), and after a time she would blow out all her feathers and stand completely at ease. Oddly enough, though the shed door was often open she never once attempted to escape by flying out. Instead, when she had had as much as she could stand she always flapped back to her favourite perch on the topmost shelf in the corner. A home-keeping soul, I must say.

After a fortnight there was no longer any evading the moral issue. The weather remained as severe as ever, but the time had come for her to go. If anything it was already overdue. Secretly I was beginning to feel not a little disturbed at the change that had come over her. For one thing, she seemed to have lost any desire for freedom. Worse still, though she was as good-looking as ever, she had lost the fine-drawn condition of the wild hawk, so slow and heavy and lazy that a flight of even a few yards left her gasping. In this state she would never be able to hunt for herself: slowly but surely the killer-instinct in her was being blunted, as were the points of her talons with scraping about on the concrete floor. Worse of all, she was growing to be far too accustomed to the human presence for my liking. *And it was all my fault!*

It began to look as though the wisest course might be to present her to one of the zoos or, failing that, to keep her indefinitely. But no, the temptation had to be resisted. Kill or cure, she would have to take her chance.

The first attempt at release turned out to be an ignominious failure, ignominious for both of us. The place I had chosen was ideal, a stretch of moorland with wooded slopes and a range of hills in the middle distance, and all swarming with rabbits. Everywhere the snow was criss-crossed with their tracks. Rabbits in twos and threes all over the place, bobbing about against a background of dazzling whiteness. Sitting targets. Easy meat. She could hardly miss.

Alas for my plans! When I took her out of the box all she did was to hop up on to a boulder and sit there looking at me with a half-helpless, half-witless expression. Maybe the change from the darkness of the shed to the brilliance of the snow-covered wasteland had been too abrupt? Taking her back on to my hand, I tossed her high in the air, only there was no strength in it—she stalled and flounced down again, spreadeagled in a deep drift. The third try was rather more successful: this time she beat off low across the rise, scattering rabbits to right and left of her as she flew, only to alight in the first available fir tree and wait for me to fetch her! By the time I reached the foot of the tree half a dozen Carrion Crows had gathered around shouting abuse at her—and derision at me. There she sat, forty feet up, staring into space, lost in a day-dream, apparently. I could hardly leave her in a predicament of this sort. If I did, the chances were that she would go on sitting until she dropped: so, at the risk of life and limb I shinned up as best I could, with the brittle stubs breaking off under my weight and brought her down. On the way back, against my better judgement, I tried her again, this time with consequences that were very nearly disastrous: she made a three-point landing on the main road in front of a double-decker bus! Mercifully I got there in time to rescue her, an escapade that left the pair of us gasping.

It now appeared that the process of weaning her back to the ways of the wild was going to be far from easy. Each day for nearly a week I took her out and exercised her over the same stretch of ground, hoping against hope that she would gain in confidence and aerial mastery. At first she made little or no progress. Like an invalid who has lost the use of his legs, she floundered about in a way which would have been pathetic had it not been so completely apathetic. Several times I was within an ace of losing her, and on each occasion I was more than half inclined to leave her to her fate, being thoroughly out of patience with her for being so infirm of purpose. Once she came down, all of a heap as usual, in the middle of a frozen lochan, and it was touch and go retrieving her, with the ice creaking and rumbling underfoot at every second step. Twice she chose to perch out on a limb where there was simply no reaching her and it was only by dint of shaking the top of the tree that I managed to dislodge her. Next she blundered to rest on a face of crag, pitching in the most awkward of all spots—a nook in the rocks with a grassy over-hang immediately above it.

As a pupil she was well-nigh hopeless. One day she would show signs of improvement and the next she would be as feckless as ever. Gradually she took longer and longer flights, but still she showed no great inclination to fly off when approached. How could I possibly leave her so long as she was so trusting, so inert? The first lout who came along could have stoned her to death and she would have watched him do it. Would she never regain her old resolution, I wondered? Was the attachment between us (such as it was) to be permanent? Had I left it too late?

The trouble was that she was too well fed, I decided. Maybe a day or two on short commons would help her to lose some of this fatal complacency. Nothing like hunger to bring her back to her senses. And so it proved. (A good thing, too, for I was beginning to find this business of climbing trees and scrambling up rock-faces just a little trying.)

Eventually there came an afternoon when at last her independent spirit reasserted itself. There was a new look in her eyes, mistrustful and bold. She was edgy, cantankerous, clutching at my sleeve and getting herself tangled upside down when I opened the box. With relief, and at the same time a certain feeling of sorrow at the thought of losing her, I saw her take off into the wind and fly off purposefully towards the wooded crag. The moment she let go of the glove I knew that it was for the last time. She settled in the crown of one of the tallest firs about a quarter of a mile away, still within sight. Then as I drew nearer she took one look at me and breasted the air again, swinging round on the updraught rising higher and higher until she disappeared behind the breast of the hill: and as she went she uttered the cry I had waited so long to hear—the clear, ringing *pee ayah!* of her kind—a fitting note of triumph to end this chapter in her story.

VI. The Yeoman's Hawk

GOSHAWK

FALCONRY, BEING AT least as old as Babylon, may fairly
claim to be the most ancient of all sports; and the fact that it is at
present enjoying something of a revival, not only in this country
and on the Continent but also in America, is only one proof of its
perennial fascination.

This revival, it may be thought, is a sign of the times. In a
push-button age, bemused by Sputnik and the prospects of inter-
planetary travel, there are a number of reasons why some of us
should find hawking more truly satisfying than a host of other
pursuits. There is, first, the natural beauty of the predator itself,
its "fearful symmetry", to say nothing of the joy and pride of
possessing one of these princes of the air. From the Golden Eagle
down to the tiny Merlin, all the birds of prey are singularly
handsome, exquisitely cut out for the work for which they are
intended. Man's first guided missile, one likes to think, was a
hawk—not so accurate as the super-gadgets of today, perhaps,
but far more admirable because living. Again, there is the
genuine sense of achievement which comes of training the
wildest of wild creatures to answer one's bidding and, above all—
the end of it all—the fierce thrill of seeing it in action, flying free,
yet always under the remote control of a human will.

For myself, I have long been a distant admirer of the
austringer's art. Despite all the advances that have been made
in the scientific study of animal behaviour, it seems that no one
has yet found a way to improve upon his age-old methods.
Apart from a few modern refinements, the tricks of his trade
are much the same as ever they were, and the tackle, too, for
that matter. Broadly speaking, the hawk-master's secret may be
explained as a strict adherence to the principle of the conditioned

66

reflex, but, clearly there is more to it than that. As anyone knows who has watched him at work, the task of transforming his "haggard" (a wild-caught passage hawk) into a reasonably trustworthy and manageable companion is one which calls for endless loving care and attention. The relationship between man and hawk is delicate at the best of times, quite unlike the bond between a man and his dog, for example. Any affinity that may exist is highly tenuous, a touch-and-go affair which is all too easily destroyed. First the wildling must be "manned" accustomed to taking its place on the fist without flying off the handle: "manned", yes, but in the process it must not lose one jot or tittle of its independent spirit. If the partnership is to be successful, the master must be prepared to sacrifice some of his own personal freedom, so much so that at times it is hard to say which is master and which is servant; and when at last some kind of mutual understanding has been reached the hawk is still quick to take offence. Anyone who ignores the well-tried tested ways soon finds himself in difficulties. Given the right treatment, the young eyas usually becomes an apt pupil. One false move, however, and tempers really fly! Any attempt to force the learner against its will leads to bad blood on both sides as readers of T. H. White's nightmarish account of his experiences with the Goshawk will recall.

Though the Goshawk has recently regained its status as a British breeding bird it is generally classed as a rare vagrant in these islands. Just why it should be so casual in its visits, seeing that it is tolerably common throughout the rest of Western Europe, is not clear. No less obscure is the question of its former status as a British bird. Thirty years ago, Mr. E. M. Nicholson formed the opinion that the Goshawk, often counted among the "lost" species, probably never was indigenous. He noted that the older English naturalists, almost to a man, were under the impression that it bred extensively in Scotland, and added somewhat censoriously, that the Scots "hearing this so persistently referred to as a fact, did not like to forfeit the honour by pleading the ignorance they undoubtedly suffered" [!]. It is true that many of the early records either referred to the Peregrine or were based on hearsay. But to reject *all* the historical evidence as worthless is neither sensible nor very fair, unless we are to write off our forbears as liars and fools without exception. Even supposing that Holinshed, Boece, Sibbald and Pennant were all guilty of treating rumour as if it were fact, there still remain several eye-witnesses whose reports carry the ring of truth. Thus, for example, the Rev. John Lapslie of Campsie, said to have been a naturalist of some repute, writing in 1795, declared that, "The Goshawk, which builds its nest upon trees in sequestered places, is likewise a native of this parish"; while in Thornton's *Sporting Tour*, published about the same time, it is stated that, "in the forest formed by Glenmore and Rothiemurchus . . . are also some eyries of Goss-hawks, some of which we saw". Fifty years later the redoubtable Charles St. John said that it bred regularly in the forest of Darnaway, though it is clear from what he says that by 1850 the species was on the verge of extinction. The last Goshawk eggs to be taken in Scotland, apparently, were obtained as late as 1883 by one of J. G. Millais' keepers.

All in all, then, there seems to be little doubt that the Goshawk was a resident and well-distributed species throughout the old Caledonian Forest, and that it remained so at least until the end of the eighteenth century. Thereafter a combination of circumstances, on the one hand the wholesale destruction of trees (which had already reduced the native stock of Capercaillie to vanishing point), on the other, the indiscriminate persecution of birds of prey (which removed the Kite, the Sea Eagle and the Osprey from the Scottish list), ensured that the survival of this outsize woodland hawk was virtually impossible.

Will the Goshawk ever return as a Scottish breeding bird? On the whole, it seems improbable. The precarious bridgehead which it has established for itself in South-East England (and there only under the most rigorous protection), is doubtless due to colonisation by passage-hawks from the Continent, more particularly from Holland. There the narrow seas offer no great barrier. Further north they do. Possibly the best hope lies in the reafforestation schemes now going forward in many parts of Scotland, though when one considers how everyone's hand (to say nothing of the law of the land!) is against the little Sparrowhawk it has to be admitted that the prospects facing the much bigger Gos, supposing it attempts a come-back, are decidedly bleak.

For myself, I have to confess that I have only once seen the bird in a wild state in this country and even then, I fear, there was a question-mark attached to it. Years ago, with a fellow sixth-former, I was watching passage migrants on the South Gare breakwater at Teesmouth when a huge brown hawk drove in from the sea. Hurrying in low across the dunes it gave us both excellent views of its markings. Greatly excited we sent off the details to *British Birds*, only to receive a polite note from the editor (the late H. F. Witherby), explaining that he was unable to accept the record since the description we had given might have fitted the Honey Buzzard equally well. At the time, I remember, we felt rather sore about it. (Honey Buzzard my foot!) Still, knowing how easily tyros can be mistaken, there is no denying that the decision against us was correct. (All the same, it *was* a Goshawk!)

Textbooks invariably describe the Goshawk as looking like a giant Sparrow-hawk: a pity, this, for though the description is the obvious one it can be very misleading. Certainly the Gos belongs to the short-winged hawks, and its proportions are much the same as its smaller cousin's, but in flight the impression given is that of a jet-propelled buzzard. One can appreciate the startled comment of the beater at a Pheasant shoot when this monster shot through the coverts: "A most awful-like bird, many times bigger than a hawk". Awful-like, certainly, is the glare of the Gos's stony eyes. Its legs are proportionately much shorter and thicker than the spindly shanks of the Sparrow-hawk, and its talons are immensely powerful, worthy of a small Eagle's. The long curve of the hooked bill, so slender yet so assured, bespeaks the ruthless efficiency of a born hunter.

Just how impulsive and how deadly a marksman the Gos can be I had never realised until I handled one. Gregarach, as her owner called her, was a fine young female imported from Germany. To begin with she was as wild as any wild cat (the result of being cooped up in a box on a journey which lasted more than twenty-four hours), but after being left to herself for a day or two she quickly regained her composure and eventually proved to be quite tractable. Within a week she had learned to answer the lure. Time and again, to be sure, she "baited", threshing her wings and threatening to strangle herself, caught upside down in the tangles of her leather jesses—but patience is the answer to every tantrum and a tit-bit of raw meat works wonders when misunderstandings of this sort arise and tempers are ruffled. Today she sits on her master's wrist as placidly as a pet budgerigar, eyeing strangers without fear.

On one of her early trial flights, Gregarach surprised everyone by nailing a full-grown rabbit at the first attempt. It was all over and done with in a twinkling. She heard the dog yelp in front, saw the white scut bobbing in the bracken thirty yards away, and in a flash went after her quarry. Her response was instantaneous, her aim unerring, her grip deadly. The rabbit never knew what hit it. Transfixed through the head and heart together it never even squealed as she shrouded it, glorying in her first kill.

Now came a tricky moment or two—for one of the surest ways of losing a hawk is to interfere with it while the prey is still warm in its clutches—but after a time the Gos relaxed, looked up and returned obediently to the lure. We breathed again. With a sliver or two of raw meat by way of reward she sat on the gauntlet looking as pleased as Punch, as well she might—an old hand at the game could hardly have accomplished the feat more adroitly.

No matter how well trained a hawk may be, various precautions have to be taken before it can safely be taken on a hunting expedition. One is that the bird must be "sharp-set". This means that the hawk must be carefully weighed to see that it does not exceed a certain weight. Given a full crop, Gregarach weighs two and a half pounds, but the chances are that if she were flown in this condition she might take it into her head to go off, and not come back. If necessary, then, she must be starved for several hours in order to lose the ounce or so which may make all the difference between triumph and disaster. In any case, quite apart from the dreaded possibility of its getting lost, a sluggish hawk is a hawk off-form, apt to miss chances that it will take with both hands when trimmed for action. Hunger is its spur. Avian digestion being as rapid as it is, the delay in setting out is never more than an hour or two, but if there is any doubt about the bird's condition the wisest thing is to wait. Hawking is no sport for those who lack patience and look for quick results.

Goshawk, first year female

"The longer she waits, the more venomous her glances"

Even to the inexpert eye, the difference between the Gos's demeanour when she is well-fed and when she is sharp-set is too obvious to miss. Off duty she looks tranquil, almost kindly. Only her eyes are on the *qui vive*, forever darting glances this way and that at objects which attract her attention—a loose feather blowing in the grass beside her, or the lark in the sky overhead. Each morning a Buzzard sails over the wood mewing all the while, as if thinking that the captive on the ground were one of her own kind, but Gregarach never answers. The longer she waits, the more venomous her glances. Sometimes as the urge to have a fling grows on her she keens to herself, a plaintive whistle which is faintly reminiscent of a Curlew in spring.

At last she is ready to go; and if the whinny she gives as she hops on the gauntlet is anything to go by, she is as eager as the rest of us to be on the move. All the way down the lane she keeps on cocking her head at this or that—here a Blackbird turning over the leaf-mould in the hedge bottom, there a Wood Pigeon bursting out of the ivied oak. Often she cannot contain herself and makes a mad dash for it, only to be pulled back by the straps which hold her. More than once excitement gets the better of her and she "baits", a bad habit which she has yet to overcome. Sometimes she does this for no apparent reason, presumably because she has detected something which the human eye has failed to glimpse. Nothing escapes that merciless stare: nothing within striking distance, that is, for the Gos's range of action is strictly limited. Thus Gregarach shows no interest in the Rooks in the tree-tops, or the Redwings at the far end of a long field, and she knows better than to plunge head-first into the bush by the roadside where a Robin is singing (though she gives it one of her nastiest looks as we pass). The targets she likes are those that present themselves at a distance of twenty or thirty yards.

Out on the open moor the jesses are untied, and from now on it is up to her. Not that she needs any prompting. Without warning she casts off abruptly and flies straight as a bolt from a cross-bow, thumping into the dried bracken with a crash. Another rabbit? The dog yelps distractedly and before the hawk can look up a cock Pheasant rockets into the air. Missed by a yard! All credit to the Gos, though: at least she spied her quarry long before anyone else had the least inkling that it was there.

71

Now the lure is swung, the whistle blown and, sure enough, the great Gos returns to settle on the outstretched arm. Heavy, powerful, she looks positively satanic as she beats low over the ground with a graceful upward loop as she alights. Over distances up to a furlong her speed is electrifying. As yet, however, she lacks the judgement and the finish of the nature hawk—which is just as well for the Grouse. One day, soon, no doubt, she will create havoc among them.

A few more headstrong rushes to show off her paces and it is time to go home. But now that she has bolted the last gobbet that her master chooses to offer her, Gregarach turns flighty and lets it be seen that she is in no mood for compliance. Instead, she swings away, beats over the rise as if bent on escaping into the next county, then perches in the branches of a tall Scots fir, from which eminence she regards us with calculated indifference. It is the sort of moment which every falconer learns to dread, the moment when it looks as though all is lost. Mercifully she consents at last, swooping down like an avenging angel on to the waiting arm. For this relief, much thanks. And so home with nothing in the bag, perhaps, but with the satisfaction of sharing the thrills and hazards of the chase. This was the sport our forefathers enjoyed, and in practising it today who can help feeling that he is following, however modestly, in a worthy tradition?

VII.   My First Iceland Falcon

EVER SINCE I was a small boy I have had a passion for Hawks. Looking back, I think it must have been Archibald Thorburn, that prince of bird-artists, who prompted this early love of mine. And how superbly he rendered the imperious looks, the general air of distinction of these aristocrats of the air! To the innocent eye of a ten-year-old by far the most intriguing of all the illustrations which adorned Coward's textbook (my *vade mecum* in those days) was the one depicting a Greenland Falcon. *Falco rusticolus candicans* ... now there was a name to conjure with, a raptor as white as the arctic ice-field itself and half as big again as a Peregrine, the kind of bird which any man might be proud to include in his life-list. Some day, somewhere, somehow, I promised myself I would see this dazzling creature. Time and again I pictured the incident in my mind's eye—a snowy hillside in the wilds of Sutherland, perhaps, with the Grouse scattering to left and right beneath the Falcon's swoop, or, more spectacular still, a frozen estuary on the east coast with the wild fowl rising in panic all over the place and the great bird high above them, resplendent, mystic, wonderful, poised for the strike, its pinions stretched against a leaden sky.

Alas for my hopes! Half a lifetime has gone by and I have still to set eyes on my White Falcon. All the same, I have had the excitement of some near misses. Some very near misses at that. There was, for example, that Easter week-end in Norfolk, 1947 it must have been, when the bar parlour gossip at Brancaster centred on the "girt white duck-hawk" which had been seen on the saltings. Again, there was the day on the Solway, far out on Blackshaw Bank (and how far from the land it is there at low water), when an outsize Falcon (too big, too lumbering for any Peregrine, surely), made a half-hearted pass at the Barnacle

73

Geese and then beat off heavily across the estuary before I could be quite positive of the identification. Admittedly, this one was nearer black than white in colour. No matter, however, for it is now recognised that the Gyr, Iceland and Greenland Falcons as they used to be called, are simply geographical races of the same species. Not only is it practically impossible to say which is which in the field, at any rate in their juvenile plumage, but in all three it is apparently not unusual to find white and dark phase individuals in the same eyrie. So great is the confusion, indeed, that one cannot help wondering whether the mere handful of reliable records for the Gyr in this country is best explained by the readiness to assign any big dark Falcon to the Icelandic race. As a rough general rule, it can be said that the latter is intermediate between the grey Gyr of the Norwegian fjell and the snowy Greenland Falcon, but immature specimens present quite a problem even when they can be handled as museum skins. In the field the only thing to do is to write them off, however reluctantly, as "possibles", as happened in the case of my Solway bird. In Orkney and Shetland, of course, the chances of seeing an immaculate adult are rather better: at any rate on one famous occasion the farm-servants at Halligarth, in Unst, were startled out of their wits at breakfast time—and on the Sabbath, of all days—by one of these white bolts from the blue which chased a Pigeon through the open door, slew it at their feet and made off before anyone could raise an outcry.*

By far the most exasperating of these near-misses (hard-luck stories, if you will), occurred quite recently. On this occasion the place was Loch Leven, the time of year early November, and my companion Maury Meiklejohn, widely known to ornithologists as the author of an erudite paper on that most elusive and tantalising bird the Hoodwink. From the roadside, the two of us were watching the hordes of Pink-footed Geese on St. Serf's Isle, intrigued by the presence of a solitary white goose in their midst. Was it a Snow-goose, we wondered, or just another wretched albino? In order to get a closer look and on the off-chance of putting the geese up, I left the road and walked down to the

* No doubt it was the regularity of these occurrences which led the eighteenth-century systematist, Gmelin, to state that the White Gyr "habitat in Islandia et in Scotia borealis"—a mistake as it turned out, but an excusable one.

My first Iceland Falcon

lochside. Sure enough, the Pink-feet rose in their thousands, wink-winking at the tops of their voices, and with them the all-white bird. No black primaries, worse luck . . . it was an albino after all.

When I got back to the car Maury was all smiles. Less than five minutes after I had left him, he said, an Iceland Falcon had shot overhead, hotly pursued by a heckling Peregrine. For the moment he had been so taken aback by the discrepancy in the sizes that he had almost mistaken the pursuer for a Merlin: then he caught a glimpse of white on the other's head and saw its streaky underparts.

This news fairly took the wind out of my sails, I must say. The most maddening thing was the thought that if only I had happened to look up at the time I could hardly have failed to see my long-sought Icelander as it made off across the loch towards the distant hills. Hoodwinked again! Needless to say, I kept my eyes skinned for the rest of the day and, needless to say, the miracle was not repeated.

Nevertheless, by an extraordinary coincidence, within a week I *did* see an Iceland Falcon. Unfortunately, when it came, the great moment turned out to be a sorry anti-climax. Indeed, were it not that the chain of events which led up to it was so ludicrous, the story would scarcely be worth telling. Tucked away on one of the inside pages of a Sunday newspaper was a four-line news item which caught my eye. According to this, a large hawk "with a wing span of over five feet" had been captured aboard a weather-ship stationed in mid-Atlantic. For several days violent north-westerly gales had been blowing and the bird had alighted in an exhausted condition. As it showed no inclination to leave the vessel it had been kept alive and eventually brought ashore when the weather-ship returned to its base. A quick telephone call to the port authorities elicited the information that the vagrant had been handed over to the Society for the Prevention of Cruelty to Animals. Further enquiries revealed that for reasons which scarcely do credit to the intelligence of this worthy organisation's officials a home had been found for the castaway in one of the Scottish zoos. There at last I tracked the lost one down.

My first Iceland Falcon, and what a beauty she was! To

all apearances she was a typical young Gyr in her first plumage, so bulky that she made the biggest Peregrine I have ever seen look puny, a pigmy by comparison. She was powerfully built, compact and chunky and her bluish feet would not have disgraced an Eagle. Her eyes were darker than black grapes. The feathers of her mantle were gun-metal colour, finely edged with white, with a patch of white the size of a snowball on the nape and the underparts silvery, boldly spattered with blackish markings.

There she sat, between a Great Horned Owl and a crochety old Raven, looking quite docile, or at any rate impassive. But the raw steak which had been left for her remained untouched. Turning her head suspiciously she watched me sidle up to the stump on which she was perched, ready to dash herself against the wire walls of the aviary if I dared to raise a hand against her. At close quarters she looked less like a Peregrine than ever, altogether more massive and thickset, broader in the beam, hornier billed: a Falcon fit for the wrist of an emperor. Face on, she already looked decidedly white about the head and neck, with just a trace of a moustache, so that it was easy to envisage her a year or so hence in the full-blown glory of the Iceland Falcon's kenspeckle white and grey. In profile, I decided, she looked rather less distinguished—the features not so finely chiselled as the Peregrine's—but what a magnificent figure she cut when she bridled, her shoulders hunched like a heavy-weight's and her pinions so long that they almost reached the top of her tail.

Quietly, guardedly, she allowed me to photograph her in various attitudes, one of which, I am glad to say, reproduces the pose that Thorburn hit off so well. Only when I made the mistake of touching her (an indignity which no wild-born blue-blooded hawk can endure) did she take offence, whirling round and round in tight circles until at last she alighted, gasping, in a corner. Wide-eyed, bill gaping, she reminded me of an athlete who has just run a hundred yards flat-out, still fighting to regain his breath. Clearly, in this state, she was not fit to be released, though personally I should have preferred to see her given the chance of freedom.

The trouble is that in captivity most birds of prey very soon lose their fine-drawn condition, and young ones especially

are soon in difficulties if they are called upon to undertake anything like a sustained flight. Indeed, the regularity with which
passage hawks avail themselves of a lift on board ships suggests
that for all their speed and adroitness in the air they tire sooner
than other migrants on a long sea crossing. At the same time, it is
hard to say why this unlucky bird should have been so distressed
by a strong north-west (that is, presumably, following) wind.
But, then, the ways of the Gyr are always unpredictable.

The upshot of it all is that I now live in hopes of finding
a second Iceland Falcon in happier circumstances. If only the
first could have figured in some heroic exploit—like the Halligarth bird, for instance, cutting a dash and retrieving its prey
before anyone knew what had happened—instead of being
cooped up, alone and disconsolate, in a shabby cage!

VIII.   The Case of the Short-eared Owl

WITH THE CLOSE of the holiday season a great quietness falls upon the Highlands. The busloads of tourists, the caravanners at the lochside, the youth-hostelers traipsing over the hills have all, or very nearly all, gone home. Gone too, are many of the birds whose presence enlivens the moorland waste during the summer months. As early as the beginning of August the Lapwings, Oystercatchers, Curlews, Dunlin and Golden Plover begin to move out, flocking in their thousands to the estuaries and the shore. In September, sad thought, the Greenshanks that wakened the wildernesses of Sutherland in June are probably puddling around on the filter-beds of some L.C.C. sewage-farm. The lochan where the Red-throated Divers roused the echoes with their crazy love-making is empty: a mirror for the clouds. Most of all, one misses the tinkabell voices of the Common Sandpipers, wagging their tails and flitting along the burns. The show is over, it seems. Nothing for it but to face the prospect of another winter of discontent.

October is the Month of the Roaring. Now after weeks of lying up in the birch coverts, the stag turns moody and restive. Shorn of their last strips of velvet, his antlers are full-branched again, the tines bone-white and hard. From time to time as he browses on the slopes, he raises his head and stands at gaze, staring into the distance in a lost sort of way, as if trying to take his bearings, then stretches his neck and utters a belly-raking roar. The sound rumbles sullenly through the emptiness of the glen: a gruff, leonine utterance that is in keeping with the beast's lordly appearance; and yet, despite the halo-effect with which Scott and Landseer and the whisky advertisements have surrounded it, the red deer strikes me as being a singularly unromantic creature, not half so attractive, nor so mettlesome as the spring-heeled roe. Let those who will, then, study the love-life of the muckle great stag and his harem: for me, the Roaring marks the end of an off-season as surely as the first snow on the high tops marks the onset of winter. Now, when the Fieldfares and Redwings in their droves crowd the scarlet rowans one can take to the hills again with fresh heart, untroubled by the midges that all too often make summer days in the Highlands intolerable, free of the haze that clouds out the distant ranges.

Too often, unfortunately, the winter hills have little to show in the way of birds. Once the heather has faded, the Twites disappear and there is a steady thinning out of the multitudes of Meadow Pipits, Larks and Linnets. Small passerines being in short supply, many of the predators are hard put to find a living. The Merlin, nippiest of all bird-hunters, goes south about the same time as the Swallow, while the Peregrine, true to its name, takes to a wandering life. But no matter how bleak the outlook, or how bare the hillside, there is one predator which can always be counted on: the Short-eared Owl. Biscuit-coloured, it wafts on its roundabout course, as uncertain as a will o' the wisp, tilting aside here to peer into rushes, lost in view for a moment behind a hummock, appearing again in the place where it was first seen, and all the while fairly lolling on the air as if it intended to keep on going indefinitely. For patience and concentration, for meticulous care and attention to detail the Short-eared Owl has few equals. No other predator makes hard work look so effortless. Intent on its search, it often crosses the path of the lonely hill-walker, its yellow eyes turned upon him inquiringly as it wafts by. Often, too, it is pestered by the Hooded Crows which take a plaguy delight in mobbing it. When that happens, the Owl may be forced down, facing the spoil-sports with squinteyed fury; or, if it chooses to, it mocks its tormentors by soaring far above them.

South of the Border the Short-eared Owl nests regularly in parts of East Anglia, the Pennines and the Cheviot countryside, otherwise it is known chiefly as a winter visitor. In Scotland, despite the *Handbook's* statement that it breeds "locally and sparingly", it now seems to be the commonest of all the owls, no matter what the season. In the absence of any sort of nation-wide census, it may be thought that such an opinion needs to be treated with reserve, but when one considers the nature of the terrain there are good grounds for believing it to be correct. Quite apart from the periodical increase in the vole population—and in some areas the increase in recent years has been phenomenal—the planting of many hundreds of square miles with conifers has created conditions which are ideal for the Short-eared Owl. Whether or not the species will find things quite as much to its liking in years to come when the plantations have grown to maturity, is an open question.

But, then, an ornithologist is the sort of person who is constantly left guessing. The problems with which he is presented have a way of remaining unsolved because it is only rarely that he is in possession of all the relevant facts. Indeed, there are occasions when he is given the chance of observing his birds at close quarters and still finds himself at a loss to understand what is happening. If the following account reads like a mystery story, therefore, let it be said at the outset that it is up to the reader to provide his own solution, since his guess is likely to be as good as the author's.

As early as February, it was clear that 1956 was going to be a Short-eared Owl year in the Southern Highlands. Flapping and gliding, they hunted low over the heather, meandering this way and that in their tipsy-like inconsequential way as they inspected every square yard of the ground. Here and there they poised and plunged head-first into the grass. Sprawled in a heap, they waited a moment or two before lifting into the air and carrying on as before. Often there would be as many as six or seven together in view at the same time; and on one occasion, crossing over the Campsies from Lennoxtown to Fintry, I counted no fewer than twenty-three in a single morning. The reason for all this activity was plain to see, of course, for everywhere the ground was riddled with vole-runs, tiny brown forms scurrying across one's path at every third step. If these movements were visible to the human eye, how much easier it must have been for the eyes of an Owl to pinpoint them.

Easy living makes for prolific breeding, and throughout April and May these Owls indulged in the most ecstatic of courtship flights. On calm evenings they beat solemnly over their territories in mazy slow-motion, almost as if they were intent on marking time in mid-air. This courtship-flight has been described often enough, to be sure, but for the sake of accuracy it is worth pointing out that the performance follows a regular sequence, a set pattern which allows of little or no variation. From a height of two hundred feet or so (considerably higher at times), the bird first utters a series of low barks, *Uh uh uh uh uh.* Next, with wings outstretched and motionless, it sails forward like a soaring Buzzard. Then, with a sudden, convulsive moment, it wrings its wings and claps them together seven or eight times with the utmost rapidity, the tips meeting beneath its tail. In doing so, the Owl falls several feet, after which it resumes its normal slow-flapping flight.

Anyone seeing this aerial stunting can be assured that there is a nest not very far away. Long before the end of March, then, I had a rough idea of the location of at least half a dozen nests. Ascertaining their precise whereabouts, unfortunately, proved to be a much more difficult business—and in the event my original good intentions were sidetracked by a pair of Merlins and a pair of Hen Harriers which occupied the same ground. As a result, honesty compels me to say that I have never yet found a Short-eared Owl's nest with eggs, and the chances are that I never shall unless I stumble upon one by accident. Once the chicks are hatched, of course, it is a relatively simple matter to track down the nest: the constant to-and-fro-ing of the parent Owls provide the necessary clues.

Eventually I was shown a nest by Dugald, the keeper. According to him it contained nine eggs, rather a big clutch but in vole-plague years as many as thirteen or fourteen have been recorded. The situation was a little unusual: a heathery clearing deep inside a spruce plantation. As usual, there *was* no nest, not so much as a scrape even: just a space between two tussocks screened over by a spray of heather. The date was May 25th.

The sitting bird waited until we were ten yards away and then flew off without a sound. Dugald, who had not visited the nest for over a week, was surprised to find that all nine owlets had hatched out in the meantime. All shapes and sizes, they ranged from one lusty youngster which was already sprouting feathers to a tiny mite scarcely two inches long. Huddled together, they lay on their sides, their orange-yellow eyes glaring up at us from their black faces. When approached they whickered angrily, huffing themselves up and sneezing defiance; and on being handled they made curious little cracking noises in their throats.

The day being windless and warm, there seemed to be no harm in putting up a hide on the spot. To erect it was the work of a few minutes. With Dugald as my "going-away man" I crouched inside, confident that the old bird would soon return.

No such luck. Once, twice, she flew overhead and barked peremptorily—*kwowk!*—but without venturing to alight. Give her time, I told myself: the roof and sides of the hide were well covered with heather—before long she would come to accept it as part of the scenery.

Left to themselves the owlets shuffled into a pile and fell asleep in the shade. Occasionally one of the bigger ones would raise its head and whicker softly, rather like someone suffering from an acute attack of hiccoughs. Otherwise, as far as I could see, there were no signs of any activity.

After an hour and a half of this I began to feel vaguely uneasy, and when the smallest chick of all started to hitch forward into the open sun, using the stumps of its wings for leverage, I decided to call it a day. Quite clearly the old bird was not going to stand for this wretched hide of mine; and, anyway, it was not fair to keep her away any longer. Better to acknowledge that I had taken too much for granted. Better to remove the offending object altogether, I decided.

Before leaving, however, I picked up the little one, which was now in danger of falling into a ditch, and placed it back on the pile. It was only then that I noticed that the nine owlets had somehow or other reduced themselves to six. The discovery left me gaping. But this was impossible! After all, I had been watching them at a distance of only a few feet, never once taking my eyes off them for the best part of two hours. Still, there it was: instead of nine there were now only six.

A hasty search of the ground near the nest revealed no trace of the missing ones. No doubt, there *were* hiding places where they might conceivably have concealed themselves, but if so I could not find any: besides, the heather was so thin that this hardly seemed possible. In any case, if they had wandered off by some back exit without my seeing them surely I would have heard them moving? The only alternative explanation—cannibalism—seemed to be as unlikely as it was unpleasant. How could any owlet swallow one of its lesser brethren without causing an upheaval in the nest?

The whole thing was puzzling, not to say, perturbing. Whatever the explanation, there was no doubt that human interference was at the bottom of it, which left me feeling not a little guilty.

Next morning I visited the nest again. As before, the old bird waited until I was almost upon her before leaving, only this time she behaved as if she were quite distracted. Squawking hoarsely, she perched on the topmost point of a spruce sapling, her wings all a-quiver, her face set in a ring of white feathers.

Sure enough, there were now only five owlets!

Not daring to stay a moment longer, I made off as fast as I could. That same evening, however, curiosity got the better of me and I returned to take a second look. At this time of day, I argued, both parents would be away hunting. My worst fears were confirmed when I saw that yet another owlet had disappeared. Knowing that young Short-eared Owls are incorrigible wanderers, I now carried out the most thorough search, parting the grass clumps and poking into the heather, going over the ground in circles again and again. All to no purpose. If the lost ones had been moles they could not have disappeared more effectively. In the circumstances, it was difficult to believe that they were somewhere around in hiding. In any case why should half of them wander off like this, one after another, while the others, snug in the nest, showed no inclination to do so?

If it had not been for my experience in the hide, I might have jumped to the conclusion that the old bird had secretly removed her offspring one by one, as Woodcocks sometimes do when their nest is discovered. As it was, it began to look as though cannibalism offered the only plausible explanation.

For the next two days I left the nest severely alone, content to watch any comings and goings from a distance. Until the early evening there was nothing doing: then, about seven o'clock, one of the parents (the male, I fancy), appeared from nowhere carrying the usual vole.

In some trepidation, I visited the nest on May 29th only to

find that things had gone from bad to worse during my absence: of the original brood of nine there now remained only a single owlet. Gnome-like of visage, this little wretch spread its wings and lay back ready to defend itself to the death when I stood over it. Could it be that this handful of fluff and feathers was the villain of the peace, I wondered? For all its show of hostility, it was inconceivable that this puny creature could have harmed its weaker nestlings let alone eaten them alive. Inconceivable— why, this sole survivor was no bigger and no heavier than the two big owlets which Dugald had held in his hand for me to photograph only a few days before.

Within the week the nest was completely deserted. Since the last of the nine could hardly be accused of having eaten itself, there was nothing for it but to conclude that all the fledglings had scattered after all. But remembering those hours in the hide when three of them had vanished under my very nose, I found it difficult to believe that this was, in fact, what had happened. Normally the tendency to wander off manifests itself only after brooding has ended, that is, when the fledglings are about a fortnight old: whereas in this case the ones which were the first to disappear were not the big fellows, nor the tiny-tots, but medium-sized owlets still in the downy stage.

Whatever the true explanation was I can only say that it escaped me. If this account reads like the nursery rhyme of the Ten Little Nigger Boys, my excuse must be that at the time I felt as helpless and as baffled as a stooge in the presence of a master-illusionist. Obviously there was a catch in it *somewhere*, but just where I was never able to decide. Not for the first time, it was borne in on me that Owls are cryptic creatures, not to say queer. Very queer.

GAME BIRDS

BLACK GROUSE
PTARMIGAN
CAPERCAILLIE

IX.   A Tournament of Blackcocks

BLACK GROUSE

FOR MILES THE road wanders up and down through the forest, climbing the sides of heathery knolls, dipping into birch dells where the roe deer lie up in the daytime, losing itself in the gloom of plantations where the Owls hoot at noon, getting stonier and stonier the farther it goes. A quiet, secret road, the sort that leads from Nowhere to the Back of Beyond. At the far end, where the last gate is left behind, the fir trees thin out, giving way to open moorland: and here, right at the roadside, is a patch of rushes and bleached grass where the Black Grouse come to hold their strange rites. From early in February until midsummer they assemble at this out of the way spot in the early morning and again in the late afternoon, regular as clockwork. A full session will see thirty or more of them crowded into an arena less then twenty yards in diameter and when passions are aroused it goes without saying that the fun is fast and furious. During the day the display ground, or lek, is deserted, but one has only to look at the loose feathers left lying around and the way the grass has been trodden flat by the constant stamping of the birds' feet to picture the scene when the excitement is at its height.

To imagine what happens at these gatherings, however—or even to be distant spectator—is no substitute for being actually in the thick of things. To gain any appreciation of the finer points of the game—for a game it undoubtedly is—one needs to be in the position of a combatant oneself. In the ordinary way the bird-watcher has no occasion to use a hide, but in a case like this there is something to be said for following the example of the bird-photographer. As it happened a tumbledown drystone dyke skirted the very edge of the lek, so close that the Blackcocks frequently perched on it when they were not engaged in fighting, and to knock in a few poles and slip on a loose-cover of canvas was the work of a few moments. Promptly at five o'clock on the sunniest-ever afternoon of mid-April I ensconced myself inside.

Prompty at five-thirty, the first party of five Blackcocks flew in, uttering a peculiar sneezy note—*tsheeari!*—and at once, without any standing on ceremony, they began running and chasing each other all over the place.

The sound of this preliminary fracas quickly summoned the others which had gathered together on the moorside a quarter of a mile or so away, waiting for the signal to begin. They arrived with an almighty rush, splaying their lyre-tails and erecting their white coverts the moment they touched down, and immediately began to strut this way and that in the most extravagant of attitudes, stiff and proud as peacocks. Thirty feet from the hide, two fiercesome cocks faced each other in hot blood, squaring for action like wrestlers looking for a catch-as-catch-can hold: and in a flash they were at it hammer and tongs, bills jabbing, wings drumming as they met breast to breast, until one fell back and scuttled off with its tail down. At this the other sprinted after it, worrying it from behind; while several of the bystanders left off parading to join in the pursuit of the routed bird, eager to get in a peck or two on their own account. The victorious cock came bustling back, all importance, only to be challenged in turn by another champion—a veritable Lord High Executioner of a Blackcock—which came charging through the lists hell-bent on a quick knock-out. Once again the pair manœuvred, face to face, one looking sideways to the right, the other sideways to the left— rather like duellists taking their guard, I thought. With their wattles inflated and sticking up in fiery points, they crouched, glowering at one another—as irascible as colonels suffering from high blood-pressure. They shook their heads in annoyance, crowing defiance. *KorkerÁRR! KorkerÁRR!* But this time, though spoiling for a fight, the rivals thought better of it; at least one of them did for at the critical moment it turned away, proferring its white vent with a touch-me-if-you-dare expression. Instead of seizing the opportunity to attack it from behind, its opponent also turned away, whereupon the first bird plucked up courage again and it was the other's turn to yield ground. And

Blackcock
displaying

Ready for the fray

"Squaring for action
like wrestlers looking
for a catch-as-catch-
can hold"

so it went on, first one then the other acting the part of aggressor without either of them venturing to strike the first blow. Among Blackcocks, apparently, the art of keeping one's nerve (*and* one's tail), up is essential if one is to preserve one's dignity, to say nothing of one's social status! "Be bold, be bold, but not too bold", seems to be their motto. Observe the proprieties. Beware of being over-impulsive. The longer I watched the more inclined I was to think that for all their going through the motions of threat-displays, the birds were really taking part in what could best be described as a ceremonial dance. All over the lek they were arranged in partners, each performing a *pas de deux*. So long as the pairs did not put a foot wrong honour was satisfied: it was only when one or other of the partners overstepped the mark that tempers got out of hand and the feathers flew. One cock stood on a hummock, dozing in the sun and taking no part in the proceedings. Another kept strutting all over the place as if it owned it, butting in on the dancers and causing all kinds of mix-ups.

This initial burst of activity was short-lived. While it lasted, the free-for-all was so confusing that it was difficult to make head or tail of it. After a few minutes, however, all the birds relapsed into a state of comparative calm, indifferent to the near-presence of neighbours with whom, only a moment before, they had been eager to pick a quarrel. The swollen, huffed-up appearance and the grotesque postures gave way to more normal attitudes. Most of them stood at gaze, as if waiting for the next fit to begin. Suddenly they all flew up with a roar of wings—one of those curious, inexplicable "dreads" which occur periodically on bird-communities. Maybe it was a stoat in the grass that had caused it, or the Harrier there beating low across the moor or the yodelling of the Redshanks. There was no telling.

Away they whirled over the rise and out of sight except for one bird which alighted on the skyline and stood there looking back at the vacant lek.

Nothing happened for a whole hour. Getting on for seven now and across the glen the long blue shadows were beginning to feel their way up the mountainsides. Shrews twittered in the grass. Pipits fluttered up from the wall beside me spilling their songs in the bright air. Over on the right a pair of Red

Grouse were enjoying a dust bath, the cock grovelling in a scrape of gravel on one side of a rock, the hen on the other. Evidently they came here regularly, for the scrapes were well worn: and a charming sight they made, lying there side by side, scrabbling away with their feet, fluffing out their feathers and wriggling their bodies to make themselves comfortable. How different, this married state, from the chancy mating of the Black Grouse! Once, twice, the cock looked up to keep an eye on the Short-eared Owl as it wafted uncertainly overhead. White-faced and staring, the owl lifted aside, alternately flapping and gliding, and headed straight for the hide, its yellow cat-eyes darting an inquiring look at the tell-tale peep-hole as it sailed past.

All this time the solitary Blackcock in view had not moved. Now from somewhere over the rise there sounded the sneezy challenge note. *Tsheeari!* The sentinel repeated it, at the same time giving a little jump and hitching its wings. Without further warning the whole company returned in a body, tumbling down on to the ground in front of me and at once beginning their posterings all over again with renewed vigour. As before, the excitement reached its climax in the first few moments, with birds sneezing, crowing and "rookooing" for all they were worth. Before long the centre of the arena had become a battlefield. Two cocks in particular had a rare dust-up buffeting each other so furiously that not only did they lose several body feathers but also two or three primaries (one of which I picked up afterwards, snapped off half way up the quill). The speed with which they chased one another—always with their tails fully spread and their necks outstretched, of course—was quite astonishing, but not half so astonishing as the determination with which they pressed the contest to a conclusion. Until now I had been more than half convinced that the whole business was rather perfunctory, or at any rate not to be taken very seriously—a sort of glorified shadow-boxing, full of sound and fury, perhaps, but for the most part signifying nothing. But from a ringside seat there was no mistaking the deadly seriousness of a full-blooded contest when it *did* occur. It was noticeable that these cocks made no attempt to use their feet when fighting. Instead, they tried to seize their opponents by the scruff of the head, jabbing away with their bills and drumming their wings as they clashed. Since it was impossible to watch all the birds at the same time, being surrounded on all sides by threat-displays of one sort or another, it was hard to say just what was the occasion of an outbreak of hostilities. As often as not one of the contenders held back and the affair petered out inconclusively. It seemed that for all their "looking big" and the officiousness of their showing-off, these displays were sustained by a kind of Dutch courage. Occasionally, however, the sparrings (interspersed with angry *KokerARRs* on both sides) would lead to a real set-to; and in the breach of the peace which followed several birds would come charging in from the side lines to join in the fray. More than once I saw a bull-necked cock come running at the double to settle the issue between two evenly matched fighters, almost as if it had been waiting off-stage for the opportunity. Bowled over by a flank attack, the unfortunate victim had no option but to turn tail and run for it, with three or four birds prodding and pecking its hindquarters. About half the birds on the lek, I noticed, had had the tips of their white tail coverts snipped out in this way.

Once again there came a lull in the proceedings. Tails began to droop, sure sign that they were losing interest. One left off parading to preen. Another dozed. Something was worrying them, it seemed, for now the low anxiety-note was sounded on all sides—*uk uk . . . uk uk uk . . .* and away they went again. But this time, instead of waiting at a distance before flighting back, they all returned post-haste on foot, striding along with their heads down between the tussocks, fairly tumbling over themselves in their eagerness to re-enter the lists. The queer thing was that once they were away from the lek any aggressive impulse was repressed. Maybe an odd bird would strike an attitude on another part of the moor but when it did it seemed to leave the others quite cold. It was only here, on this charmed plot of ground, that the Blackcocks could summon up the enthusiasms and the passions which decided their arguments.

This communal display of the Blackcocks has been written up and filmed so many times that there may seem to be little point in trying to add anything to the accounts which have already been given, still less in pretending that the significance of the ritual has been misunderstood. Nevertheless, though there is an undeniable likeness in the various accounts, each of them differs from the others not only in detail but also in certain essentials. In view of this it may be as well to break down the whole into its parts, so to speak, before venturing to put forward a new interpretation.

There are three distinct "figures" or, rather, "steps", each having its appropriate vocal accompaniment. To begin with there is the "Crow and Jump". Almost invariably this is the opening gambit, the spark which touches off the internal explosion. With head erect and wings held loose, the cock leaps vertically in the air, brandishing its flight feathers and uttering a strained, Partridge-like crow: *tsheeari*. This action gains in intensity the more often it is repeated. The jumps become higher, the wings beat the air more frantically. By way of variation, the crowing may be accompanied by a genuflection instead of a jump. The head-erect attitude is the same, that is, but the neck is jerked violently downwards. Either way, the bird behaves as if it were a clockwork mechanism which never fails to produce the appropriate noise and gesture once it is well and truly wound up. Indeed, the resemblance to a piece of clockwork is strengthened by the fact that before beginning the bird wrings its head almost as if it *were* winding itself up. The "Crow and Jump" seems to serve both as a challenge and as an invitation to fellow cocks to come to the lek. At least the sneezy note is always the first sound uttered by incoming birds, and whenever the lek is temporarily deserted it is the call-sign which heralds their return.

Once the protagonists are assembled, it is only a matter of seconds before they assume the special display-posture which is *de rigueur* at the lek. In this, the Blackcock's curly tail feathers are loosened and spread open on both sides of the body and the under tail coverts fluffed up to form a silky white rosette. The wings are drooped, exposing two circular spots of white at the shoulders. At the same time the scarlet wattles are distended and the neck swells to twice its usual thickness. A goatee beard protruding beneath the chin indicates that the bird is dressed for action. The general effect is certainly imposing, not to say intimidating: if the Blackcock were to turn itself inside out it could hardly look more fantastical or more overbearing than it does. In a moment, its appearance is entirely transformed, so that when the mood passes and it returns to normal, the bird has a curiously deflated appearance. Now and then a non-displaying bird will put in an appearance, but though the presence of these spectators is tolerated it is invariably ignored. On one occasion I tried the experiment of placing a stuffed Blackcock *and* a Greyhen in the middle of the tourney-ground only to find that they received no attention whatsoever.

According to some observers, each Blackcock has its own station on the lek and holds it against all-comers, in the same way as other birds occupy and defend a "territory". This is only partly true. Admittedly, the cocks spend most of their time standing still in the same position, so that after watching them for several days one is able to distinguish one individual from another. This bald-headed fellow, for example, always takes his stand within a foot or two of the quartzite stone yonder, while his neighbour (the one who is chiefly responsible for his ragged appearance) mounts guard among the rushes there to the left. To the right, in a slight dip in the ground, there is a group of ten, each of which clearly knows its place and keeps to it. Indeed, many of the scuffles which arise are the result of incoming birds overshooting the mark when they alight—a common enough error on windy days. Any Blackcock which touches down in the wrong places commits a serious offence and has to face the music on the spot or else run for it. This probably explains their frantic haste to get back "home" after their periodical sorties, and the wild scrambles which take place before they sort themselves out. Yet when things begin to happen there is plenty of movement and the positions on the field are very soon changed. Not only that, but as the season draws on it will be found that the composition of the groups is no longer the same and that many of the birds have shifted their ground. About the middle of May the attendance begins to fall off, leaving the die-hards to fight it out among themselves. Whether this is because the absentees have lost interest or because they have been eliminated in the earlier rounds of the competition is anybody's guess, but the result is a noticeable rearrangement of the pieces on the board.

And now for the second move in the game. *En grande tenue*

the Blackcock cranes forward, and with neck inflated and bill pointing at the ground, begins his well-known bubbling. Heard in the distance, it sounds exactly the croodling of a domestic pigeon. At close quarters it becomes a rhythmical phrase with a rising and falling intonation which is distinctly musical: "A stoop of sherry for Charrlie, a stoop of sherry for Charrlie, a stoop...." That, so far as an inarticulate burbling can be rendered phonetically, is the way it goes. So long as it continues—and when the bird is well and truly "wound up" it may last for over a minute—the body is tense and tremulous with effort, the tail feathers all ashiver with ecstasy. At each inflation of the syrinx the feathers on the sides of the neck are parted, exposing the naked flesh. This bubbling, surely, is the Blackcock's song. It is a mistake, I feel sure, to regard it as primarily aggressive in intent. For one thing, it does not seem to be addressed to rivals, and for another the effusion has all the appearance of being self-stimulating and self-gratifying. No doubt at the same time it serves both as an advertisement and as an invitation to any Grey-hen within earshot. Certainly when three of four cocks are bubbling together the whole moorside trobs with its rhythm, a rhythm which, even to the ears of a human being, is as stirring as any drum-beat.

The third note, an angry *Korker ÀRR!*, is reserved for the war-dance proper, a sort of battle-cry. It heralds the outbreak of hostilities and is to be heard wherever and whenever two or more birds engage in fisticuffs.

After eight now and the light fading. The nearer hills had bloomed over and the distant ranges were shading off into the haze of evening. Back in the plantations a late thrush was singing. After the bustle and commotion of the last three hours it was almost a relief simply to sit back and appreciate the beauty of a Blackcock in all his glory. At any time he cuts a fine figure of a bird. The blue lustres of the neck and back, set off with a brilliant red comb above the eye, not to mention the curious cut of the tail, are extremely handsome in themselves, and when he decks himself out in his full finery, he certainly makes the most of himself.

So far not a single Greyhen had put in an appearance. Rather surprising, this, in view of the fact that it was generally agreed

Three moves in the Blackcock's display

(1) The opening gambit

(2) Neck inflated, the bird cranes forward and begins to croon

(3) The battle-cry heralds the outbreak of hostilities

that mating took place at the lek. Another time, perhaps. . . .
It was almost dark as I came away, and a thin slip of a moon was
coming up behind the shoulders of Ben Lomond. Sure enough,
on my way home through the forest I passed several Greyhens.
In ones and twos they were out taking a stroll in the twilight,
picking up seeds and grit from the roadside. Sturdy and sober-
looking they were, I must say, these grass-widows. Maybe it was
only a passing fancy, but from the way they carried themelves
it was plain to see that they were perfectly capable of raising a
family without the assistance of those good-for-nothing consorts
of theirs. For the time being, at any rate, the goings-on at the lek
were no concern of theirs. One of them stood to attention, tossed
its head, and flew back into the trees, muttering softly to itself as
it flew.

Blackcocks indeed!

Subsequently I visited this same lek on a number of occasions,
but never once did any Greyhen deign to grace the proceedings
with her presence. Yet the local shepherd assured me that Greyhens were always present at the early morning performance.
Could it be that, thanks to being a bit of a slug-abed I had missed
seeing the "real thing" through not watching at dawn? Unfortunately, the lek was thirty miles away from my home and to
one who had never distinguished himself as an early riser the
prospect of driving such a distance, most of it over stony hill
tracks, was less than alluring. In any case, if these late afternoon
gatherings were exclusively confined to the male sex—and there
was no doubt that this was the case—it hardly seemed credible
that no one had remarked on it before. During the daytime it was
not uncommon to see odd Blackcocks and Greyhens keeping
company together as if they were, in fact, paired. Away from the
lek, too, I occasionally came across a single Blackcock showing off
in front of his lady-love, or dutifully following her as she went
about her business in the plantations. But as the evening drew
near segregation between the sexes became the general rule.
Far from showing the least interest in the activities at the lek,
all the Greyhens in the vicinity remained in retirement. Within
a yard or two I could say where several of them had their hide-
outs, the places where the eggs would eventually be laid; and I
knew that I could rely on finding them there in the evening just

as surely as I could count on the Blackcocks mustering on the lek at the same time.

It was all very puzzling. Maybe the discovery was only a very minor one, but the discrepancy between what I had been led to expect and what I had actually found left me wondering whether some of the long-accepted theories about this communal display could be trusted. For that matter, could the evidence of my own eyes be trusted? In order to leave no room for doubt, I visited the lek again and again, hiding away like Diogenes in his tub, all through May and well into June. Still the stately cavortings continued, interspersed with the usual cock-pit tussles, though by this time many of the contestants were distinctly the worse for wear and others were beginning their summer moult. After the end of May the attendance was not so good, yet the behaviour of those which did turn up was as boisterous and pugnacious as ever. All to no avail. Too late, now, of course, to look for Greyhens: by now they were all tucked away in their nests in the undergrowth.

The statement that black-game are polygamous has been made so frequently and so confidently that one hesitates to question it, particularly as it has the backing of no less an authority than the *Handbook of British Birds*. For all that, the evidence for it is somewhat inconclusive. Short of colour-ringing a number of birds, it is hard to see how it can be proved that one Blackcock regularly mates with several Greyhens, or *vice versa*. When there are so many birds bustling about and mix-ups are the order of the day, it is next to impossible to keep track of individuals for any length of time, so how can anyone be sure that polygamy, rather than promiscuity, is the rule? Since the females are in the habit of cutting the afternoon performance, is it safe to interpret the antics of the males on the display ground solely in the light of the sexual-selection theory? It may be that we need to think again.

From what I saw, then, I concluded that this nightly tournament of Blackcocks served no obvious purpose in bringing the sexes together. If anything, the motives which inspired it seemed to be social rather than sexual. Rightly or wrongly, I was reminded more than once of the ritual dances and initiation ceremonies of primitive tribes, and from that point of view, if from no other, the solemnities were not entirely meaningless.

When all is said and done, "lekking" and "laiking" (that good old Lancashire word) both derived from the same root. Doubtless the shared excitement which is generated at these gatherings helps to bring the birds into breeding condition and to keep them fighting fit. The lek, too, is the one place where the youngster who has yet to achieve adult status can win his spurs. Apart from this, however, the lekking habit affords a striking example of the strong hold which routine exerts on non-rational behaviour. The attitudes which are struck—the dumb-shows and the nervous tics—are repeated long after their original stimulus has ceased to be compelling, with the result that in the end the display becomes formalised, almost a sportive occasion, in the sense that it is indulged in for its own sake. Certainly if the birds' efforts are meant to impress the opposite sex, as the books say, there is nothing for it but to confess that

> "What they fought each other for
> I could not well make out".

X.   Upon a Peak in Mamlorne

PTARMIGAN

THE THIRD AND last pitch of the gully was a brute, its walls gleaming with blue-black ice. Immediately overhead the chock-stone bulged out, jagged with icicles as thick as a man's arm. Before tackling it we decided to dig in and take a breather.

After climbing for an hour or more we now found ourselves unexpectedly in the strong white light of the sun, looking across layer after layer of filmy cloud to the distant summits as, one by one, they thrust their heads clear, Stob Gabhar, Clachlet and Buachaille Etive Mhor (with Bidean and its satellites behind), and away to the west the cone of Cruachan "sharp as a pen". Detached from their bases, the mountains looked like islands in a frozen sea. Somewhere below was the Moor, the one and only Moor of Rannoch, but there was no sign of it now, only the mist-wraiths curling up from the mouth of the chimney through which we had just emerged. How odd to think that down there the day was still overcast whilst here, a mere two thousand five hundred feet higher brightness was all, the radiant brightness of sun on snow. Jack, surely, must have felt like this when he reached the top of his beanstalk and stepped off into the landscapes of Fairyland.

We were alone in a lifeless world. Vaughan's World of Light. The silence was sacramental. Neither of us spoke. Now and then tufts of snow would topple from the overhang, whispering to themselves as they rolled down the chute of the gully, faster, faster and faster, to burst upon the air at last in a smother of spray. It was a perfect spot in which to smoke a pipe of peace, windless and warm, one of those rare moments when everyday thoughts and feelings take on an aspect of otherworldliness.

As we rested, letting our minds go blank, feeling the ache in our finger tips turn to a fiery, comforting glow, there was a movement on one of the ledges below and the head and shoulders of a white bird appeared, then another. Ptarmigan! It was as if the snow had suddenly crystallised out and transmuted itself into living form. At first the two birds were much too preoccupied to notice us. With their heads down, they kept plucking at the sprigs of crowberry which grew from the rock face, occasionally turning aside to sample the seed heads of the *Festuca* grass. The air was so still that the regular snip-snip of their bills was audible at twenty yards and as they moved along the ledge they kept brushing the snow aside.

The nearer bird was obviously a cock. His stouter bill and bigger head, not to mention the prominent scarlet wattle, easily identified him. His carriage, too, was the more upright—his gait the jauntier—and as he paced forward the jerking of his tail kept time with the nodding of his head. By contrast, the hen looked much more sedate, a demure little thing who followed in the steps of her lord and master with an air of quiet submission. Once or twice she ambled up the tilted slab to join her partner she missed her footing on the glazed surface and had to use her wings to recover her balance. The cock had left off feeding and was now preening, muttering softly to himself—a low *nup nup nup*, so low as to be nearly inaudible yet somehow expressive of the utmost contentment.

Karr ikrikrrikrrrkrrr . . .

A dry rattle in his throat announced the fact that he had seen us at last. Facing about and upending his tail he repeated his warning. Without waiting, the hen crouched and gave a gutteral *uk uk*—the usual signal for the take-off—and away they whirred, scattering the snow behind them with their quills.

"Ptarmigan," wrote Pennant, "are very silly birds, so tame as to bear driving like poultry," and anyone who has gone hill-walking in the Highlands in summer will agree that the description is not inapt. Like the Dotterel, another bird of the high tops, the Ptarmigan can be very confiding on its breeding ground. Early in April, before the eggs are laid the pairs often appear to be quite oblivious to the presence of human beings, the hen creeping about on the screes quite unconcernedly while the cock, apparently tied to her tail, escorts her and fusses after her with all kinds of gesticulations. But the Ptarmigan in winter is a very different bird, unpredictable in its behaviour, and often quite unapproachable. Though rarely shot nowadays, the coveys tend to break cover at sight unless, of course, there is an Eagle in the offing, in which case it hardly needs saying that they lie very close indeed.

Outside the breeding season the habits of the Scottish Ptarmigan have not been studied in any detail and for reasons that are not far to seek. For one thing, comparatively few bird-watchers have the opportunity and those who have do not always feel inclined to scorn delights and live laborious days on desolate mountains. After all, merely to *see* a Ptarmigan in January or February, to say nothing of watching it for any length of time, is an achievement in itself, calling for energy, determination and a certain readiness to accept disappointments. In most cases it means a longish walk, several miles of soggy going, perhaps, followed by a stiff climb with the prospect of seeing little or nothing for one's trouble at the end of it all. The sheer birdlessness of the Highlands in winter has to be experienced to be believed: a few Red Grouse on the lower slopes—an occasional Hoodie, otherwise the only bird one can rely on seeing once the 2,500 contour has been left behind is the Raven. Once in a while the tinkling voices of Snow Buntings may be heard or a Golden Eagle will wheel out above the skyline, soaring in its pride of place, but it is as well not to count on either. The mountain world is a dead world. The Ptarmigan, to be sure, is the exception to the rule, but whether or not you see Ptarmigan among the snows depends very largely on luck.

Having already said that they are so wary it may seem a contradiction to say that there are times when they creep about in much the same way as they do in summer, with the result that one observer misses them altogether while another, only a hundred yards away, perhaps walks straight on to them. The truth is that they react differently in different conditions. In mist (and as often as not the summits are lost in the clouds) they will allow a fairly close approach. In clear, windy weather they are always much wilder. A good deal depends, too, on their numbers. Where there are only two or three in a party, they may be quite tame, especially after a thaw. The larger the covey, however, the sooner will the alarm rattle be sounded—the curiously suppressed croaking of the cock—and when that happens it is usually only a matter of seconds before they take wing. Like so many white doves, they race off in tight formation close to the ground, fairly nose-diving over the blind side of the crag for fear of being taken by surprise.

It is a mistake to suppose that Ptarmigan invariably pack during the autumn and winter months. In the Cairngorms, no doubt, packing is the rule but in the Western and Southern Highlands it is much commoner to find them in small parties or even in pairs throughout the winter. As with the Red Grouse, which musters by the hundred when the moors are snowbound only to split up into small groups as soon as conditions improve, the Ptarmigan's way of life is largely determined by the weather. Snow conditions, in particular, play an important part; and in this respect it seems that the West coast birds find themselves at a disadvantage compared with those in the East. It is not so much that the semi-permanent snow-beds are disappearing as that the new falls are of uncertain duration and slushy by comparison with the fine, dry snow which comes with an east wind. Of all the factors controlling the existence of this species, one of the most significant, undoubtedly, is the length of the period of *continuous* snow-cover. A glance at the map at once reveals that the areas where snow lies for more than a hundred days in the year are precisely the areas in which most Ptarmigan are to be found. Where the winter is milder the birds are thin on the ground and do not pack, either because they are not forced to by hard weather or simply because there are not sufficient numbers. The difference between East and West is so marked, indeed, that anyone living in Aberdeenshire is likely to form an impression of the birds' habits which hardly agrees at all with that gained by a watcher in Argyll.

In a general sort of way it has always been recognised that the Ptarmigan becomes rarer and somewhat local the farther west one goes in Scotland. What is not generally realised is that the Scottish race is gradually retreating along a line which may be drawn roughly from Ullapool to Callander. East of this line it continues to hold its own. South and west of it, the species appears to be fighting a losing battle in the struggle for existence.

This contraction of the Ptarmigan's range in Scotland is taking place so very slowly as to be almost imperceptible, which explains why it has been overlooked, or at any rate unremarked, hitherto. It cannot usefully be compared with the case of the Corncrake, which has disappeared from many of its haunts in England during the lifetime of many watchers, who still like to think of themselves as middle-aged, nor with that of the Wryneck which for some reason is withdrawing no less rapidly in the opposite direction. On the contrary, it appears that the Ptarmigan has been on the retreat for several centuries, possibly throughout the historical period.

Consider the evidence. If the remains found in the cave of Inchnadamph are anything to go by, the bird was much more numerous than the Red Grouse in prehistoric times, when low-arctic conditions prevailed not only on the high tops but also over the country as a whole. While its actual status must remain conjectural, it seems likely that the Ptarmigan was first driven to find its present niche as a mountain-top species during the period known to the climatologist as the Sub-Boreal, that is, between 3000 and 2500 B.C., when the tree-line in the Central Highlands is believed to have reached as high as 3,000 feet. Thereafter its restricted habitat must have remained fairly constant, for though the tree-line was lowered by as much as 1,000 feet somewhere about 500 B.C., most of the lower ground which might otherwise have been suited to the bird's requirements was at that time being overlaid with its present mantle of peat.

Coming down to more recent times, the evidence is at best so slight as to be inconclusive and at worst so untrustworthy as to be better disregarded, though there are a number of chance references which show that the Ptarmigan was prized as a table bird in places where it is practically unobtainable today. A letter written by King James VI in 1617 to the Earl of Tullibardine, commanding him to provide "capercallies and termigantis" has been widely quoted, but it is not clear whether one of the sentences in it ("The raretie of these foules will . . . make their estimation the more pretious"), is to be interpreted as meaning that these birds were uncommon or simply that they were uncommonly good to eat.

But if the old records are neither here nor there, the modern ones leave no room for doubt. In Galloway, and the Southern Uplands, where it was formerly well established, the Ptarmigan was extinct before 1840. It disappeared from Arran by 1860 and from Rum, despite several attempts at re-introduction, by 1890. In Islay, Jura, Mull and Skye (which topographically and climatically may be treated as parts of the Western Highlands), the birds have survived, but in such small numbers that it is clear that their eventual demise is only a matter of time. Indeed, the position today in these islands is similar to that which the indefatigable Harvie Brown noted in the Outer Hebrides in 1879 when he scoured every hill in Harris and Lewis without finding a single bird. True, Ptarmigan *were* seen there long after this—yet his experience was an indication of the shape of things to come, for by 1938 there were none to be found anywhere in the Long Island.

On the mainland, too, the net has been closing in. From Sutherland to the Arrochar "Alps" there has been a noticeable withdrawal all along the line during the past fifty years. Before the Second World War it was quite easy to see Ptarmigan with chicks on Ben Lomond. There are none there now. I have trudged up and over this popular hill a dozen times without ever seeing more than a singleton—and the same is true of neighbouring three-thousanders which are nothing like so frequented by youth-hostellers and steam-boat trippers. According to one shepherd who has spent the greater part of his life on Ben Vorlich (Dunbartonshire) the handful which linger are the merest remnant: in his boyhood, he is sure, there were five or six times as many.

At one time it was supposed that regular shooting was the surest method of ensuring a healthy stock. Where the coveys were not thinned out, the effects of constant in-breeding made themselves felt sooner or later. Plausible as it may have been as regards the artificial rearing of Pheasants and Partridges, it is clear that the sportsman's theory does not hold good in the case of the Ptarmigan. We need to look elsewhere for the real cause of the decline: and in doing so we may remind ourselves of the old Highland saying that "High and dry appears to be their motto".

That the Ptarmigan, essentially an arctic species, should be adversely affected by the so-called amelioration of climate now affecting the higher latitudes is only to be expected. It is true that the recession of the glaciers in Iceland and Spitzbergen provides a much more spectacular demonstration of the change which has occurred than anything which has been so far observed in Britain, but that is no reason for supposing that *no* corresponding effects have been felt in this country. In fact there is a good deal of evidence to show that during the past fifty years the tendency has been towards milder winters and wetter summers; and so far as the West of Scotland is concerned the meteorologists (who are the last persons to put their trust in hypotheses) are agreed that the records for this same period show an increase of about one degree in the mean annual temperature and an increase of the order of fifteen per cent in rainfall. Whether or not these changes represent anything more than a temporary oscillation, and whether or not it is safe to call them a trend, cannot be said. But if it is true that an increase of three degrees Fahrenheit would be sufficient to raise the heather line to 4,000 feet in a few years, and the tree-line, eventually, to 3,000 feet, it is easy to see that the Ptarmigan's *lebensraum* may be seriously threatened. As it is, the bird is restricted to a narrow moss-lichen zone which does not allow of any adequate safety margin. In the Western and Southern Highlands, where these climatic changes are most pronounced, the mountain's are more peaky than the broad and level plateaus of the Eastern Grampians. Inevitably, this means that there is a tendency for the birds to be confined in isolated "pockets". The actual acreage of suitable ground between the 2,500 and 3,800 contours (which may be taken as the vertical limits), is much smaller on a conical hill, say Stobinian, than it is on such table-tops as Lawers or Braeriach.

In its arctic habitat the Ptarmigan is free to move about from high to low ground as conditions dictate, thus ensuring a change of diet as well as a healthy intermingling of stocks. In Argyllshire, by contrast, the bird appears to have become almost entirely sedentary. Again, according to Salomonsen, the hen is the first to assume the cryptic pepper-and-salt spring plumage in Greenland, while the cock suppresses the moult. In the Western Highlands the reverse is very often the case, which may perhaps be taken as an indication that the life-cycle of these

Ptarmigan, cock (*above*), hen (*below*). Photographed in December. In the southern and western Highlands the assumption of the pure white dress is delayed and ptarmigan in various in-between plumages can be seen as late as January

Ptarmigan is out of step, so to speak, with the conditions now prevailing in this sector of their range.

All things considered, then, we may take it as proved that the Scottish Ptarmigan is steadily decreasing and that many parts of its former range are no longer occupied. It remains to ask why this should be so. This is the kind of question which the thoughtful ornothologist is wont to pose only to admit in the end that he can find no satisfactory clue to the answer, let alone an answer. The case of the Ptarmigan is particularly interesting, however—in some ways unique—in that the decline must be attributed to causes which are entirely natural. Among a number of conceivably inimical factors which can be listed, human inter-ference can for once be ruled out, for there is no bird on the British list which has been left to itself so much as the Ptarmigan. As a sport, Ptarmigan-shooting (like Ptarmigan-watching) seems to be a shade too strenuous for the modern taste. Dis-turbances caused by drilling and blasting in the development of hydro-electric schemes can also be ignored, as can the effects of these schemes once they are in operation, since the bird's habitat is well above the drainage areas concerned. Admittedly, hill-walking is much more popular than it used to be, but there is no point in pretending that this has seriously interfered with the birds on their breeding grounds—Ptarmigan are not unduly sensitive creatures—and, besides, they have vanished from many hills on which human beings scarcely set foot from one year's end to another. If human interference is to blame, how are we to account for the fact that the birds vanished from such remote and inaccessible summits as Corserine and the Merrick over a century ago ? And if we are content to suppose that they have been driven from the Arran range and the Cuillin ridges by well nigh ceaseless processions of climbers what are we to say of Rum which is, to all intents, closed to the public ?

It may be retorted that the decline may nevertheless be due in some way or other *indirectly* to human intervention as, for example, through the increased protection afforded to the Golden Eagle, or the preservation of the Red Grouse or the introduction of large numbers of hill sheep. As to the first of these it need only be said that, other things being equal, Ptarmi-gan are perfectly capable of maintaining their numbers in districts where they are regularly preyed upon by Eagles. Of the other predators, only the Hooded Crow need be taken seriously. No doubt the Fox, the Wild Cat (now much commoner than it was at the turn of the century) and the Peregrine take their toll also, but the percentage destroyed in this way must be relatively insignificant. If anything, one would have thought that the man-made deer forests of the Highlands provided an ideal sanctuary for a species like the Ptarmigan, but it is clear that things have not worked out that way. Can it be that the presence of other competitors which owe their existence in one way or other to man is inimical? On the face of things, of course, the hill sheep look harmless enough, though it is possible that the long-term effect of grazing on the upper slopes is to bring about changes in the plant-life of the moss-lichen zone besides reducing an already precarious food supply. As for the Red Grouse, which are frequently found as high as 2,500 feet, they may act as carriers of disease or—and this seems the likelier conjecture—they may oust the less progressive Ptarmigan from places in which it might otherwise eke out a living of sorts. Co-existence between two closely allied species is never easy, and may be impossible where the two habitats overlap: sooner or later the more successful one begins to crowd out the other.

As yet there are no marked vegetational changes on the high tops—though there *are* signs that the upper slopes are becoming choked with grass—so that on the whole it seems unlikely that the decline is due to any failure in the normal food supply. Typical Ptarmigan ground is easily told: firmly packed stones or scree, an alpine rockery, carpeted with moss (chiefly *Rhacomitrium lanergonisum*), lichens (*Cladonia sp.*), dwarf ferns (*Cystopteris fragilia*), Heath Bedstraw, the Saxifrages, and Crowberry, Bilberry and Cloudberry in the crannies. Because of its rapid run-off this zone is comparatively "dry" and has its own distinctive ecology. Below a certain level, usually between 2,500–2,800 feet above sea-level it ends rather abruptly and is replaced by the various heath grasses and rushes (*Carex rigida et al*), which may give the ground a less naked look but which are certainly not to the liking of the Ptarmigan. So long as the moss-lichen zone is not entirely blotted out by snow the bird can subsist without much difficulty, but when the summit is drifted over it may be that the lower ground to which it then resorts does not provide the kind of food required.

It is more probable, however, that the factors responsible for the changing status of the Scottish Ptarmigan are meteorological rather than ecological—always recognising that the two go together. Whereas changes in vegetation may be slow in making themselves felt, changes in the weather can be cataclysinic in their effect. It cannot go for nothing, for example, that June and July (the period when most Ptarmigan chicks are hatched) used to be regarded as dry months and that since 1881 there has been a gradual and almost continuous rise in the rainfall figures for these months in the West (*but not in the East*) of Scotland.

Another factor which has to be reckoned with is the amount of light, particularly sunlight. It has been shown experimentally that length of daylight not only controls the complicated moults of the Rock Ptarmigan, but that it serves to regulate the sexual rhythm. It is well known, too, that Ptarmigan prefer the sunny side of the hill and that they are most active on bright, clear days. To say the least of it, bright, clear days are in short supply in the Western Highlands! If it is permissible for the archaeologist to attribute the decline of certain primitive cultures to the excessive wetness of Early Iron Age weather it ought not to be entirely out of the question for the ornithologist to argue that persistent low cloud and wet-blanket summers may have a depressive effect on a bird.*

To say that many of the hens are lost in the murk for nearly half the year may sound like an exaggeration: if so, then the exaggeration is pardonable. In this respect the West coast summits are by far the worst offenders. Those which stand only a few miles farther inland are not affected to anything like the same extent. Thus, Ben Buie is a cloud-compeller of the first order and the chances of viewing the panorama from its summit cairn are few and far between compared with those offered by Ben More though the latter, only fourteen miles away to the East,

---

* Such an argument may not carry much weight when it is recalled that in the high arctic where the bird flourishes the breeding season is no less fog-bound. Nevertheless the fact remains that the Scottish Ptarmigan is more numerous in the east where the summits are clearer. There is, besides, a great difference between being fog-bound in snow (which reflects what little light there is) and being fog-bound among wet rocks!

happens to be nearly 800 feet higher. Whether we adopt the jargon of the animal behaviourist and write in terms of light-deficiency and "releasers" which fail to function as they are designed to do, or whether, as observers in the field, we are content to say that the birds appear to be understimulated and leave it at that, the meaning is much the same.

It is possible, too, that the factor which we are trying to pin down may be connected with atmospheric conditions themselves rather than with such things as temperature or rainfall. In this connection it is as well to remind ourselves that the first places to be abandoned were Galloway, Arran, Rum and the Outer Hebrides. Evidently exposure to the Atlantic air-stream has *something* to do with the problem, but it is not enough to state this as if it were somehow self-explanatory, for when all is said and done these places were once capable of supporting a flourishing Ptarmigan population. What has happened that they are no longer capable of doing so? The best answer seems to be that in recent years (recent, that is, in the meteorologist's reckoning) there has been a more vigorous circulation of North Atlantic air and that this has produced a more oceanic type of climate. Naturally, the islands have been the first to bear the brunt of the great depressions. Not only does the West of Scotland lie in the track of the storm-belt and its associated warm fronts, but the lie of the land ensures that the maximum effects of these are felt. The main sea inlets (Solway, Firth of Clyde, Loch Linnhe, etc.) and many of the larger freshwater lochs (Awe, Ness, etc.) are more or less in line with the prevailing South West winds and act as funnels for them.

> "On this side lay the ocean and on that
> Was a great water. . . ."

Tennyson's description applies to many of the mountains in this region. It follows, therefore, that the kind of atmospheric conditions experienced in the islands are to some extent duplicated over large areas of the Highlands. Sea breezes circulate freely on all sides of the hills. Humidity is high. The incidence of severe frost is mitigated. Thaws are more frequent. To pretend that the Ptarmigan dislikes these conditions in much the same way as some people avoid certain West coast resorts because they are "too relaxing", would be to introduce an anthropomorphic note unnecessarily. But if the thorn turns from the sea and the bracken shrivels at the touch of salty air, it is arguable that the Ptarmigan also is adversely affected.

In short, everything points to the conclusion that this species is finding life increasingly difficult in the softer, unsettled climate now prevailing over large areas of the Highlands. Difficult as it is to pin down the precise factor, there cannot be much doubt that climatic changes have something to do with it. "Amelioration" spells deterioration for a species which cannot adapt itself to new conditions. That being so, the prospect facing this, one of Scotland's most distinctive birds, is less than promising; and those of us who love nothing better than to share its company in the corrie and to hear its cautious eructation from the rocks must take comfort in the knowledge that the cosmic forces which decide our weather may yet bring about yet another reversal in its fortunes.

XI. Cock of the Woods

CAPERCAILLIE

WHEN THE WIND is from the north the waters of the loch can be rough enough to make the crossing to Inchconnachan quite an adventure. The little dinghy slops along, bouncing awkwardly in the troughs of the waves and the oarsman is hard put to prevent one blade ploughing too deep while the other rakes the air at a crazy angle. A drake Goosander surfaces almost under the bows and scutters off in alarm. Ahead lies the island, its sandy bay as smooth as glass behind the promontory.

To land on Inchconnachan is to set foot in a private world. Its hollow dells where the fallow deer stray like phantoms are strangely hushed, out of the snatch and pluck of the wind, and yet (like Prospero's) the island is full of sweet noises. Wherever you go the spinning-wheel ditties of Goldcrests are sure to accompany you: tiny shapes, half-seen, they flit among the birches and the scrub oaks. Long-tailed Tits go whispering by and Tree Creepers, zee-zeeing to themselves as they dart from bole to bole. In places the heather is head high and the bracken so matted that you have to fight a way through. There are ferns actually growing from some of the tree trunks and all the lower branches are draped with grey-green moss. Mossy, too, are the hollows where the going suddenly becomes spongy and you sink in up to the knees. Untamed, untrimmed, the place has a primeval air. Here in the centre of the island the birch-oak woods thin out and give way to a grove of tall Scots firs, thrawn, old trees, their roots clutching for a foothold on the bare rock. No need to be told that this is a sanctuary—you sense it as surely as if you were about to enter the porch of some ancient cathedral.

In a moment the secret is out. From the nearest tree a hen Capercaillie breaks cover, slipping out so unobtrusively that she hardly makes as much noise as a Wood Pigeon. *Uk uk!* she calls softly, showing her red-roan tail and the bronze boss on her breast as she bustles across the clearing—followed immediately by a mighty cock which crashes out right overhead. Neck outstretched, away he goes like a ship in full sail, his bowed wings beating hurriedly, then gliding as he cants and swerves among the branches. Then everything happens at once. To left and right, the tree tops fairly explode as three, four, five more hens burst from their hiding places. A silence, followed by the biggest bombshell of all as another huge fellow (surely the patriarch of all cock Capercaillies, this one!) makes a dash for it. *Kek kek!* he cries, not half so loud as a Jackdaw.

Though they are rarely or never disturbed, these island "caper" are extremely wary, so wild, indeed, that unless you are lucky you will get no more than a fleeting glimpse of them in a day's jaunt. On the ground they are invisible until the last moment, and in the trees, despite their size, they are no less hard to find. Their flight, which is deceptively fast, gives the impression of controlled power and follows a near-level trajectory. The take-off is nothing like so noisy as it is often made out to be. Here and there, no doubt, a cock may find himself caged in at the critical moment and be forced to breakout in bull-at-a-gate style—and then what a crackling of twigs and fluster of wings there is—but usually he is well aware of the approach of danger and ready for a clean getaway. As for the hen, her departure is best described as surreptitious.

On second thoughts, to say that Capercaillies are wary is perhaps misleading. Unless they have been disturbed and are already on the alert they wait until the intruder is within a few yards of where they are feeding before flying; and even when they are taken by surprise they go out singly, rarely or never in a body. Maybe it is an over-simplification to say that the rule is one bird, one tree, but in the ordinary way each bird keeps itself very much to itself. Being the most arboreal of all the game-birds, the social life of the Capercaillie is apt to be somewhat tenuous: there is none of the tight formation of a Partridge covey or a pack of Red Grouse. The cock, in particular, is nothing if not an individualist. Indeed, so far as their social behaviour is concerned, it is hardly an exaggeration to say that the difference between the two sexes is no less striking than the differences in their size and appearance.

Like the Greyhen, the hen Capercaillie is something of a sober-sides, discreet and matronly in her ways. The cock, on the other hand, as might be expected of an exhibitionist, can be quite unpredictable at times. Normally secretive and undemon-strative, he sometimes goes out of his way to make himself obstreperous during the breeding season. Just as in English newspapers one reads accounts of Swans holding up the traffic, so in Scotland one occasionally hears of cock Capercaillies breaking up picnic parties or behaving officiously in the presence of human beings. Not all these stories are apocryphal, either. Harvie Brown tells of one redoubtable cock which lay in wait for any woman or girl (apparently the men-folk were immune!) who used a path through a wood in which two hens were brood-ing. Here on Inchconnachan, too, there used to be one old grey-beard who refused to budge from his favourite perch on the lowest branch of a spruce even when two or three people were immediately beneath him. When the spaniels were snuffling around and a walking stick was pointed at him, he still continued to sit. Unmoved, and apparently immovable he would look down, never batting an eyelid—and this in December when the snow was on the ground.

Such indifference to danger, nevertheless, is exceptional. Normally the birds wait until you are almost on them before giving the game away; and when they do, it is hard to say whether you or they are the more surprised. A sudden crashing of sticks, a bulky shape that hurtles off through the half-light of the tree tops and the cock of the woods is gone.

That is the trouble with Capercaillies: you can see them a hundred times and still feel that you are little the wiser. Cer-tainly they know how to look after themselves. Resting or feeding, they keep well under cover and in flight they are as tricky as Woodcock in putting obstacles between themselves and the enemy, so that by the time they are under way and in the open they are out of sight.

Fortunately this colony is entirely sedentary. Occasionally the birds may fly across to one of the neighbouring islands but for the most part they stay put here on Inchconnachan. Any day,

Capercaillie. Cock and hen on the look-out

"Aloof as ever, the cock of the woods keeps vigil"

in any month of the year, you can be sure of finding them at home in the fir woods which crown the rocky head of the island and fringe its shores. There are stands of conifers on the "mainland", less than half a mile away, old trees, too, which look suitable in every way, but you will be lucky if you ever find a Capercaillie among them. More so than any other birds, the Wood Grouse must have peace and quiet. For them the narrow strait which separates Inchconnachan from the rest of the world is the great divide.

It is a hard thing to have to say of Europe's largest game bird, but the truth is that the Capercaillie's way of life is just about the dullest imagineable. He has his favourite trees, one for roosting and one for sitting in during the day, and he sticks to them. Sedate and stolid as a barnyard fowl on its perch, he seems to spend a good deal of his time doing nothing in particular. He is a bit of a hermit, too, for though the hens and the young birds of the year remain together until the end of the year, the cocks seem to prefer to keep themselves apart.

But if his behaviour is unexciting he is a magnificent creature to look at. Once disturbed, he has a habit of standing erect on the top of a Scots fir which, judging by the way its upper branches have been flattened, has been used as a look-out by generations of Capercaillies. The feathers hang loose at his throat like a goat's beard and when the sun catches it, his breast is glossed with a band of peacock-green. The horny hook of his bill and the profile of his head and shoulders are reminiscent of an Eagle rather than a Grouse. In a good light he looks slate-grey, not black, with a conspicuous white spot at the shoulder. Try staring him out and see which of you is the first to tire! With his head askew and his neck thrust out at an inquiring angle he will remain statuesque like this for a whole hour, longer if necessary—the very picture of suspicion.

There are a number of these look-out trees on the island. They can be told at a glance by their peculiar shape—the way the branches are bent over to form platforms and open spaces among the foliage—though whether this is due to the natural tendency of the Scots fir to "round-off" as it nears the century mark, or whether the birds themselves are responsible for it, it cannot be said. Time was when the silivculturist did not hesitate

to accuse the Capercaillie of inflicting serious damage on growing timber. It was said to nip out the terminal buds of the young
saplings, causing them to die off or to become malformed
as a result. Today most foresters consider that any damage
caused in this way is negligible. Unlike the Black Grouse which
may, locally, create havoc among newly-planted seedlings, the
Capercaillie's range of action is limited by the necessity of
keeping within easy reach of old trees. Where new plantations
are accessible he is not above raiding them, and when that happens it is likely that some of the tender shoots of the imported
soft-woods suffer. But his own special tree, the Scots fir, is a
tougher proposition. Even under the weight of the stoutest
cock (which may be as much as twelve pounds) it will bend
double without breaking, and observation shows that the birds do
not usually select the all-important top-most shoot. For one thing
they are not sufficiently agile, preferring a sure foothold where-
ever possible, and for another there are plenty of equally succu-
lent shoots on other parts of the tree. In any case, the proportion
of trees affected must be exceedingly small compared with the
total number: for every stunted, bare-topped fir which has been
trodden down and stripped of its needles there are a hundred or
more which look as if they had never been touched.

Capercaillies are by no means entirely confined to conifers,
of course. At least half of the island is covered with deciduous
trees and from March to November the birds may be found anywhere among them, often on the ground. Though their diet
consists mainly of pine needles, they vary it with such items as
bilberry leaves, moss, birch buds, grasses and even lichen. Occasionally they are to be seen grubbing around the mounds of the
wood-ants, probably looking for the eggs. In summer and
autumn they spend whole days among the heather clearings.
The hens in particular show a marked seasonal variation in their
habits. The cocks, probably because they take no part in the
rearing of the family, are much more conservative: apparently
bed and breakfast up aloft is their motto even in June and July
when the undergrowth is thickest and leafiest.

Though the Capercaillie is once again a common enough
bird in central Scotland its haunts are so difficult to work that its
private life remains very much a closed book. While the fighting-

cock antics of Black Grouse at the lek have frequently been photographed and filmed very few people in this country can claim to have witnessed the full courtship display of the cock Capercaillie or heard his cacophonous song. At most times of the year he is an extraordinarily silent bird, reserved and quite undemonstrative. Even in March, when the Wood Pigeons are building their flimsy nests in the larches and the Woodcock's eggs are laid in the birch glade, he seems slow to shake off his apathy. Only towards the end of the month or early in April does he begin to show signs of awakening interest. Prominent on one of his look-outs, he stands at gaze, waiting, uncertain how to begin. Then, ruffling out his beard like someone clearing his throat before making an after-dinner speech, he mutters to himself *kek-kek-kek* . . . and stops, evidently at a loss as how to go on. Once more he stands at gaze, then tries again. With his wings held loose at his sides and his turkey-tail arched he looks (and doubtless feels) a little surer of himself. *Kik kek, kek kek, trik trak trik trak* . . . and again the unwound clock stops ticking. This time he waits five minutes before he can summon up the necessary enthusiasm. Then he crouches, head up and rigid, tail stiffly fanned, in a curiously trance-like attitude, and at last gets it off his chest: *kik-kek kik-kek* . . . *kikkek kikkek*, a glug, a gobble, a whoosh. The opening statement is deliberate, the rest so run-together and inarticulate as to make any attempt at a phonetical rendering quite impossible. The gobble sounds rather like the sound of water going down a plug-hole at an incredible rate, and the final whoosh resembles nothing so much as the noise of some heavy body, say a polar bear, splashing into a pool.

Possibly because they are left entirely to themselves, these island "caper" are no longer polygamous. If anything, the cocks outnumber the hens, with the result that their courtship performance seems to have lost some of the intensity which is displayed in colonies where competition is fiercer than it is here. Though it cannot be proved, it is at least conceivable that where polygamy is the rule it has been brought about by human intervention. It is perhaps significant that both the Red Grouse and the Ptarmigan, in which the sexes are not readily distinguishable at a distance, are monogamous. The Blackcock and the cock Capercaillie, on the other hand, are instantly singled out by the sportsman: they offer a more tempting target, and in the past it has often been considered the done thing to pick off the males while sparing the females. On Inchconnachan, where there is no shooting, it looks as if the natural ratio between the sexes has been restored.

Restored. The word itself is a reminder of the fact that had it not been for the enterprise of a Norfolk man, the Capercaillie might not have succeeded in re-establishing itself in Scotland, As things turned out, the introduction in 1837 of forty-eight birds from Sweden was so singularly well timed that within the space of half a life time they had multiplied and spread to many parts of their former range. Evidently all that was needed was the opportunity. The niche was there for the taking and they took it gladly. From the original centre on the Taymouth estate they quickly spread outwards, following the river valleys and using the larger woods as stepping stones in their advance. At first the bare hill passes served to block any extension westwards, but it was not long before the birds found their way round these obstacles. Between 1838 and 1878 there was no stopping them. Since then the advance has continued though at a much slower rate and it is clear that the initial impetus had already exhausted itself by the turn of the century. There are still areas south of the industrial belt which might prove to be suitable for colonisation, and with new plantations growing fast (and with the Forestry Commission to protect them) a further increase in the numbers of Capercaillie might seem to be assured. As it is, there are probably as many birds in Perthshire and Stirlingshire as ever there were. Yet a county-by-county comparison of the present position with that given by Harvie Brown in his monograph *The Capercaille in Scotland,* published in 1888, shows that the limits of the advance had already been reached at that time and that not a few of the places occupied have since been abandoned.

Idle as it is to speculate about the causes of the extinction of the species during the eighteenth century, the success-story of the Capercaillie during the middle and later decades of the nineteenth century asks for some sort of explanation. It is generally assumed that the bird did, in fact, become extinct after 1760, though the evidence is by no means conclusive. In the troubled days which followed the '45 there must have been plenty of places where it might conceivably have survived without anyone knowing, or at any rate without anyone troubling to report its existence. Nevertheless all the records agree that by the middle of the eighteenth century it has become extremely rare. Pennant, not the sort of observer to miss much in his travels, only saw one specimen in his tour of Scotland in 1769, a bird which had been shot near Inverness. The interesting thing is that it had apparently been rare for a century or more before this. Much of the historical evidence is as unreliable as it is contradictory, but the Game Laws of the Scottish Parliament would hardly have found it necessary to impose fines of up to £100 for poaching offences had the Capercaillie been at all common. There is, too, a letter written by one Jo. Dickson to the Laird of Glenorchy in 1651 which suggests that the bird was considered to be a notable trophy: "I went and shewed your Capercailzie to the king in his bedchamber who accepted it weal as a raretie for he had never seen any of them before." Even allowing for the fact that the king (the prospective Charles II) was a newcomer to Scotland and no great countryman this speaks for itself.

Though burning, felling and general neglect must have been contributory factors, it seems likely that the gradual wasting away of the old Caledonian Forest (remnants of which still exist in Glen Falloch, Abernethy and Rothiermurches) is best explained as being due to climatic changes. Whatever the cause, it was the loss of thick cover rather than any serious reduction in its food supply which sent the Capercaillie into a decline. There are, even now, many more pines in Glen Falloch than there are on Inchconnachan, which is three parts deciduous, but the trees are too scattered, too exposed for the bird's liking. Reafforestation on any large scale did not begin until it was too late to save the indigenous stock which had been reduced to a few isolated pockets. But the fifty years which elapsed between the time when the original Scottish race is presumed to have died out and the time of the re-introduction from the Continent allowed the late eighteenth century plantations to mature and so provide the kind of environment in which a new race might thrive. The releasing of those forty-eight birds at Taymouth, then, may best be compared with an operation in which the patient's life is saved by a blood transfusion after the heart itself has left off beating. Strictly speaking, no doubt, the Capercaillie's claim to rank as a genuinely British breeding species is no better than the Red-legged Partridge's or the Pheasant. For all that, it is impossible to think of the Wood Grouse as an alien. It belongs to Scotland's avifauna as surely as do the Eagle, the Crested Tit and the Ptarmigan.

Across the loch the snow-speckled ben is hung with low clouds. The wind has abated and a soft rain is setting in as the boat puts out from the bay and heads for the shore where the evening lights are beginning to show along the roadside. Looking back, the mixed woods of Inchconnachan are full of subdued colouring—the vinous pinks and crimsons of the birches, the russet oaks and straw-yellow larches, the black of the pines—and there, crowning the topmost tree of all is the figure of a bird silhouetted against the heavy sky. Somewhere a Robin sings. A pair of Hoodies fly over, calling hoarsely as they make for their roost-wood. The plip-plop of the raindrops increases to a hiss as the downpour begins in earnest. Beside the boat-house stands a Heron, waiting to begin his night's fishing. Away over on the island the figure has not moved. Only the head and neck show. Aloof as ever, the cock of the woods keeps vigil as the darkness closes in.

WILDFOWL AND WADERS

WHOOPER SWAN

GREY GEESE (1)—(BEAN,
WHITE-FRONTED AND
LESSER WHITE-FRONT)

GREY GEESE (2)—(GREY-LAGS
AND PINK-FEET)

BARNACLE GEESE

RED-THROATED AND BLACK-
THROATED DIVERS

RED-NECKED PHALAROPE

XII. Way of the Wild Swans

WHOOPER SWAN

THAT SWANS ADD a touch of dignity to any landscape goes without saying, whether it be the Thames at Hammersmith or the Tweed at Berwick, a brick-pond in the Potteries or the ornamental water of some gracious country house. For all its graces, nevertheless, the familiar Mute Swan looks more at home in a man-made landscape: there is something about it which assigns it to that class of bird aptly styled by Charles Lamb as "tame, villatic fowl". For the field naturalist, at any rate, the Mute Swan lacks the appeal of the wild-born Whooper. Whereas the one conjures up mental images of summer days— the Avon at Festival time, Abbotsbury in spring, municipal parks in August with schoolchildren scattering their bread on the waters: the other calls to mind sterner scenes—grey days in winter when the faraway bugling of these great white birds is the only sound to break the silence of a snowy world.

Though not uncommon, the Whooper is best known in the south of England as an occasional hard-weather visitor. In Scotland, on the other hand, the winter population of Whoopers rivals that of the mutes and in places exceeds it, so that it is no exaggeration to say that for six months in the year these magnificent birds may be reckoned an everyday sight. Here and there, of course, odd pairs remain to breed—and the historical evidence suggests that in Orkney at least they bred regularly until the end of the eighteenth century. Discounting this minute handful of permanent residents and the rather bigger handful of stragglers that can often be seen on our north-western lochs in summer, ninety-nine out of every hundred Whoopers are immigrants. In the Lowlands the main contingent arrives in mid-October and from then until Christmas there is a good deal of local movement before the Swans settle in for the winter. In places—Loch Leven is a notable example—they assemble in mighty heads, as many as two or three hundred at a time, but these gatherings are not altogether typical. More commonly the company will consist of not more than a dozen or a score, and on migration they frequently travel in parties of four or five. Often, while climbing in Western Argyll, I have seen Whoopers making their landfall after the sea-crossing (presumably from Iceland) and almost invariably the flight formation has been made up of a pair of adults with two or three juveniles, the latter easily identified by their putty-coloured bills. Indeed, the more closely one watches them the more obvious it becomes that the family rather than the flock, is the basic unit in the wild Swans' social life; and so strong are the ties which bind the family together that the same four or five birds which travelled south in autumn will usually remain together throughout the winter—and even make the return trip together, too, when the time comes to leave these shores in April. True, on the larger lochs these family parties join forces with others of their kind, but in doing so they are always careful to retain their separate identity; and wherever possible, they seek out some private water where they can keep themselves to themselves.

For the past three years I have watched such a family of Whoopers from a window seat, so to speak, since the little lochan they frequent is virtually on my doorstep. Situated as it is in a residential suburb, surrounded on three sides by houses, this stretch of water is hardly the sort of place where one would normally expect to find wild Swans, and at first the newcomers are understandably nervous. After a day or two, however, they come to accept the situation, possibly deriving a certain amount of confidence from the resident Mutes and the imperturbable Coots. Even so, it only needs someone to show himself on the roadway— or worse still, a dog frisking at the waterside—to start them nodding their heads in alarm and uttering their musical call-notes. Unlike their companions, they are never, under any circumstances, to be tempted to the edge with bribes of food! Unapproachable, aloof, mistrustful, they always keep their distance. Out in the middle or at the end of the lochan which is protected by a wind-break of reeds, they lead a quiet, uneventful existence, up-ending in the shallows to dredge weeds from the bottom, preening themselves and, for want of anything better to do, just dozing and drifting.

Side by side with the semi-domestic Mute the Whooper, to my mind, cuts much the finer figure. A cob Mute in all its glory, with its wings arched like a ship in full sail, looks a shade too conscious of its own importance to be truly impressive, but there is never anything in the least pompous or ridiculous about the Whooper. The erect carriage of its neck, folded back at the base with the upper half held stiffly vertical, gives an impression of effortless strength. The profile of the head, too, though less obviously handsome than the Mute's, is more striking—the solid, black bill inlaid with a wedge of golden-yellow skin: gooselike, perhaps, yet having a kind of raw-boned, barbarous beauty. For the rest, the difference between the two can best be expressed by saying that the Mute Swan sits the water as if it meant to be ornamental, the Whooper as if it meant business.

Until early in the New Year the two species lived together in perfect harmony, neither interfering with the other. Occasionally odd Whoopers would drop in to share the company of the five "regulars" but never for any length of time for it was evident that the family did not welcome the intrusion of strangers, preferring to have the lochan to themselves. Whenever their voices were raised after dark—and how tunable and eloquent they sounded in the frosty starlight!—I guessed that some outsider had turned up to disturb their peace of mind. (Either that, or it was some prowling cat that had made them find their tongues.)

Then, in February, the resident Mutes, sensing the spring in their blood, began to be officious, not to say truculent, towards the inoffensive Whoopers. Inflating himself with righteous indignation (after all, this *was* his territory!) the cob charged up and down, pursuing his mate hour after hour and threatening anyone who got in his way. Undemonstrative as ever, the Whoopers bore all his affronts with quiet patience. Rather than take any chances, however, the parents sailed in line ahead, one of them leading, the other bringing up the rear, ready to fend off any attack on their young ones if it came to a clash—and with territorial disputes coming to a head clashes soon became the order of the day—the Whoopers showed that they were more than capable of defending themselves. The old cob Mute would come surging on, breathing fire and defiance, only to be met, the moment he ventured within reach, by a vicious dig that very soon sent him about his business. Never was an aggressor so quickly or so thoroughly deflated.

How the feud would have ended had the Whoopers chosen to stay is anybody's guess, though personally I have no doubt as to who would have had the better of the argument. Certainly where non-breeders remain behind to spend the summer in Scotland, experience shows that they have no difficulty in overcoming the resentment shown by Mute Swans which share the same water.

As it happened, the issue was decided by a sudden change in the weather. Towards the end of February a two-day frost sealed the lochan with three inches of ice and for nearly a week there was skating in one corner. In the far corner, the five Whoopers worked night and day to keep open a black puddle of open water crowded out with Coots and Tufted Ducks. Unable to take off, the Swans cruised this way and that, their necks jerking anxiously up and down, their voices raised in mournful clamour. Meantime, the Mutes plumed themselves disconsolately on the bankside in front of the houses, ousted from the pool that rightly belonged to them.

After the thaw the Whoopers were strangely unsettled. Facing each other in the manner of courting Grebes, the two oldsters would engage in a high-pitched, quavering conversation. Clearly, the urge to be on the move had begun to assert itself. Clearly, too, the Swans were in two minds whether to go or stay. Their voices proclaimed their uncertainty, now loudly exultant, now muted in softer undertones. Possibly they sensed the approach of another cold spell, for though the first crocuses were already brightening the lochside gardens and the days lengthening, there was still plenty of time for winter to show its hand.

One morning, after a more than usually noisy colloquy, the Whoopers made their decision. In full cry, belling and trumpeting, they taxied over the surface, kicking up a long furrow behind them and took off into a stiff wind. Heading south, they oared their way over the city, ghost-white figures against a darkened sky, their voices lingering in the distance long after the birds themselves had disappeared from sight. That night it froze harder than ever and we had the heaviest snowfall of the winter.

Whooper Swan

"The profile of the head, though less obviously handsome than the Mate's, is more striking—the solid, black bill inlaid with a wedge of golden-yellow skin—goose-like, perhaps, yet having a kind of raw-boned barbarous beauty"

Mallard drake preening

Next morning it happened that I was on the "Flying Scotsman" *en route* for King's Cross: one of those cut-glass winter days when the world seems to be all brightness and sparkle. Just south of Berwick the railway line runs parallel with the shore and close to it. As the express roared on past Holy Island I spotted five Swans flying steadily along the line of breakers. With their long necks straining in front and their wing-beats methodically keeping time, they remained abreast of the train for nearly five minutes before the sand dunes hid them from view, during which time their air-speed cannot have been far short of sixty miles an hour.

To suppose that these were in fact the same five Whoopers which had spent the winter near my home would, of course, strain coincidence to the point of absurdity. As in late autumn, so in early spring there is a good amount of local movement, and when their inland waters are iced up, many Whoopers take to the tidal flats and the estuaries. Nowadays indeed, it seems their relative, Bewick's Swan, only visits this country in any numbers when the Ijselmeer is frozen over, that is, in periods of protracted hard weather. At least this is the explanation which is usually given for the decline in the numbers of Bewicks wintering in Britain, and it is as plausible as any. As recently as fifty years ago, Bewick's Swan was a well distributed, regular winter visitor to many parts of Scotland, especially in the West. Today, a whole winter may go by without more than a dozen individuals being reported—a sad miss, for after the Whooper, Bewick's Swan is the most heart-stirring of all British wildfowl.

In the event, my home lochan had not seen the last of its wild Swans after all. At the end of the first week in April, when the Mutes were busy piling up their outsize nest beside the boat-house, two Whoopers returned and spent a week there: the same old pair without a doubt—I recognised the cob by the warty protuberance on his bill—only during their absence they had somehow contrived to part company with their cygnets.

Without fuss or effusiveness, the pair lazed around on the glassy water, indifferent to the quarrelsome Coots and the Tufted Ducks that kept bobbing up alongside. Evidently their courtship days were over and they were simply biding their time, taking things quietly before the long journey that lay ahead.

One morning when I looked for them they had gone. In their

place a swarm of Sand Martins was twittering over the surface and at the bottom of the garden the first Willow Warbler was lilting. Curled on her nest beside the boat-house the Mute Swan slept on her eggs while her lord and master kept guard in solitary state. A tranquil scene and a pleasing one, now that warm days were at hand. And somewhere, steering resolutely across the northern seas, two other Swans were heading homeward, to a destination only they could know of, perhaps to Myvatn or some glacial lake in far off Novaya Zemlya, that legendary country which is forever fated to remain for most of us a name on the map.

XIII.   To the Dark Tower

GREY GEESE (I)

THE LORDS OF GALLOWAY, I fancy, must have had more than a touch of high romance about them. Thanks to them the map of the Stewartry is richly inscribed with the poetry of place-names, many of which look as if they had been taken straight out of the Arthurian legends—as Gatehouse of Fleet, the Long Loch of the Dungeon and the Round Loch of Glenhead, Cairnsmore of Deugh and Rigg of Millmore, the Black Water of Dee and many another. Whereas the average Low-lander is content to call his place the Mains, the Kirkcudbright-shire farmer prefers something rather more imposing, say Shiel of Castlemaddy or Airds of Kells or Grange of Bladenoch or Lodge of Kelton or (a dreich one, this) Blackhill of Bush. What more natural, then, than that a hill with the resound-ing name of the Drum of Threave should turn out to be a singularly modest eminence not much above the size of a long barrow?

I came to it first in early February, a day when the countryside was still patched and streaked with snow and the air sweet with the smell of raw turnips out in the fields. First impres-sions, I must say, were disappointing. On Salisbury Plain this hummock might have been reckoned a landmark: being where it was it hardly seemed worth a second look—and yet, come to think of it, there *was* something about it, something not unlike the mental picture of that "green hill far away without a city wall" which is framed in the imagination of every Sunday School child.

From the roadside I took a quick look at the hill through the telescope. Yes, the Geese were there alright, between three and four hundred of them at a rough guess. To be sure, there was nothing very remarkable about that—there are many places in Scotland where Geese muster in flocks far greater than this. If the Drum is unique it is not for the numbers of Geese which it attracts but the variety. There have been times when as many as six different species have crowded on to its few green acres at the same time, a record which it is safe to say is unequalled anywhere else in Britain. That morning I had to be content with five— Grey-lags, Pink-feet, Bean, Greenland and Lesser White-fronts (not counting a party of Canadas which flew over honking their heads off later in the day).

The Grey-lags were strung out in a loose phalanx, six or seven deep, on the breast of the hill. Chuntering softly to themselves as they grazed, they advanced slowly up the slope. Among them was a conspicuous white Goose (a Snow, by all that's wonderful!) which on closer inspection proved to be nothing more exciting than an albino. Further over on the right, a company of Pink-feet was taking things easy, most of them snoozing with their heads tucked in between their shoulders. The White-fronts were in a huddle on the wet ground at the foot of the Drum where they were partly concealed by the rushes. One or two of them had wandered off on their own, however, so as to offer a head and shoulders view. Gloomy as the light was, the white blazes of their foreheads stood out clearly, as did the orange-yellow of their bills, and when they turned face-on several of them showed stomachers of solid black. Greenlanders beyond a doubt. Best of all were the Beans, the birds I had travelled a hundred miles and more to see: a hefty-looking lot, so dark that they appeared to be almost soot-coloured. They too, had got down among the rushes and were quietly feeding. Now and then a neck was raised as first one then another took stock of the situation, but for the most part they kept their heads down, satisfied that all was well.

Presently they left the swampy ground and moved out into the open, snipping away methodically at the short grass as they strayed; and just then a hint of brightness—it could hardly be called sunshine—broke through the cloud layers. A mercy that it did, for of all the geese the Bean is the one that most needs to be seen in a good light. Instead of looking uniformly dingy, they

Bean Goose

Pink-footed and
White-fronted
Goose

Grey-lags

now showed up in their true colours, warm brown with paler barrings across the back and legs of the most vivid orange-red. Was it an optical illusion or were their necks *really* longer than those of the Grey-lags and Pink-feet, more swan-like in their curves? In this bunch—between sixty and seventy all told, with more to follow—the yellow-billed variety predominated, but there were so many black-billed birds mingling with them and so many intermediate types that there seemed to be no point in trying to discriminate between them. One or two had bills which were entirely yellow, except for the nail, and in every case it appeared that these were also the biggest individuals with traces of white feathering on the forehead. Was the yellow (orange) bill simply the mark of the oldster? And could it be that all the learned, never-ending arguments for the existence of separate races—*arvensis, segetum, et al.*—were specious after all? Was Abel Chapman right when he wrote that: "These variations are purely individual, dependant on age and sex, and have no systematic value?"

As the leading Bean moved steadily uphill it reached forward and prodded a small dark Goose which had fallen asleep in its path. Until now I had not noticed this solitary one. When it stood up, with the burly Bean head and shoulders above it, the bird showed a patch of white that extended up on to the crown. Lame on one foot, it hobbled forward a few paces and then sat down again, only to be moved on yet again as the others crowded around. A Lesser White-front . . . and fifty yards further up the slope was another, this one fast asleep too. Later on, after scrutinising the ranks of the Grey-lags, I discovered a third. Curiously enough, each of them had attached itself to a different gaggle and showed no signs of wanting the company of its own kind.

Three Lesser White-fronts!—yet until 1954 this rare Goose had never been recorded in Scotland. It is just possible that it may have been overlooked, of course, though it seems unlikely. In all probability these three were genuine newcomers, out-riders of a westward extension of the species which has been taking place since the early years of the century. In a way the presence of Lesser White-fronts and Bean Geese side by side was symptomatic, for while the one is well on the way to becoming a

I

regular, if thinly disturbed winter visitor to Britain, the other seems destined to become a *rara avis*.

If the Irishism is allowable—and presumably it is seeing that the bird is invariably referred to as "the brownest of the Grey Geese", the Bean is much the rarest of the commoner wild Geese. Greylags, Pink-feet and White-fronts may be seen in their thousands in the right places, but a flock of as many as a hundred Bean is something to write home about nowadays. Their winter distribution in these islands has become more and more sporadic, and many of the localities in which they were formerly reputed to be both regular and numerous are no longer visited. In fact, it was the knowledge that this plot of rising ground on the outskirts of Castle Douglas was one of the few remaining places where one could be certain of finding Bean Geese in any numbers which first brought me to the Drum of Threave.

The curious thing is that until comparatively recent times the Bean was regarded as the typical Grey Goose in many parts of Scotland where it is now practically unknown. No doubt some of the old records need to be treated with proper reserve, for time was when the name "Bean" was applied more or less indiscriminately to any of the Grey Geese—and the fact that it was even said to have bred indicates that the bird was confused with the Grey-lag as well as with the Pink-foot. Allowing for this, however, the indications are that during the past century, and more particularly during the last fifty years, there has been a definite and progressive decrease in the numbers of Bean Geese wintering in this country. Thus George Bolam, writing in 1910, "after considerable pains to make sure that they were of this species", reported considerable flocks on the Northumbrian Loughs: and in Sir Hugh Gladstone's time there was no lack of Bean Geese in Ayrshire. Today the bird-watcher may scour either of these counties without coming across more than a handful.

How to account for this change of status? There is, first, the strong probability that the Bean population has decreased at the source, thanks to industrial developments in its northern breeding grounds. Alternatively, it is possible to argue that so far as their winter haunts in Great Britain are concerned they have been displaced by the Grey-lag and the Pink-foot, both of which have undoubtedly increased during the same period. Whatever the reason, fewer and fewer Bean are crossing the North Sea to winter in this country. It is significant that their arrival used to coincide with that of the other Grey Geese whereas today they rarely appear until after the New Year, the inference being that they prefer to spend the autumn and early winter on the Continent. In this respect, incidentally, the Bean Goose resembles the Bewick's Swan, another species which has become much scarcer in Scotland within living memory.

It goes without saying that the range of any species is never entirely static but subject to periodic contractions and expansions; and there is reason to believe that the winter ranges of all the wild Geese in the Northern Hemisphere are at present in a state of flux. Taking place as they do on so vast a front, the changes cannot easily be detected by the solitary observer, but perhaps some inkling of them may be gained by focussing attention on the sort of thing which happens in a single area. Thus, in the Island of Bute, the Grey-lag was reckoned an infrequent and irregular visitor until the end of the First World War. By 1938 its numbers had increased to 200 and in 1946 as many as 9,000 were reported. Yet in Islay during the same period the number of Grey-lags has steadily declined and their places have been taken over by Greenland White-fronts. Since it is unlikely that a powerful and rather aggressive species has been forced to give way in the face of increasing "foreign competition" the conclusion must be that the change of locale has been brought about by a change in the habits of the birds themselves—and there is evidence that this is the case. A century ago the Grey-lag was pre-eminently a goose of the saltmarsh: today it is very largely a bird of the pasture-lands. Whether it was originally driven to forsake the saltings because of the disturbance caused by shore-shooters or whether it did so of choice (assuming that the word has any meaning in such a context), it is clear that some adaptation to a changing environment has occurred. A hundred years may be an almost negligible space of time from the point of view of the evolutionary process, but it is long enough to bring about changes of habit which are of far-reaching importance.

The relationship between species and species is akin to that between the pieces on a chess-board: move one and sooner or later all the others are affected. With the big battalions of Grey-lags moving in to occupy their feeding grounds the Beans may have found themselves in a situation which, if it was not actually impossible, was at least uncomfortable. Though Geese are not above hobnobbing with other species for a time (Pink-feet will join up with Grey-lags when it suits them and an odd Lesser White-front will tag along with any of the big fellows for want of any better company) they have their own social hierarchies and these do not allow of any long-term or wholesale intermingling. As a consequence, relations are apt to become strained where two similar species have to exist side by side. It is not simply a question of there not being enough food to go round, nor is there necessarily any question of open conflict between the two. It is as though the presence of the "others" creates a tension; a tension which may not amount to positive uneasiness, perhaps, but which sooner or later leads to one species taking itself else-where. Maybe this sounds slightly far-fetched. If so, it is the wording which is at fault. Anyone who has watched Whoopers and Bewicks when they are together on the same stretch of water must agree that the two do not "get on" at all well. The Bewicks have a faintly apprehensive, inhibited look: they keep themselves to themselves almost as if they were conscious of being outsiders—and this without any hint of resentment from the Whoopers. Is it so far-fetched to say that Whoopers are stolid creatures and that the Bewick's temperament is, by comparison, nervous and sensitive? If not, and if, as seems probable, the numbers of Whoopers have increased, it may well be that the Bewick's Swans which formerly wintered in Scotland have been impelled for the sake of their own peace of mind to seek other resorts. And by the same token it is conceivable that the Bean Goose has withdrawn from its old haunts because of the advance of the Grey-lag.

But how often does any bird-watcher bother his head with this sort of problem when he has his eye glued to a telescope and the Geese are there in front of him as large as life? What is it that makes him watch their every movement so intently, as if his life depended on it? What does he expect to learn? What can he *hope* to learn? And why, after gazing admiringly at Thorburn's book-plates (in which the dowdiest bird is invariably glossed and groomed for stardom), does he gain this intense satisfaction in seeing a lumpish-looking figure of a goose with nothing very distinctive about it except a black bill picked out with yellow? Can it be that most of us are not really bird-watchers so much as bird-viewers and that any scientific pretensions we may have are no better than a cover for the same kind of interest which prompts other people to become philatelists or connoisseurs of *objets d'art*?

Come to think of it, the spell which the wild Geese have cast upon the present generation of bird-watchers—and not only bird-watchers—takes a deal of explaining. The mystique which has been built up around them owes much to the enthusiasms of a select band of writers, illustrators and broadcasters who know how to appeal to the imagination of the general public. The wild Geese have had some very efficient publicity-agents, and their reputation has been boosted sky-high as a result. They have become good "copy" for the city millions who have never pulled on a pair of gum-boots, let alone endured the hardships of six or seven hours of bog-trotting. The Pink-foot has been billed as "the most wonderful bird in the world", the White-fronts have their television show, and the Snow Goose has been the subject of a best seller. And yet, so far as looks are concerned, Geese are not particularly attractive creatures. If not drab, their plumage can hardly be termed colourful. A Grey-lag with a nose that shines like Bardolph's is not unhandsome—and let no one dare to call him ungainly!—yet for all the dignity of his carriage (between a roll and a swagger) it is not easy to say wherein it is superior to that of any barn-yard gander. The communal life of the wild Geese, too, is apt to be uneventful. They feed, they converse, they doze in the sun, they move about from place to place as occasion demands (though by no means so regularly as some writers would have us believe). Left to themselves they soon settle down to tranquillity—and inactivity. They have their occasional squabbles— some despot pushing the others around as like as not or maybe a tiff between neighbours cheek by jowl in the press—but for the most part their social behaviour is so well ordered that watching them for half an hour at a time tends to become monotonous. Only in the air do the wild Geese become spectacular.

On the ground their language can only be described as an incoherent gabble: on the wing it becomes eloquent, a clangorous music which never fails to send a tingling through the blood and moves the heart "more than with a Trumpet". Their fascination, too, owes something to the lonely places into which they lead us. Their wariness acts as a challenge. Whatever its secret, there is no resisting the spell of the wild Geese once it has taken hold.

GAR Goggogogg! . . . The nasal klaxon of one of the Grey-lags sounded the alert. In a second every head was erect, watching. Over on the far side of the marsh a man and a dog were approaching across the fields. Presently they disappeared behind the railway embankment. The Pink-feet tucked in their heads again. The White-fronts returned to their grazing. Only a false alarm, evidently.

Only the Grey-lags remained on guard. *Kar GOG!* For some reason the portly old gander was not satisfied. Calling the others to order, he stood at the ready, stiff-necked with suspicion. The entire flock had now halted in their tracks, waiting for the signal. There was no fuss, no hurry, no last-minute panic before the take-off. Even to the human eye the flight-intention movements were perfectly obvious. Perfectly timed, too. A nervous waggle of the head from the birds in front and the phalanx began to move off in formation, at the double, rising upwind and filling the sky with their deep-mouthed clamour.

At once the roar spread to all parts of the hill, altos, falsettos and basses blending and yet not blending in a babel of sound. The uprising was now general. Springing up almost vertically, the White-fronts were off to a flying start. *Winkink OKOKOK* barked the Pink-feet. *Gzank gzank* said the Beans (always the most taciturn of the Geese even in an emergency) as they swished over, heading inland towards the marshes of Loch Ken. By this time the roar of the crowd had resolved itself into a confused murmur, almost a buzz, as the skeins sorted themselves out and set course for their several destinations. Now that the pandemonium had subsided a little it was possible to distinguish between the registers of the different voices, the shrill whinny of the White-fronts, the cheerful bibble-babble of the Pink-feet, the stertorous intonation of the Grey-lags, the hoarse monosyllabic

utterance of the Beans. The chorus had died away and some of
the Geese had already settled again in the fields beyond the river
before first the dog and then the man appeared on the top of the
hill. I might have guessed as much.

Seeing that the damage was done and there was nothing
to be gained by concealment I decided to take a stroll that
way myself. Everywhere the ground was strewn with droppings. Even now that I had set foot upon it, though, it was
by no means obvious why this hillock should be such a favourite
gathering place for the Geese. True, it had certain advantages.
For one thing, it was partly surrounded by bogland so that
the likelihood of anyone sneaking up without being seen or
heard was more or less ruled out. Better still, it commanded
an uninterrupted view of the surrounding district, a countryside of farmlands and unreclaimed marshes into which a strategic
withdrawal was possible in almost any direction. The grass
looked sweet and tender, but no more tempting than the
grass in many another field—at any rate to the uncritical eye
of a non-vegetarian. As for the disadvantages, not only was
the hill exposed to view from the main road but it could easily
be approached on the blind side from the railway line which
ran behind it: and believe it or not there was a gasometer only
three fields away. Evidently the certainty of being forewarned
of the approach of danger and of having a safe getaway in the
event of a crisis meant more to the Geese than the possibility of
their whereabouts being discovered. The sound of the town clock
chiming the hours and the quarters, the washing blowing about in
the back gardens of the nearer houses, the buses trundling along
the road below, the factory hooter—so far as the Geese were concerned these sights and sounds belonged to another world and
could safely be ignored. Provided that they were not disturbed,
they did not mind living at one remove from the affairs of men.
Wise birds!

Shropshire folk have a jingle which proclaims that:

"Clunton and Clunbury, Clungunford and Clun
Are the quietest places under the sun."

Galloway is just such a land. Serene and gentle, this stretch of country between the Solway shore and the hills has much to offer those who, like the wild Geese, want nothing better than peace and security. But this does not, in itself, explain why so many different *kinds* of Geese are to be found here. In general the distribution of Geese in Scotland answers to a definite pattern, each species having its own "sphere of influence" and keeping to it. In much the same way as it was once possible to lay one's finger on the map and say that this was the Campbells' country and this the territory of the Mackintoshes so it can be said that each of the Geese has its special grounds. Thus, in the East the Pink-foot is much the commonest goose. In the Clyde area the Grey-lag has a virtual monopoly. The White-front's zone lies further west still, in the islands. The gathering of the clans in this corner of Kirkcudbrightshire can be understood, then, as being due either to its position at the convergence of three fairly clearly defined zones, or simply to the natural advantages of the terrain. The latter seems to be the likelier explanation. It cannot be entirely accidental that the rarest of the Geese, the Lesser White-front, singled out this delectable spot when making its first appearance in Scotland.

From the marshes that lay on the far side of the hill came the clonking of many Whoopers, forty-three of them herded together on the ice. At my approach their ululations grew louder and heads began to nod in alarm, but for once they stood their ground and made no attempt to fly.

The river was chock-a-block with floes after the late thaw. A bunch of Goldeneye surfaced close in by the bankside (the drake with a spot of white the size of a shilling on his black face), only to splash off in a hurry when they realised their mistake. The whistling of their pinions sounded more tunable than ever in that wintry silence, like a string that goes on twangling long after it has been plucked. A thin, cold sleet had begun to fall. Grey as the spectre of famine, a Heron unfurled its wings and went honking across the fields where the hulk of Threave Castle stood foursquare on its island. Jackdaws were cackling about the broken battlements, Pigeons crooning on the block of masonry above its portal (the Hanging Stane of which the Douglas was pleased to boast that it "ne'er wanted its tassel"). Time had brought in its revenges. Never again would these castle walls resound with deeds of derring-do and the strains of minstrelry. Hero and dastard alike had come to the dark tower and had had their day. Now there was only the fifing of Wigeon from the riverside, the forlorn swansong of the Whoopers out on the marsh, and in the distance, the heart-warming chorus—the "music nighest heaven"—of the wild Geese on their nightly errands.

XIV. Grey-lags and Pink-feet

GREY GEESE (2)

DRIVING NORTH TO Aberfoyle and the Trossachs the
motorist often remarks on the abruptness of the contrast between
the Highlands themselves and the great stretch of low-lying
country at their feet. Ahead, the mountains rise in a solid, unbroken rampart, Ben Ledi's broad back and the camel-humps of
Ben Venue rising above the wooded foot-hills, with Ben Lomond
away to the west standing aloof from the others. To the east there
is a seemingly endless prospect of cottongrass, peat-hag and
heather through which the young Forth finds its hidden way
towards Stirling and the sea. On a clear day the view is nothing
if not extensive, the tower of the Wallace Memorial, nearly
twenty miles away, being a prominent landmark. Here and there
a clump of birches helps to break the monotony of these dead-
level perspectives, a landscape which at times reminds one of
Shakespeare's "blasted heath" and at others of the primeval fen.

Flanders Moss is the name given to this area of unreclaimed
bogland on the border of Perthshire and Stirlingshire. Low-
lying as it is in comparison with the hills that flank its northern
and southern extremities, the moss is, in fact, a perfect example of
what the botanists call a raised bog. In England and Wales this
type of natural habitat is to be found in one locality only—
Tregaron Bog (Cors Coch Glan Teifi) in Cardiganshire. In
Scotland, of course, such bogs are not uncommon, though it
would be hard to find one larger than this or with a more pictur-
esque setting.

The name, Flanders Moss, is distinctly appropriate: it derives
from the eighteenth century when a local landowner, Lord Kames,
employed Dutch engineers and a gang of Flemish labourers to
improve his estate. The names of two farms, Easter Polder and

Wester Polder, also bear witness to this venture. Methods of drainage and land reclamation in those days were inclined to be somewhat rough and ready, it seems: once removed, the surface peat was simply dumped into the river, with the result that the stuff piled up in the lower reaches of the Forth, where it interfered with the fishing to such an extent that protests were raised and the scheme had to be abandoned. No wonder, either, for although its fringes have been converted into pasture and arable land by these nibblings, the greater part of the moss has proved so intractable as to defy any attempt at wholesale reclamation. The heart of it is still untamed, a vast sponge, covered with sphagnum, juncus and, bog-myrtle, with patches of thin heather in the drier sections. Bog-trotting may have its delights, but after an hour or two on this quaky ground, sinking in up to the knees at every step, it is apt to prove an exhausting business.

The depth of the peat cover varies considerably. Borings show that in places it is not less than thirty feet deep. Because of this, the watercourses are visibly lower than the general level of the bog, tucked away in secret channels where they cannot be seen until the last moment—a fact which the newcomer, intent on making a point-to-point crossing soon learns to his cost.

At first sight Flanders Moss strikes one as being a sportsman's paradise, the ideal rough-shoot. Certainly it is rough! Being so acid, however, the peat moss cannot support a rich animal population, at any rate not during the winter months. It is significant, perhaps, that this is one of the few localities in Britain where the arctic flowering shrub *Ledum groenlandicum* has established a foothold. According to one theory, this plant is indigenous, a genuine relic of the Ice Age: according to another, its seeds were brought here accidentally by the Pink-footed Goose. Whatever the correct explanation may be, it needs no great stretch of imagination to see a certain resemblance between the Greenland tundra and a Scottish bog, especially when the latter is ice-bound. Even the hardy Red Grouse fail to thrive here and one may plough around, ankle-deep and deeper in water, for hours at a time without flushing more than an occasional pair. Snipe, too, are few and far between. Black Grouse are plentiful in the rushy corners where cover is available and there are Pheasants and Capercaillie in the neighbouring woods, but the moss itself is too exposed, too wet and too barren for most birds. In some of the drier sections sheep and cattle can be seen grazing, but even they cannot be turned loose in a quagmire. Of the wild mammals, the one most often seen (apart from the ubiquitous field vole) is the roe deer which lies up here in the open during the day-time. Oddly enough, the mountain hare is also quite common. For the rest, it seems that for nine out of the twelve months the peat-bog is such a God-forsaken place that neither bird nor beast has much use for it. In summer, of course, it is another story, for then the air rings with the shrieks of countless Black-headed Gulls, the whistle of Redshanks and Curlews, the stutter of Sedge Warblers and babble of White throats along the riverside. For a time, in May and June, the white acres of silky cotton-grass look almost gay. But in the depth of winter the scene can be cheerless enough, and whole days may pass without much, or anything of note being seen—a solitary Hen Harrier toiling into the wind, perhaps, or a bunch of Goosanders fishing their way upstream, but little else.

Little else, that is, except for the Geese. For the Grey-lags, the wide spaces of the moss offer a sanctuary as safe as any that is to be found inland, and from the end of September to the end of April, when the last stragglers pass through on their way north, never a day passes without a skein or two dropping in to rest or feed. Though the numbers vary a good deal from year to year—in mild autumns they may be slow in coming in—the total is usually not far short of a thousand by the middle of November, but this is not to say that they are always to be seen together in a single flock. Companies of fifty and a hundred up are constantly coming and going; and especially at the week-ends when the local sportsmen blast away at them on all sides a thousand Geese can make them-selves very scarce indeed. No sooner are the guns silent, how-ever, than they invariably return, cackling and gabbling on their way from the Endrick marshes or from lower down the Carse of Stirling.

For all their wariness, Grey-lags are noisy feeders. As often as not, their presence can be detected long before the birds them-selves can be seen. In fact, if it were not for the almost ceaseless buzz of conversation which they keep up—the kind of back-ground noise which is the more noticeable in the wintry silence

of the peat-bog where the only other sound is the wind's swish—
a man might be hard put to find them at all. In the small hours,
and whenever the coast is clear, they prefer to graze in the surrounding fields, for there is nothing they like so much as sweet,
green grass, but during the day when the chances of getting it
without being disturbed are not so good, they congregate along
the sides of the sunken watercourses below the level of the bog
where they are not to be seen. Here, thanks to the nasal chanters
and raucous grunters among them, it is possible for the watcher to
steal a march (if crawling on all fours through a morass can be
called stealing a march) and spy on the phalanx as it goes about the
serious business of feeding. For the field ornithologist there is
no sport half so exhilarating as this.

Portly, leisurely, deliberate in all its movements, the Grey-lag
has the homely air of a goose which looks as if Nature intended it
for the farmyard from the beginning. Its mannerisms, its expostu-
lations, even its voice are strongly reminiscent of those of the
domestic goose. When it stretches one leg behind it and luxuri-
ously ruffles out every feather of its wing to preen—a trick most
birds perform but one which Ducks and Geese seem to take a
special delight in—the watcher knows that he has seen the same
action many a time on the village green. When a gander, too
ponderous to move out of the way, digs its neighbour in the
midriff and then stands, stiff with indignation, while the other
stretches its neck on the ground and hisses defiance it is hardly
possible to restrain a smile. Not that there is anything in the least
ludicrous about the Grey-lag's behaviour. If hullaballoos and high
words are often to be heard, actual squabbles are infrequent: most
of the birds are too busy feeding, heads down and all in the same
direction, snipping the turf methodically with a left-and-right
sideways movement. Invariably, however, several of them will
stand and stare, their necks raised in suspicion. If one does so for
any length of time, others take the cue, the regiment is halted
in its tracks, ready for the alarm to be sounded—and away they
go, with a Hampden roar as they take off. In the sunlight the pale
lavender of their fore-wings and shoulders look almost white. As
the main body disappears into the distance, splinter groups are left
circling high overhead, as if reluctant to leave their grazing
grounds while there is any chance of returning to them safely.

Five minutes later, their honking is renewed as they settle in a far corner of the bog.

Unlike the shore Geese, these inland Grey-lags keep no regular hours. On calm nights they may roost in the sheltered bays of the Lake of Menteith nearby, or take a short flight into the hills. Wind and weather, not the tide, regulate their movements. Wherever they spend the night there is always the danger of being stalked by foxes (and the half-eaten remains that one occasionally comes across indicate that the danger is not always avoided), or by prowling otters.

At the turn of the century, apparently, the Grey-lags had Flanders Moss more or less to themselves. In recent years, however, their monopoly has been increasingly challenged by the arrival of large numbers of Pink-feet. Previously, the latter had only visited the moss on their return passage in April. Pink-feet, it hardly needs to be said, are more strongly represented on the East coast, possibly because they relish the kind of feeding which is to be had on stubble fields and arable land. The west, being so much wetter, is more given over to the green pastures which Grey-lags prefer. In 1955, a good year for all the Grey Geese, the numbers of Pink-feet were so phenomenal that even Loch Leven and Tentsmuir, their traditional gathering grounds in October, could not accommodate all-comers. As a result, an overspill of something like a thousand birds settled on the moss about the same time as the newly-arrived Grey-lags.

An interesting situation now developed. At first the two species joined forces. If not actually intermingling, Pink-feet and Grey-lags could be seen feeding side by side—and a fine sight they made, strung out in irregular lines across the length of the field. Darker necked, neater and more compact than the Grey-lags, the newcomers were obviously quite at home. But only for a time. In November the hosts parted company, the Grey-lags keeping to the northern side, close to cultivation, while the Pink-feet settled in on the moss itself. Whether this separation was brought about by a shortage in the food supply—not enough turf to go around for two thousand once the grass had stopped growing—or by an unconscious rivalry between the species is anybody's guess. Certainly the Pink-feet managed to grub up a living from the wet peat which the less frugal Grey-lags left severely alone. Hard work and hard diet digging for the shoots of the white-beaked sedge or tearing off the brittle stalks of molinia and juncus, yet they seemed to thrive on it . . . until the turn of the year when the urge to be on the move again reasserted itself and the gaggles dispersed. By February many of the Grey-lags had gone, too, leaving a hard core of some three or four hundred in possession. Hard weather put an end to any further competition between the species; for when the snow lies deep in the fields and the squelchiest parts of the moss are sealed with ice there is nothing for it but to look elsewhere.

Still, as events have proved, the Pink-feet have established a precedent and staked their claim. Though there is, of course, no question of open hostilities between the two, it is clear, as the years go by, that these infiltrators from the east are gradually taking over from the stolid Grey-lags; a struggle for supremacy, no less dour than the struggle for survival itself, and one which adds its own touch of drama to the bleakness of the tawny peat-bog.

XV.   The Last of the Barnacles

BARNACLE GEESE

FOR THE WILDFOWLER and the watcher of wildfowl there is no place like the Solway: the north shore of the Solway, that is, for the Cumbrian side has not altogether escaped the disfigurements of industrial development and the urban sprawl. Anyone who has asked himself what estuaries looked like before men got to work on them will find the perfect answer in the mouths of the Nith and the Lochar, just as surely as anyone who hankers after the widest of wide-open spaces will find himself lost in wonder on Blackshaw Merse. Solway never does things by halves. Empty-looking as its windswept landscapes often are, the memories one carries away are of birds *in the mass*: a thousand Scaup diving together in Carsethorne Creek, an array of six thousand Pink-footed Geese on the Annan saltings, a cloud of Knots flickering across the sands of Southerness, Shelducks in the bays and, of course, Oystercatchers. . . . Oystercatchers digging for worms in the fields behind the sea-wall, Oystercatchers crowding on to the mussel beds as the tide turns, Oystercatchers piping their heads off everywhere on the grey mudflats.

For myself, the Merse has always had a special appeal as being one of the few places where Barnacle Geese can still be seen in their big battalions. Granted, there are Barnacles in plenty in some of the Islands—the machair of the Atlantic beaches is ideal for them—but so far as the mainland is concerned, the Merse might almost be described as the last out-post of this, the most elusive and (to my mind) the most handsome of our wild Geese. I have sought them here in all weathers from early October to the end of March, in driving rain and wind, in genial sunshine and in hard frost when the brash ice was piled along the tideline and the foreshore was as hard as iron. If only I could say that as a result of

Wigeon drake whistling

Pintail drake

all these miles of slouching through muck and mire I had come to understand the ways of these admirable little Geese, but the truth is that I cannot: to me they remain as enigmatic as ever. And so I go on seeking them lured by a desire which cannot be satisfied. Odd, is it not, how a man's interest in a bird can become a ruling passion? By trial and error I have come to know the spots far out on Blackshaw Bank where the ooze quakes like a jelly, ready to suck the unwary down, the channels where the sneak tide comes swilling in behind your back, the gutters which can be crossed and those which cannot—but of the Barnacles themselves I am almost as ignorant as when I began. For all that, I cannot think that the quest has been entirely wasted. *Something* remains from those world-well-lost days, something which is too indefinable to be set down in terms of matter of fact, yet none the less meaningful for that. It is the sort of meaning which cannot be stated outright but only hinted at, and I can think of no better way of attempting to evoke it than by describing one of these wild-goose chases.

According to the calendar it was the first day of Spring. The Nith never ran more briskly beneath the bridges of Dumfries than it did that March morning when I boarded the nine o'clock bus for Glen Caple. A sprinkling of snow had salted the hills afresh overnight. The air was biting. The Lesser Black-backed Gulls had returned, the first time I had seen them in any numbers since the late autumn, though one or two had hung about the river all through the winter. Maybe it was too early in the year to be thinking of spring migrants: all the same, it was clear that things were on the move. The fields were crowded with Common and Black-headed Gulls, with Lapwings, Golden Plovers and Curlews, all resting or waiting about on their way inland for the breeding season.

Glen Caple. It sounds as if it ought by rights to be somewhere in Perthshire. In fact the village is typical of the Solway scene, its houses lining the river front, facing towards the marshes and the hump of Criffel: the kind of place which old W. H. Hudson would have delighted in, for here on a winter's day one can take one's ease in one's inn and listen to the inspiring gabble of Greylags and Pink-feet as they pass over in their chevrons, up-river in the early morning, seawards in the late afternoon.

From the village to the open Merse is getting on for three miles, and having got that far one has done no more than reach a starting point, for though the Barnacle's haunts are not so exclusively marine as those of the Brent they are far out on the saltings and beyond—and when Blackshaw Bank is uncovered it stretches more than half-way over to the English side. At first the road hugs the riverside, and a pleasant road it is, fringed on one side with alders and reedbeds, on the other with hedges and fields, so that the bird-watcher gets the best of both worlds—estuary and farmland.

Redpolls twittered in the alders, hanging upside down among the catkins and showing their pinks and crimsons to the sun. Corn Buntings jingled on the tops of gate posts. Partridges craked in the fields, sprinting this way and that in pairs and suddenly pulling up short to stand and crow. Wood Pigeons clapped their wings and flew out of the ivied oaks, mounting steeply to breast the air and mounting again. Across the river some thirty Greylags were quietly grazing and on the bankside beneath them was a company of sleepy Wigeon. Neither Ducks nor Geese bothered to raise their heads as I passed by. (So much for the sense of security which comes with the close season.) Out in midstream a flotilla of Red-breasted Mergansers were disporting themselves, the drakes shooting up their heads one after another as they displayed.

Further on I was faced with one of those happy dilemmas which so often present themselves in places like this where land- and sea-birds are to be found side by side—the choice between watching a charm of Goldfinches in a bramble patch or a bunch of Scaup close in to the nearer bank. Before I could make up my mind the Goldfinches prattled and danced up in alarm as a falcon Merlin, cutting in from nowhere, shot through them—a near-miss if ever there was one. And then, as if to cap the unexpectedness of the incident, a Woodcock rustled up from tangles of the bramble patch, slanting its stick of a bill to eye me as it jockeyed into the breeze.

And so to the saltings and their endless vistas broken only by the gaunt poles erected by the stake-net fishermen. Skiddaw and Saddleback glistened austerely to the south above the haze which hid the distant coastline. Larks sprang and sang and kept on singing. Lapwings wheeled and tumbled over the sea-wall, crying *wee willukaweeuk willukawee*: the unmistakable voice of spring, and from the black wood which screens the red ruin of Carlaverock Castle from view came the soft cawing of many Rooks. Out here on the Merse, though, it was still midwinter except for the glad shrilling of the Larks, and after a time even they were left behind. Then the only sound to be heard was the low grunting of Shelducks far out on the flats, the sudden squealing of Redshanks, a Curlew bubbling over with excess of gladness. As far as eye could see there were Shelducks standing in twos and threes, the drakes tossing their bills in the air or bowing profusely with neck outstretched.

But no Barnacles! Their favourite gathering ground, a green spit at the edge of the saltings was deserted; and the dried husks of their droppings showed that it had not been visited for several days. No wonder, either; for it was not long since the hard spell had ended. Six weeks of snow and ice had left the grass bleached and chaffy. Poor stuff at the best times, one might think, yet the Barnacles seemed to like it well enough. Until recently, at any rate, the flock (nine hundred strong when they first arrived) had remained faithful to this spot all through the winter. Even when they were disturbed they invariably returned to it as soon as the coast was clear. Just why they favoured this particular stretch of saltings it was hard to say, unless it was that this spot of land offered one of the few places where they could walk straight off the mudflats and begin feeding. Elsewhere the saltings ended (or began) in a miniature cliff about three feet high—no great obstacle, perhaps, but big enough to prevent a clear field of vision for a bird standing only eighteen inches high. Barnacles are often said to be more approachable than other Geese, but I have never found them so. On the contrary, their psychology seems to be shaped by one overriding necessity, the avoidance of danger. In their Arctic breeding haunts they nest on inaccessible cliff-faces, in situations more in keeping with an eagle than a goose; and in their winter quarters they seek out the dead-level coastlines where there is little or no fear of their being caught napping. Grey-lags and Pink-feet, wary as they are, flight inland to feed and where the lie of the land allows of a stalk it is possible to surprise them. Not Barnacles.

Judging by the numbers of dead Oystercatchers lying around

the Geese were not the only ones which had been feeling the pinch. Many of the corpses were still quite fresh, showing that the birds had survived the long cold spell only to succumb to general weakness after it had ended. Why so hardy a species as the Oystercatcher should have suffered such heavy losses—in the course of an hour I must have picked up thirty or more—was a mystery. And talking of mysteries, why was it that some of these birds had short, "sawn-off" bills while others had long, pointed bills? It was common knowledge, of course, that there was considerable variation in the length and shape of the Oyster-catcher's bill and that, as a general rule, the male's was stouter and shorter and the female's longer and slenderer. Time was when the systematists tried to separate the species into Continental, Icelandic and British races using bill measurements as taxonomic characters, but it is evident that so variable a feature is quite unreliable for such purposes. Arranging a dozen of these Solway birds in a series, I found that they varied from 63 to 83 millimetres in length and from 10 to 12.5 millimetres in depth. The shorter the bill the more obviously worn it was; and in one or two cases the upper mandible had actually snapped off at the tip, the result, no doubt, of prying open some intractable sea-shell. And here was an interesting thing, in some cases it appeared that the outer sheath was in the process of being shed. Half-way along it, the bill had a wrinkled appearance as if the skin were being pushed off by the new growth underneath. Did this mean that the Oyster-catcher, like the Puffin, renewed its bill each spring? It looked rather like it.

But to get back to the Barnacles, wherever they were. After three hours of heavy-footed slouching over the flats it began to look like a vain quest. Maybe the Geese had left earlier than usual this year and were already on their way north? At long last, though, I heard their excited buzz of conversation in the distance, like the yapping of a kennelful of puppies—and there they were, all seven hundred of them, strung out in a line along the fringe of salt-marsh. As usual, they had seen me first, but for the moment they were not unduly worried. At both ends of the phalanx a few Geese had put their heads up, leaving the others to carry on feeding.

What a smart fellow the Barnacle is, to be sure. The face

and forehead are milk-white or creamy and in some (presumably old) birds, the palest of golds. The bill is a tiny stub (shorter than a Wigeon's!). The neck is jet black "shining like the coal" and the upper parts Air-force blue, barred with black and white. But it is not the fetching pattern of its plumage, nor the pleasing colour-scheme which lends this little goose its air of distinction so much as its trim lines and dainty carriage. In any case, there is no point in describing the individual Barnacle: it is the *flock* which counts and which provides the special thrill.

At first the eye sees nothing to choose between the closely-packed birds: they all look alike, just as sheep or, for that matter, human beings tend to do in a crowd. Before long, however, it becomes apparent that there *are* differences, not least in size. Some of the little ones really are diminutive, the bigger ones much heavier and more thickset. (How long will it be, one wonders, before the pundits decide that these undersized specimens are a race apart, hailing from a different quarter of the polar regions, and call them Lesser Barnacles?) Gradually, too, the eye begins to discern certain family and group relationships within the great collective. When they are busy feeding they are amicable enough, and in a crisis, needless to say, they act as one, but in their off-moments they can be as quarrelsome as schoolboys. Tiffs of one sort or another are constantly blowing up, no sooner begun than forgotten. Here a lordly gander barges its neighbours aside, snatching the grass from under their feet. Another here, a youngster apparently, gets a hot reception when it strays too far from the side of its parents, one of which rushes to the rescue with wings raised, ready to fend off its assailants. The youngster returns, looking thoroughly chastened, only to wander off into bad company again soon afterwards. But this time, as if unsure of its welcome, it abases itself in suppliant attitude, creeping forward with neck outstretched. Once again the unwanted intruder is driven off and again the jealous parent has to chivvy it back where it belongs.

And now, for no apparent reason unless it was that they did not care for the glint of the telescope, the watch-dogs began to nod their heads, calling the others to orders. Left, right and centre the regiment closed its ranks and moved off, stepping purposefully towards the sea. *Owka owka!* The murmured talk took on a more urgent intonation, the walk became a run, and suddenly the shore resounded to the dull roar of their uprising. In a long, irregular line they straggled across the flats, heading for Southerness and the old lighthouse, keeping low all the way until they dwindled into the nothingness of the horizon. Useless to follow them now that the tide was running. . . .

But what was this? Looking back to the spot from which the Geese had just risen, I saw that one of them had been left behind. A lame Barnacle—and instead of making a run for it in the open where the chances of cutting it off single-handed would have been rather slim, the foolish creature limped off up the narrow creek like a Duck entering one of the pipes of decoy. Even so, the cripple dodged about so desperately that I was hard put to keep up with it, let alone lay hands on it—and the bed of a creek is hardly the place for a flying tackle—until it found itself in a side-channel from which there was no escape and squatted down with its head in a corner. The last, unavailing subterfuge of the wounded goose. Poor thing, it hissed abominably, fighting to get free; and then lay still without struggling. It was an immature bird, all skin and bone, and riddled with shot as like as not, though as far as could be seen there were no external marks of injury. In all probability it would never fly again. For all that, this bundle of energy was so full of pluck that the idea of putting it out of its misery, as the saying is, was not to be thought of. Instead, I carried it for a couple of hundred yards and set it down on the tideline. With great dignity and without undue haste, it paddled in and swam off out to sea, never once looking back.

A fortnight elapsed before my next visit to the Merse. Outwardly the landscape was the same as before, only now that the Geese had gone it seemed to have become stale, flat and unprofitable. Criffel was no longer hoary. Larks sang and Lapwings tumbled and in the Carlaverock woods the first Chiffchaff of the year was softly lisping. From the mudflats came the far-off titter of a Whimbrel. And somewhere out there a solitary goose was left to while away the summer that lay ahead. The last of the Barnacles. For its sake as well as my own I could have wished the summer over and gone so that once again I might listen for the glad tidings that are borne on the winds of October and take heart anew.

XVI.   Voice of the Kelpie

RED-THROATED AND BLACK-THROATED DIVERS

SPRING DAYS REJOICE the heart more keenly the farther North one goes. At least so it seems. Whether it is because warm days are so few and far between and therefore not to be taken for granted as they are in softer climates, or because the dead season tends to be long drawn out in the higher latitudes and the year's return to life the more welcome on that account, there is no saying. Certainly there *is* a difference. Crocuses that light their candles along the crazy-pavements of Dorking in early February call for no comment and receive none : in Inverness they may still be reckoned a bit of a miracle at the end of March. In the Home Counties May means the song of the Nightingale and the voice of the Turtles from the elms around the cricket-field : North of the Border it means the bubbling-over of Curlews out on the moor, the whim-wham flight of Lapwings, the sharp *pleet-pleep* of Oystercatchers flying overland in the darkness. For large areas of the Highlands it means the difference between utter desolation and a wilderness which is no longer entirely God-forsaken. Down South the smaller passerines are abundant throughout the year : one never misses the Meadow Pipit, say, or the Linnet. In Scotland one has to resign oneself to the virtual disappearance of many of the small birds after October so that one learns to appreciate having them around in places where they are not to be looked for in winter.

Spring comes slowly up this way and most of the higher bens carry traces of white until the beginning of June. Often there is little or no cover for the "leaf-warblers" when they arrive, and at first the fiery Redstart looks singularly out of place in the black sticks of the woods; but with all promises which are long delayed in their fulfilment, the heyday of a Scottish

Spring is the more radiant when it does arrive. Eventually there comes a morning which seems to have been borrowed from high summer,

> When drop-of-blood-and-foam-dapple
> Bloom lights the orchard apple
> And thicket and thorp are merry
> With silver-surfed cherry
>
> And azuring-over greybell makes
> Wood banks and brakes wash white like lakes
> And magic cuckoocall
> Caps, clears, and clinches all.

On such a day my thoughts invariably turn to a dubh-lochan in Knoydart, one of the countless, nameless little tarns that brighten the dun wastes of the Rough Bounds, and to a hill loch nearby. This loch, they say, used to be avoided by the local clansmen because it was believed to hold a kelpie, and anyone visiting it in grey weather when the mists are trailing might be forgiven for thinking that it does so to this day. Strange noises out of this world, are to be heard there at times—demoniacal cries that strike no less wonder in the mind of the bird-watcher who recognises them as the "song" of the Black-throated Diver than they once did in the imagination of the superstitious Gael.

After a fortnight of wet, blustery weather came the Glorious First of June. In the lower glen it was hot and silent. The hills looked strangely solemn. A muscular adder, coiled like an ammonite, lay on the stony track, squirming away into the bracken at my approach. (No use tip-toeing by in clinkered boots!) Grasshoppers churred and the clegs (those objectionable dirt-coloured flies which settle unbeknown on the less accessible parts of one's anatomy and wait a moment before making up their minds to sting) were out in strength for the first time: and when clegs are out for blood there is no stopping for a breather or admiring the view. Whinchat after Whinchat sputtered into song along the deer-fence and then flew around, ticking in alarm from sprays of bush heather. The bare slopes were embroidered with flowers: quatrefoils, bed-straws and milkwort (the blue lobelia of the mountains), bog asphodel where the going was soft, yellow saxifrage in clusters under the wet rocks, and the butterwort raising its violet head among the mosses.

Above the tree-line it was a perfect morning, less sultry than it had been lower down, with just a lick of cooler air blowing off the sea. The lochan had never been bluer. Hidden away in the hills and surrounded as it is by moraines, this little stretch of water is not easy to find, even with the aid of a one-inch map, and having once found it its whereabouts are apt to remain as much a secret as they were before. Somehow it is the sort of spot which needs to be discovered afresh each time it is visited. Had it not been for the Common Gulls which flew out to meet me long be-fore the lochan itself came in sight I might have passed within a hundred yards without seeing it and spent half the day wan-dering up and down in among the peat-hags. *Klea kleea*, they called, fretfully at first, then *kak kwak*, more peremptorily, as I kept on: not without good reason, either, for their nests were here, there and everywhere along the waterside—among the green mare's-tails, in the heather, on the tops of the boulders by the outflow. Several of them contained eggs which were already chipped.

The colony was a new one and still quite small, not more than thirty pairs at the most. All the same, it was too big for my liking. If the numbers went on increasing the way they had done during the past two years it would soon be good-bye to the Divers. As it was, it looked rather as though the Red-throats had taken the hint and gone elsewhere this year. There was no sign of either of them.

Without much hope, I made my way round the edges of the pool, keeping a sharp look-out for any depression among the rushes that faintly resembled a nest. The circuit was almost com-pleted when, within a yard or two of my starting point, I saw it. The egg! No beachcomber unearthing treasure-trove ever whooped with as much delight as I did at that moment. A matchless *objet trouvé*! It was a very nugget of an egg, elongated and perfectly symmetrical. Copper-colour and blotched all over with black it shone with the patina of a rare metal.

So the birds were here after all. And now it was just a matter of retiring a little way and waiting for one or other of them to return. If only those know-all Gulls would leave off squawling! Making oneself scarce on an open moor can be quite a problem, but for once the moraine came in handy and after a time the clamour died out. Except for one querulous individual which refused to leave me alone, all the Gulls soon returned to their nests and settled down again. Out of sight out of mind. . . .

There was no shade, and hardly a breath of air to ripple the water. On a warm day like this, I told myself, the Red-throat might be away for hours—and a moment later found myself sitting up with a start. Surely the sun was playing tricks with my eyes? But no, it was not the sun that was playing tricks: it was the Red-throat. The bird had been there all the time! How on earth had I missed seeing it? It was impossible. The lochan was barely a furlong from end to end and half as wide. Incredible, but there it was.

The Diver was low in the water, sure sign that it was not at ease. Now and then it dipped its bill in up to the eyes, as if peering into the depths. After a time it left off patrolling and began to dive, surfacing each time with only the head and neck showing and staring about it with what seemed to be an anxious expression. Next it began to preen, turning over on its side and nibbling its white underparts. That done, it stretched and shook first one, then the other flipper in the air, in the offhand manner of an aristocrat waving some tiresome fellow aside. (Those *very* Common Gulls!) Anxious my foot! Before long the bird had laid its head upon its back and was fast asleep.

Divers, they say, are not very intelligent creatures. Possibly not, yet when it comes to outwitting a man they know a trick or two. This one was taking no chances, certainly.

Half an hour went by and still the bird did not move: "as idle as a painted ship upon a painted ocean." Then, when it began to seem that the best thing to do was to leave it in peace the Red-throat raised its head and mewed softly. Its attitude was now tense with anticipation, neck forward, bill pointing at the sky.

Krukkeruk! The cry came from high overhead, guttural and terse. *Krukkerukeruk!*—and with something of the speed and unexpectedness of a guided missile the second Red-throat came in with a rush. With its wings held steady and its body aimed at the centre of the lochan like an aerial torpedo, it hit the water with great force, scoring a long furrow over the surface.

The two now approached each other, rather cautiously it seemed, as if neither was sure what the next move ought to be. Face to face, they touched bills, upending in the water like Grebes, but the salutation was half-hearted and petered out just when it seemed that they were about to start waggling their heads. Instead, they half-submerged and began to cruise round the little bay, side by side, cooeeing plaintively as they swam: *sotto voce* at first but threatening to become blood-curdling at any moment. Even in the white blaze of early June the cries had an eerie, faraway quality about them. They sounded fey. No despairing lovers these, though. Suddenly the water swirled over them as they crash-dived together. After a few seconds they broke surface, cackling and caterwauling, growling and groaning—cockerel-noises and heart-rending shrieks all blended together in the wildest, unholiest *concordia discors* that ever was heard anywhere.

This passionate outburst was short-lived. When the violence of their outcry had subsided, the pair swam quietly together, necks well up and bills pointed obliquely at the surface in front of them. The greeting ceremony was over, the drama ended.

Drifting apart now, they floated at ease, doing nothing in particular. With one paddle stuck out behind them they turned in lazy circles; and as they did, the colour of their throats kept changing—robin-red in the sun, merging into dried-blood and darkest maroon in the shade. Its shape kept changing, too— a broad band when the head was lowered, narrowing to a mere ribbon whenever the neck was raised. The lavender grey of their heads, the meekness of their attitudes, their sinuous lines and slenderness—everything about them was delicate. Everything, that is, except their love-making.

Now the first diver cocked its head on one side, staring one-eyed at something up in the sky. It looked uneasy. Far up in the blue a Raven called, going over into the hills: and the bird on the water relaxed again.

Kror, it answered, a sonorous note. As much as to say "All's well". Again the other gave its soft low moan without bothering to raise its head to look.

There was no point in staying on. Even in cold wet weather and with a full clutch of hard-set eggs no Diver will think of returning to its nest until it is well and truly satisfied that the human intruder has made good his departure. These two were simply biding their time. The day being warm, the single egg could be left indefinitely. They could afford to wait. In any case, it was time to be on the way uphill again to see how the Black-throats were getting on.

Three hours without a shirt had left me well and truly roasted and long before the loch came in sight my shoulders had begun to smart under the chafing of the heavy rucksack. For another mile my eyes prickled with the salty sweat from my forehead: then the ground levelled out and the going became easier.

Fortunately the islet on which the nest was situated was on the nearer side of the loch so that it could be approached without being seen. Flopping down in the heather I wormed forward with all the care of a wild-fowler stalking a Grey-lag: but it was no use—the Diver spotted me the moment I raised my head. Crouching low among the rushes, she lay with her neck outstretched in an attitude of deep obeisance. After waiting a moment like this she shuffled forward a yard and slid into the water, disappearing beneath it without seeming to dive at all. I waited for her to reappear, thirty seconds, forty-five . . . a whole minute, and still there was no sign of her. Once there was a hint of movement on the surface, as if a salmon had changed its mind in the act of rising. Twice the top of her back showed as she rolled like a dolphin—the same snaky motion with which she had first submerged—but by then the bird was at least three hundred yards out. (To say that a Black-throat *dives* when it wishes to escape notice is to use too strong a word: rather is it drawn under bodily, as if by some hand beneath the surface. Surreptitiously, almost apologetically, the sinuous body resigns itself to the element in which it is so completely at home. The vanishing trick is performed without a trace of effort, with a suaveness which is itself liquescent. A Coot splashing about for water-weeds is the veriest bungler by comparison and even the most expert diving-ducks are made to seem clumsy.) Five minutes later she came up farther off still, away over on the far side of the loch where the waves were dancing in the sun. On this side the surface was glassy, and yet she had made her getaway so smoothly and so furtively that anyone who did not know *exactly* where to look would never have seen her.

The islet was no great distance from the shore and the channel in between shallow enough for wading. The water looked cool and alluring, quite deceptively so, for once in, its iciness quickly numbed a man's bones to the marrow. Half way across, a duck Merganser came squattering out from the fringe of bog myrtle, croaking in distress, but search as I might there were no eggs to be seen. The Diver's nest, on the other hand, was obvious to anyone with half an eye: a flattening among the rushes with the two magnificent eggs laid side by side upon it. The few pieces of sorrel which were strewn around them looked as if they might have been added by way of decoration. More probably, however, they had got there entirely by accident, broken off and shoved in front of the hen Diver as she hauled herself out of the water. As yet there was no slipway to speak of, nothing like the Red-throat's muddy slide at any rate, and seeing that the nest was right at the lochside, so close that the sitting bird might have reached forward and wetted her bill without uncovering the eggs, it seemed hardly likely that there would be later on in the season. The bottom was stony, a level pavement, shelving away into deeper water about six yards out: and the shallows were so very shallow, barely ankle-deep in places, that no one could have credited that they could cover a bird the size of a Diver. Yet somehow or other this one always contrived to prostrate herself beneath the surface and sneak away without being seen.

Having ascertained that the second egg had been laid that day there was no excuse for hanging about and keeping the bird off the nest longer than was necessary. Wading back to the shore I clambered up the bankside above the islet and stretched out in the heather. In this position there was no possibility of my being seen and with the telescope screened with bracken I could command the length and breadth of the entire loch.

So far I had seen nothing of the cock Diver. When at last I spotted him he was fishing by himself at the bottom end of the loch about half a mile away. Presently he left off diving and swam over to join his mate who was now preening herself out in the middle. Not a sound passed between them as he joined her. Nevertheless it was clear that he understood well enough what was going on, and from now on he remained at her side.

How fantastical, how impossibly beautiful these Black-throated Divers are in their summer dress! No photograph can do full justice to its weird symmetry. Other species have their fancy dresses, their extravagant displays and unpremeditated outbursts of song, but in the case of the Divers both the external and internal changes in the bird's condition amount to nothing less than a metamorphosis. Seeing them like this on their breeding loch, it is hard to believe that they can be the same birds which have spent the winter fishing their way up and down the coasts and estuaries of England and Wales. It is not simply that their appearance is so utterly unlike what it was three months ago, nor that their overt behaviour has undergone a sea-change in the interval. The difference is so absolute that it seems impossible that the birds themselves can remember anything at all of their former existence. It is the difference between the bulb in the frozen ground and the daffodil unfolding its sheath, between the chrysalis and the perfect image. To call it the miracle of spring, as the older writers were wont to do, may be to utter a common place, but if so it is only because we have allowed ourselves to become so case-hardened that natural phenomena no longer fire our wonder as they should.

It must have been getting on for an hour and a half before the pair ventured to come alongside the nest, but at last they did, diving in unison and gently tossing their bills each time they surfaced. Standing off from the islet they began to preen again. (The amount of time which a Diver spends in trimming its feathers, stretching its wings and sleeking its head on its back is nobody's business.) Neither of them, it was plain to see, had the least intention of going ashore just yet. If not actually worried, they were very far from being satisfied that everything was as it should be. Once or twice they touched bills as if minded to indulge in a bout of dalliance—or was it the cock trying to persuade his mate to return to the eggs? If so, she was having none of it, nor of his canoodling.

Close in at last, the pair came to a standstill in the narrows. In the full light of the sun, their crowns and napes looked silvery grey, smoother than sealskin, with a ruby eye placed well forward like a jewel set in velvet. The black patches on their throats (copying-ink purple, actually) seemed to have been cut out of glossy paper and pasted on, and the sides of their necks pin-striped with black and white down to the waterline. Each wore a half-necklace of white spots below the chin. The black of the upper parts was broken up with two elliptical patches of squarish white speckles arranged in regular rows. But why snatch a grace beyond the reach of art by trying to describe it? The crazy pattern was such an eye-teaser that it was impossible to take it all in at once; and the total effect was more than the sum of its parts. Call it dazzling, bewildering, eccentric and leave it at that. No doubt the Black-throat's breeding plumage provides an effective camouflage in certain lights, but (as I see it) it is inconceivable that any principle of natural selection should ever have produced this weird and wonderful design. For design it is, and no matter in what sense the word be used, design implies a purpose. True, the Argument from Design, as the philosophers once called it, has no place in modern scientific thought, which regards it as invalid. So much the worse for modern scientific thought. If the heart has reasons which the head knows nothing of, it is no less true that the life of instinct has its own ineffable logic: indeed, it is the apprehension of this subliminal life which is the very stuff of bird-watching and which alone justifies and sustains the naturalist's quest in every field. Maybe it is not longer quite in order to ask: "What the hand and what the eye?" yet in cases like this it is not easy to believe that the existence of pattern—any pattern—can be explained in terms of sheer determinism. Such rare devices argue an artificer. To say that it is in the nature of things that the diatom or the frost crystal take the form they do is to leave the spirit of inquiry unsatisfied: and so long as it remains unsatisfied, not only is the idea that purpose entered the universe by accident repugnant to good sense, but the "nature of things" itself must be called in question.

All curves, the pair continued to patrol. They sat the water more assuredly than the timid Red-throats. Even now that every detail of their plumage could be examined it was still hard to say which was which, and quite impossible when the two were apart. Possibly one *was* slightly smaller than the other though the difference was never obvious. Indeed it was only the fact of the second egg's being newly laid which convinced me that the bird which I had seen leave the nest was the female. That and the fact that she acted more shyly than the other. As yet the turn-and-turn-about business of brooding had not begun in earnest. For his part, there was an air of unconcern about the male Diver which suggested that he had nothing to lose. If it had been left to him, I am sure, he would not have hesitated anything like so long before returning to cover the eggs. Of the two, the female was much the slower to make up her mind.

Watching them closely I decided that it *was* possible to distinguish between the sexes after all. The half-necklace below the female's chin lacked a spot in the middle whereas the male's was complete. There were five pin-stripes on the sides of his neck and only four on hers, and when he stretched one wing (which he did frequently when bored) it was rather more liberally stippled than hers. Trivial differences, these, and almost certainly peculiar to this particular pair, but at least they helped to identify the birds as individuals. For most of us the joy of bird-watching may be three parts aesthetic and one part scientific, but after a time the greediest eye is sated with Beauty and the desire for Truth takes precedence. Delight is never passive: it must always be seeking new meanings. The flash upon the inward eye is its own reward, and there are moments when one does not ask for more, but in the long run it is the bird's behaviour which makes it so intriguing and keeps the watcher guessing.

Certainly these Divers had kept me guessing, and still they were giving nothing away. Quietly composed, they floated in the shallows, hardly stirring at all. Now that the weeks of incubation were due to begin it seemed that they had taken vows of silence when near the nest. A week ago the lochside had been loud with their ululations but this afternoon neither of them had made a sound.

Afternoon? Already it was past eight o'clock and the hills lost in their evening haze. If only my leave-taking could have been half as sly as a Diver's! What a clodhopper a man is, to be

Red-necked Phalaropes

Black-throated Divers

sure! Despite all my precautions—squirming along on all-fours and keeping out of sight until I was well clear—when I turned to look back from the *bealach* both Divers had retired and were swimming side by side in the far corner of the loch. Disturbed again. If ever a female was entitled to say, "*There*, what did I tell you?" to her spouse, surely it was this one; but knowing how well-attuned to each other they were, I cannot think that she did anything of the kind.

XVII. Grass-Widower

RED-NECKED PHALAROPE

THERE ARE NOT many days in the year when the Atlantic is so becalmed that you can blow smoke-rings from your pipe and watch them die a lingering death, dissolving into the gentleness of blue air. The rock on which I was sitting felt red-hot. Too warm for serious bird-watching this afternoon I decided, dabbling my feet in the tepid water: much too warm and far too many horse-flies about to be comfortable. Yesterday, according to the wireless, the temperature had been seventy-six in London, eighty-one at Prestwick, eighty-two at Oban; and today the sun had really begun to turn on the heat. (London, Prestwick, Oban . . . the very names came as echoes from some former existence, faraway-sounding, unreal places which belonged to another and a duller world.) Here in the Western Isles it must have been ninety or over, no shade to be found anywhere, either, and not a cloud in the sky: the sort of day to fetch the skin off your nose.

Across the loch the bugling of the Whooper Swans sounded querulous, belated and strangely out of place in the early July heat-wave. Whimbrels tittered overhead, on their way south across the Minch. For *them*, at any rate, the breeding season was already over and done with: so brief is the interval between spring and autumn in the higher latitudes. Out on the machair a crowd of Arctic Terns was mobbing a pony which had unwittingly strayed among their nests—and how the poor beast shied and tossed its head as they swooped and jabbed it once, twice, three, four, five times in quick succession. (I could feel for the pony. My own head was still sore from the drubbing which those same Terns had given me on my way to the loch.) Cows swished their tails at the waterside, up to their haunches in the shallows, patiently enduring the torments of the flies. Between them and the shore, not ten yards away from where I was sitting, three lark-size birds kept nodding this way and that on the surface, nimble as clockwork toys. Now the first of them half-opened its wings and darted sideways to snatch at a midge, now the second pirouetted daintily on the water with the ripples ringing around it, while the third dipped in its spillikin bill and swallowed some invisible water-mite.

Restless little sprites, it made no difference to them if I dabbled my feet in the water. Even when I ventured to wade in after them they remained quite unconcerned. Dodging along in front of me they went on feeding as busily and as fancy-free as ever, only flitting up when my shadow fell upon them and alighting again a few yards farther on. Even when the cattle suddenly took leave of their senses and came splashing towards the shore, which happened more than once, it seemed that the Phalaropes were not half as disconcerted as I was! Nothing could ruffle their composure. All three were females, so confiding that there was no point in using field-glasses, and one of them was so extraordinarily tame that there were times when it would have been quite easy to catch her with a butterfly net.

This particular bird was the handsomest in the whole colony, so good-looking that we called her the Queen. She was a jewel. Her upper parts were sooty grey, verging on black, streaked with buff and flecked with a few biscuit-coloured feathers on the shoulders. Sooty, too, her head, with a conspicuous white spot above the eye. Chin and throat were pure white, set off with an S-bend of the most vivid foxy-red on the sides of the neck. When she came ashore, either to stand and preen on the rock beside me or to trot along under the grassy bank plucking insects from the stalks of the buttercups and ragged-robin that overhung it, the spindles of her legs showed blue-grey. Often she came close enough to see the greenish-yellow lobes of her feet with the naked eye. But why attempt to make an inventory of this Thumbelina's beauty? Words are too clumsy. Enough to say that she was the prettiest, sprightliest little thing I ever saw, and that she made all the bird-book illustrations of Red-necked Phalaropes look wooden and ludicrous (as, indeed, most of them are).

It is hard to decide whether it is its rarity, its disarming lack of fear, its fetching colour-scheme, or the grace and delicacy of its non-stop movements which makes the Phalarope so captivating. Certainly it is rare—all-told there are probably less than sixty breeding pairs in the whole of the British Isles— but there are other species just as rare or rarer which seem virtually commonplace by comparison. Again the Phalarope is seemingly oblivious, at any rate indifferent, to the human presence: a great virtue, this, in the eyes of any bird-watcher, but hardly one which can be called unique. The secret of the Phalarope's special charm, surely, is to be found in a combination of two simple facts, first, that the bird is so diminutive, second, that it habitually lives on the water. To some extent the Dipper shares the same secret, only to speak of Phalarope and Dipper in the same breath is rather like saying that Ariel resembles Bottom. Light as a cockleshell, deft as a butterfly, the Phalarope looks more like one of the "wee folk" than a wading bird. To see one is to receive a faint shock of surprise, as if a fairy-tale creature had come alive.

Be this as it may, I could hardly take my eyes off those three midgets as they swam to and fro in the shallows. No birds, I think, have ever given me greater pleasure. The long, bright hours slipped by unnoticed, the heat of the day was forgotten, and it was not until the cool of the evening that the thought of leaving entered my head.

So far I had seen nothing of the males. For the time being they were lying low; and this was as it should be, of course, for it is common knowledge that once the eggs are laid the females show no further interest in them. If that exquisite poetaster, Nicholas Husk, is correct (and to give him his due he usually contrives to get his facts right):

> "The Phalarope, besides Red-Necked,
> Is also horribly hen-pecked:
> For nubile Phalaropes, I fear,
> Each mating season seems Leap Year.
> Here Nature slips a Shavian clause
> Within the usual avian laws:
> The female bird is big and bright,

The male a small and sombre sight.
Three courting female Phalaropes
Will centre all their marriage hopes
Upon one shrinking, timid male
And chase him over hill and dale."

Striking as are the differences between the plumages of the
two sexes they are not so striking as the differences in temperament. Side by side with her consort, the female Phalarope is
domineering and possessive, positively officious in the way she
follows him around, breasting the water as if she owned it. Fine
feathers are meant for showing off and she is nothing if not
demonstrative, fussing after the male—any male—whenever the
opportunity presents itself. The nature of the male is much more
retiring, his appearance dowdy and off-colour at the best of times.
A dapper, insignificant little fellow, he rarely or never chooses to
assert himself. There is the unmistakable look of the underling
about him.

The afternoon being so unusually warm the temptation to
leave the eggs to look after themselves for a while must have
been very strong. The nests were only fifty yards from the edge
of the loch, exposed to the full glare of the sun so that the sitting
birds must have had an uncomfortable time of it. Yet whenever
one of then flew down to the waterside he was invariably pursued
by one or more of the females who gave him no peace until
he returned. No matter how low he flew or how surreptitiously
he alighted they were after him in an instant. *Wit wit witcher!*
With a swallow-like twitter they plumped down beside him,
dodging about at his tail as he jerked this way and that in search
of insects on, above and beneath the surface. Since there was no
escaping these attentions the male accepted them demurely and
even gratefully—or so it seemed. All the same, it is misleading,
I fancy, to suggest that the male Phalarope is in the least hen-
pecked. If the females dance attendance on him like this it is more
for the sake of amorous dalliance than for anything else. At
times, certainly, it *looked* as thought the intention was to chivvy
the male back to the nest—not that he ever showed much inclination to delay his return for any length of time—but it is unlikely that this was the case for, as events were to prove, the

females showed themselves to be singularly lacking in any sort of maternal instinct. The female Phalarope may be a born flirt but she is hardly a martinet. Unfortunately I had arrived too late in the year to see much of the birds' courtship displays. Earlier in the season there had been at least a dozen Phalaropes present on this stretch of the loch. All day and every day they were to be seen chasing each other in the air and on the water, indulging on the maziest of ceremonial flights, but by the end of June five of them (possibly non-breeders) had mysteriously disappeared. Of those that remained four were unmistakably females, two males (one of them so very drab that at first I felt certain that it must be immature), leaving one rather doubtful, "unattached" bird which might have belonged to either sex.

Despite the most thorough search only two nests were found, though admittedly there could have been others in the vicinity which were overlooked. It was a longish walk round the loch, getting on for three miles, and on every side its shores gave on to the level machair, so that to have covered every square yard of it would have been no mean undertaking. Again, there were other lochs on the island which looked every bit as suitable as this one, to say nothing of scores of small lochans and bog-bean pools. Even so, the fact remains that Phalaropes were never found on any of them and that this shallow corner where the cattle came to bathe was the only place where the off-duty females were regularly to be seen. It seemed improbable, too, that the birds were breeding on the far side of the loch where the wave-action was so much more violent than it was in this sheltered south-western bay behind the sand dunes.

On the face of things, then, it appeared that there *was* a preponderance of females, though it would be unsafe to draw any conclusions about polygamy in this case seeing that the numbers were so small. While there was never any difficulty in recognising each of these birds as individuals, it was impossible to say whether or not a particular male was mated to a particular female. Off the nest, the male very soon became the centre of interest for any females that happened to be present. Having nothing to do, the females were usually to be seen swimming about by themselves at the lochside, never more than a few yards from the shore and never very far away from the nests, but as the days went by they absented themselves for longer and longer periods, especially during the afternoon. Where they went to, and what they did with themselves at these times, I never discovered. Possibly they were taking their siesta somewhere not far away, hidden in grass, perhaps—possibly they flew off to the sea-shore or to one of the neighbouring lochs. . . . Wherever they went there was never any accounting for their comings and goings. Many a time I set myself to watch for their return, but it was no use: while I was looking one way a bird would plop down on the water beside me, dropping in from nowhere as if conjured out of thin air. I could only guess that the fact that these visits grew shorter and more infrequent in mid-July was connected with a waning of the sexual impulse. As for the "Queen", it turned out that she was not so much a member of the colony as a hanger-on who dropped in as and when she felt inclined. Subsequently she was seen in the company of two juvenile birds, so that it may have been that she had laid her eggs elsewhere weeks before this and that her original mate had already succeeded in raising a brood, leaving her free to play the wanton here.

Both nests still contained eggs on July 8th. Rather surprising, this, seeing that laying may begin as early as the first week of June and that the incubation period lasts over a fortnight. Could it be that the original clutches had been destroyed (under the hooves of the cattle, perhaps?) or was the average date of laying later than I had supposed? Probably the latter. In Shetland (nearly three hundred miles further north, admittedly), the birds do not appear in any numbers before the end of May and fresh arrivals continue to come in during the first half of June. The earliest hatching date recorded for Shetland is June 21st and the latest July 24th, so that obviously there is considerable overlapping.

At the same time it seemed rather odd that so many of the Dunlin (there were Dunlin running about all over the place) still had fresh eggs when there were so many fully fledged young ones among them. Personally I found it difficult to believe that *all* these July eggs were the result of second attempts: it seemed simpler and more reasonable to suppose that in a "good year" some Dunlin are double-brooded—and the same may be true of the Phalarope, at least in the southernmost parts of its range.

Hitherto I had always imagined that finding a Phalarope's nest would be an extraordinarily difficult business. In the event it proved to be easy. All one had to do was to wait for one of the sitting birds to fly across to the waterside and then watch it when it returned. Unlike most ground-nesting species, the male Phalarope does not take the precaution of approaching the nest on foot, but drops straight in on alighting. The short grass of the machair offers little or no concealment and usually there is a tuft of cotton-grass, a dried cow-plat or some such landmark to take a bearing on. Make a bee-line . . . and the bird goes off at your feet. The four eggs, not unlike those of the Dunlin, only much smaller, are tucked inside a grassy cup some two inches in diameter.

For the next fortnight the island basked in perfect summer weather. The Whoopers had at last taken themselves off, though whether Iceland-bound (rather late in the year for that, surely?) or only to one of the other lochs there was no saying. By now many of the young Arctic Terns were on the wing. Each afternoon Kittiwakes from the cliffs came to wash and preen in the fresh water, bringing their newly-fledged "Tarrocks" with them. A pair of Oystercatchers which, only a week before, had been quite distracted whenever I appeared, no longer flew round "pleep-pleeping" in alarm—no cause for anxiety now that the last of their youngsters had taken off safely. Every day the Phalaropes were to be seen disporting themselves in the same old place, only now instead of three or four there were never more than two. The "Queen", alas, had vanished altogether.

A good deal of their time was spent ashore, picking about on the wet sand in typical wader-fashion or poking about under cover of the buttercups in search of insect larvae. On dry land, though, the Phalarope seems to be out of its element: at least it loses the greater part of the charm that it displays when afloat. I never tired—no one ever *could* tire—of watching their antics on the water. They rode it so lightly that at times it seemed as if the least ripple would overturn them, yet all the while they kept twisting and sidestepping, constantly turning back on their course, so erratic that from one moment to the next it was impossible to say which way they were heading.

The Phalarope's action when swimming is quite unlike that

of other waterfowl. Whereas Ducks and Gulls lie *in* the water, the Phalarope is so buoyant that it can only be said to balance *on* it, with the centre of gravity aft (if, indeed, these feather-weights can be said to have any centre of gravity). It lacks ballast. Normally the attitude is high at the shoulder, which gives it a curiously upended appearance, almost as if the bird were swimming on its tail. As a result, turning on a sixpence is a trick which it performs with the greatest of ease. The slender neck is held primly erect, the needle bill slightly depressed. Dabbing and dipping, it jinks along on the surface, as fidgetty as a kitten catching leaves.

Sometimes, by way of variation, a bird would begin to "spin", rotating clockwise first, then anti-clockwise, afterwards ducking its head in to take some trifle or other stirred up by the commotion in the water. It was noticeable, however, that this peculiar habit was not indulged in anything like so freely in mid-July as it had been earlier in the season—and for obvious reasons. Insect life was now so abundant that the birds fed more or less exclusively on surface flies. It was amusing to watch one cocking an eye at a bluebottle, darting up in a sudden flurry of wings to pick it out of the air or methodically inspecting the undersides of dandelion leaves for frog-hopper larvae.

Tame as they were, they would often fly up and away when least expected. *Wik!* they cried, an emphatic note, and off they shot. Sudden in all their movements, always in a hurry, they came and went with a rush, flouncing down on the water like shuttlecocks.

In the second week of July the Phalaropes were much less in evidence than they had been at the beginning of the month. Now that the eggs were at last on the point of hatching the males had become more furtive and rarely came to the waterside. What had become of the females was anybody's guess: except for an hour or so in the afternoon they were not to be seen. So little activity there was, indeed, that anyone walking along the lochside would almost certainly have come away with the impression that the colony was already deserted.

On July 12th one of the eggs showed signs of chipping. Sure enough, when I visited the loch next day (another scorcher) the dutiful male was there waiting for me. For once, he had crept off under cover and stolen down to the water without being seen. *Chee-wik chee-wik!* he cried repeatedly, turning uneasily from side to side, now and then, stretching his wings over his back as if about to take flight. *Chee wik!* It was a new note, quite unlike anything I had heard him utter before. Obviously the bird was worried. All a-twitter with excitement, he took wing and flew round and round a swampy patch a few yards away from the lochside, almost as if inviting me to go and see what was hidden there among the Equisetum and the marigolds. A faint *peet peet peet* from the walking chicks soon gave the game away. Exquisite little creatures, these hours-old, inch-long atomies, clad in orange-buff and gingery down, so fragile that it hardly seemed possible that they could ever survive the hazards to which they were exposed. Yet here they were, footing it bravely through the tangles, tumbling over themselves, falling into hoof-holes and struggling out again, each of the four going its own way. The temptation to pick one up was too great to resist, but when I did the parent bird flew round "chee-wicking" so distressfully that I felt like a criminal caught in the act.

Curious to see what would happen, I placed one of the cheepers in the shallows. At once it became completely self-possessed, paddling along, snatching at midges as to the manner born and even twittering like an adult! Even so, it was not long before it made for the shore again. There for a time it swam about quite happily under the shade of the bankside. Meanwhile, the attendant male tried every trick in the book to distract my attention, though it was clear that in doing so he was hampered by the need for keeping an eye on the rest of the brood at the same time. Several times he alighted between me and the kidnapped cheeper, "cheewicking" in my face. Once he came running towards me within arm's distance. Just then one of the females appeared, dropping in from nowhere as usual and plopping down on the water beside the chick. Without more ado she promptly tucked her head in and fell asleep! So far as she was concerned, evidently, the chick might just as well have been a cork bobbing up and down in front of her. The contrast between the behaviour of the two sexes could hardly have been demonstrated more dramatically than in this incident—the female completely indifferent, the male fairly beside himself with anxiety.

Enough of this cat-and-mouse game, though, for no experiment, however trifling, is justified if it causes suffering to a helpless creature. Rather than go on with it, I retrieved the precious little scrap of fluff and returned it to its place in the marsh. That done, I left post-haste, only too conscious of my misdeeds. In any case, it was clear that the parent bird had no intention of leading its brood to the lochside for the time being.

SEA AND SHORE BIRDS

STORM PETREL
GANNET
SHORE BIRDS
PASSAGE MIGRANTS
WILSON'S PHALAROPE

XVIII.   Imp of the Ocean

STORM PETREL

LIKE KEATS, "Round many Western islands have I been", from the Wee Cumbrae to Skye (which is really a land in itself, not to say a world apart) but there is one which has a special hold on my affections not so much for its isolation or its charm as because it is a breeding station of the little Storm Petrel. It is an islet rather than an island, small enough to stroll round in an afternoon, a fair meadow set down in the open sea. Call it Eilean Beag, then: the name itself is of no consequence since for all I know there are a hundred others like it in the Minch. Though not a hundred miles from Oban, where the railway ends and the real journey begins, the island is not easily reached and to camp out on it for a week or so calls for as much planning as an expedition to places much farther afield. You can fly to Los Angeles and watch the sea-birds on the Pacific coast in the time it takes to reach Eilean Beag from Glasgow. And all for the sake of a black imp of the ocean no bigger than a sparrow, a fly-by-night which only comes ashore to hide itself in a hole in the ground. A bird which is difficult to find, more difficult to watch when it *is* found, and most difficult to understand even when it can be watched.

For hours the lobster boat punched its way into the Atlantic swell without seeming to make any forward progress. The mainland hills had long since faded and fallen away behind, lost in the July haze, and with them the feckless gulls that had trailed out from the harbour after us. Now and then jelly-fishes the size of dinner plates came floating by, their mauve rings like so many upturned sightless eyes: and for a time a Fulmar circled the masthead, flickering and gliding and then heeling off out to sea again. A brown Eider, with five ducklings bobbing along at her tail, was the first indication that the low line of cliffs on the horizon was, in fact, getting nearer. As we rounded the skerries we saw the seals lazing on their slabs, many of them turning on their sides to watch us with eyes as big as penny buns.

The engine gave a last hiccough and sputtered into silence. The coble nosed cautiously into the haven and a row of Shags, oily green in the sun, stood to attention as it moved past them, almost within arm's reach, writhing their heads and grunting in disapproval. Oystercatchers yelped from the rocks and flew up in a panic as the old motor-tyre fenders went overboard with a splash. The boatman's lad, agile as a monkey, leaped ashore with a line. We had arrived, or very nearly—for in places like this there is many a slip between ship and shore. Naturally there was no landing-stage, only a shelf of rock with the waves sucking at the yellow wrack on its sides as they rose and fell. It was a fair jump from the gunnel, and with the boat rolling and bucking uneasily, an awkward one, but there was no time for dithering. Getting the stores and equipment off was a tricky business but we managed somehow, only losing a loaf of bread which rolled out of its pannier at the critical moment. A last word to the boatman, a wave of the hand and the coble turned for home. We were alone.

At first sight the island looked to be even smaller than the map had led us to expect, less than a mile from end to end and well nigh featureless. Devoid of trees or bushes, its main vegetation consisted of wiry grass and stunted bracken, most of which had already been browned by exposure to the salt sea winds. Outcrops of reddish rock provided the only shelter and in a hollow beneath one of the larger ones were the ruins of a croft. Its turf roof had fallen in ages ago, but the fuchsias were still flowering beside the doorway and, better still, the covered-in spring which served as a well was bubbling as merrily as ever. Here we pitched the tent.

The next thing was to get the primus going. The billy was on the point of boiling when the first of the Storm Petrels intimated that we were not alone among the ruins and that our presence was causing the other occupants a certain amount of anxiety.

Curr chik . . . curr chik . . . curr chik . . . The sounds seemed to come from somewhere at the back of the house but no sooner had I turned the corner than they left off abruptly. In a moment they began again, this time right beside me, as dramatically as the ticking of a time-bomb in a radio thriller. *Curr chik . . .* a low croak followed by a sharp, peremptory note on a rising inflection. *Curr chik . . . curr chik . . . curr chik . . .* always that same un-hurried rhythm, regular as clockwork, more like a batrachian than a bird.

With my nose to the drystone wall I sniffed at the crevices and there, sure enough, was the unmistakable scent of a petrel, not the strong whiff of the Fulmar's body odour, but a musty fragrance which was tolerably pleasant. Getting warm now! The ticking had now taken on an urgent intonation, as if the bird inside were thoroughly frightened, and lo and behold, a few yards away to the left another had started up. This one was higher up, nearer the top of the wall, the entrance marked with a spot of whitewash. There was a loose stone at the side. To remove it was the work of a moment. Mercifully it came out cleanly and there, cowering in a corner, was the tiny petrel covering its white egg.

A frailer, gentler, more endearing creature cannot be imagined. Six inches away, its brown eye looked into mine without com-prehension, without a trace of fear. Its high domed head was as round as a halfpenny, soot-coloured except on the forehead where the feathers were rusty and faded. Its wings and tail were lustrous black and its curious toylike bill seemed to have been carved from polished jet. The bird made no attempt to move. Silent, it crouched in the same position as before, ignoring the fact that the privacy of its secret chamber had been so rudely invaded. The temptation to hold it in the hand was difficult to resist but there are some risks (and some crimes) which the bird-watcher does well to avoid. Though the Storm Petrel is apparently quite fearless its temperament is so highly strung that it is easily upset. There is always the risk that the bird will slip through one's fingers and make out to sea in which case the egg will almost certainly be deserted. Not only that, but if this happens it is highly improbable that the bird will lay again until the following year. To have removed the stone was bad enough and great care had to be taken to replace it exactly *in situ* lest the incoming bird should fail to recognise the entrance on its next visit.

Without knowing it, we had pitched camp in the midst of a little community of Storm Petrels. There were at least five of them in the derelict building and others close by in the tumbledown walls. It was too late in the day to move to a new site, and as things turned out there was no need. Provided we behaved ourselves and did not make too much noise the warning voices of the sitting birds were never raised. Peaceful coexistence, as the politicians call it, was perfectly possible—and after nightfall, of course, the pairs were too full of their own affairs to be worried by the presence of human beings.

Towards evening the wind dropped and the weather turned cloudy. There was no sunset, only a flush of cerise in the far west. Inshore where the Eiders were crooning, the wavelets were tipped with rosy lights. The ocean had fallen asleep. The cliff tops were lined with Puffins, standing together in groups and companies and taking their ease as holiday makers do on a promenade. On being approached they turned their heads from side to side, uncertain what to do next and then, bowing to the inevitable, went spinning down to join their fellows afloat in the bay below.

Through the telescope I examined the wide sea, hoping to catch a glimpse of one or other of the returning "Stormies", but in vain. For that matter, never once during the whole fortnight did we see one at sea, though Manx Shearwaters were frequent enough. Where the small petrels went to during the hours of daylight was a mystery. Granted, the chances of picking up so diminutive a bird at any distance even on a calm day and in a good light are never very good. Still, so far as could be seen, they spent their days well out of sight of land, and their visits to the island were invariably made under cover of darkness.

Their arrival, usually between ten-thirty and eleven p.m. (BST), was preceded by a continuous churring, interspersed now and then with a hiccough, from the birds in the burrows. At close quarters it resembled nothing so much as the reeling of a distant Nightjar, but so faint and fairy-like as to be quite inaudible at thirty yards. The churring came from all kinds of situations, some of them quite unexpected—from the block scree at the base of the cliff just above the high-water mark, from bank-sides among the bracken in the centre of the island, and even from the mouths of some of the tunnels occupied by Puffins.

As the night closed in the air became alive with invisible forms, all flitting and glancing around in a mazy dance. It was an eerie experience to stand still and listen to their silken wings whispering around one's head, to hear them calling (a soft, surreptitious *wik*!) as they chased each other. Whether this nightly ritual was a survival of the courtship flight—a reunion of the pairs—or whether it was a communal celebration was never very clear. Examination of the burrows before midnight disclosed the interesting fact that some of those containing eggs had been temporarily abandoned—as if the bird on duty had taken time off for a spell in the air with its mate. On the other hand, those which had young chicks (that is, chicks less than a week old), always remained in attendance, waiting for a rendez-vous at the nest. Courtship flight certainly is kept up well into August and where there are several pairs together, all flitting hither and thither over the same territory, it is tempting to con-clude that the flight partakes of the character of a ceremonial dance. On the whole, however, the indications were that the main purpose served by these aerial revels, which lasted about an hour, was to orientate the incoming birds.

Living cheek by jowl with them, as we did, it was still not possible to be sure when or whether a change-over at the nest had been effected. The practice seemed to be for one bird to remain on duty for a period of two or three days, being visited once every twenty-four hours and relieved on the third or fourth night; but there were so many exceptions that it was obviously unsafe to formulate any sort of general rule. Not only was it impossible to distinguish between the sexes at this stage or to see much or anything of the goings-on inside the burrows, but to complicate matters still further there was a good deal of casual visiting—odd birds, complete "strangers", dropping in to share the company of the one in charge of the egg or chick. Indeed, had it not been for the existence of the chick, the suspicion of promiscuity among Storm Petrels would have been very strong.

As it happened, several of the nests were in positions which could be exposed without unduly disturbing the occupants so that it was possible to keep a rough check on their comings and goings. One bird (a female, surely), had three different companions on three different nights—and if the croodlings and purrings that issued from the hole were anything to go by, she bestowed her favours on all three indifferently. Having already admitted the impossibility of distinguishing between the sexes it may be asked how, without actually marking them, anyone could be sure that these visitors were, in fact, different. The answer is that there *are* variations in plumage, size, and behaviour which enable the observer to tell one individual from another at a glance. Thus the rusty feathering on the forehead of one is missing in another. This bird is plumper, its head noticeably bigger than the one which was here before.* Yesterday the visitor was quite docile when the burrow was opened up whereas today its opposite-number is sick with fright, coughing up oil and "mush" when the torch is flashed upon it.

It seems probable that much of this visiting is done by unmated, immature birds. There was one couple which were apparently playing at keeping house and home together. So far, at any rate, they had produced no egg, yet so attached to each other were they that they spent three or four days standing, or rather crouching, side by side doing nothing in particular, after which they both disappeared and were not seen again for nearly a week, when they turned up again, still together.

The croft wall was a miniature catacomb, riddled from end to end with creep-ways, but so far as could be seen, each burrow was self-contained and had only the one entrance. The problem was: how did birds returning from the open sea find the way-in in the darkness? By sight, by sound, by smell, or by some built-in direction-finding mechanism akin to radar? The eyes of the Storm Petrel are not specially adapted for night-flying: if they were the birds would presumably fly straight into the hole like Swifts or Kingfishers, and this they are certainly not in the habit of doing. Instead, they alight on the ground somewhere in the

* It is possible that the size of the head may be a sex-character: all the birds which were found to have numerous "suitors" and which, on that account, were presumed to be females, had small heads.

vicinity of the burrow and remain immobile for a time, apparently trying to get an exact bearing, then, as if making up their minds, they flutter-walk the rest of the way. Between eleven and midnight (when most of them were safely inside) it was common to come across "stranded" birds. There were, to all appearances, at a loss and helpless, yet before long they would scuttle off into the darkness. Sometimes they were to be seen clambering up the side of the wall outside the tent, using their hooked bills, wings and feet to assist them. At first it looked as if it was the constant purring of the sitting bird which served to guide the other in—and all things considered this is probably as good an explanation as any—but if this is the case how do the pairs which indulge in courtship flights or those which are in the process of deserting the chick find their way back to the unoccupied nest? The truth seems to be that until they are familiar with the lie of the land and unless there is at least a glimmer of light they do so only with difficulty. On moonless nights, and especially in mist, all kinds of mix-ups occur, and nothing is likelier than that the frequent visits of total strangers is accounted for by their failure to find the right entrance. Attractive as it is, the "radar hypothesis" is better ruled out. Even the Manx Shearwater which performs wonders of long-range homing will blunder into obstacles in foggy weather. If the Storm Petrel possessed some sixth sense comparable with that of the bats it would hardly be caught so easily in nets, nor would it make the mistake of flying into an open tent! There remains the slight but real possibility that the birds may be guided by the sense of smell. This idea is usually pooh-poohed by the zoologist on the grounds that the necessary organ is too rudimentary to be of any practical use to a petrel—but, against this it has to be said that the scent issuing from the nesting hole is anything but rudimentary! If a human being can be led to it quite infallibly why should it be impossible for a bird? The biological function of the tube-nose is, to say the least of it, imperfectly understood; and until it is it seems wiser to preserve an open mind. Beside, the attitude of ground—head down—rather suggests that they are waiting to pick up the scent, though here again it is as well to remember that appearances are deceptive.

It was at once disconcerting and delightful to turn in at one or two in the morning and find, at the last moment, an unfortunate "Stormy" caught in the folds of one's sleeping-bag. On such occasions one cannot help thinking that there is something to be said for the bird in the hand. Only then can you take in the exquisite details of its anatomy—the spindles of its legs (incredibly thin), the veined skin of its tiny webbed feet (no bigger than the nail of your little finger), its extraordinary lightness and suppleness. Soft and tremulous it lies in the folded palm: and then, just when you are thinking how well behaved it is, the little thing throws a fit and starts squealing in a high-pitched, elfin falsetto. Before you can let go of it, the captive retches up a mouthful of yellow oil and slivers of white fish. Put it down on the ground and the bird stands upright on its tarsi balancing itself with its wings and takes off almost vertically. In the air it suddenly seems to have grown twice as big as it was in the hand.

Handling Stormy Petrels is apt to be a messy business and not the sort of practice which is to be encouraged, if only because the birds are so extremely sensitive. There is this to be said for it, though, that at least it does provide us with scraps of information about the feeding habits of this little-known species. By no means every individual obliges by being sick on the spot—and there is no excuse for holding them until they are terrified out of their wits—but in some the reaction is almost instantaneous. Evidently it depends to some extent upon whether or not the bird is freshly returned from the sea: a bird which has been in the burrow for two or three days will often allow itself to be handled without struggling whereas the one which takes over may start screeching and vomiting the moment it is touched. Sometimes the discharge is a clear, colourless oil, some of which may be exuded through the nostrils. More frequently the oil is yellowish and anything but clear—rather like the mess in a sardine tin after the contents have been removed. In addition to the oil in which it is smothered, there is a liquid grey "mush" with solid fragments among it. The latter may include such items as roe, liver and other offal, as well as bits of white fish. These undigested remains are interesting because they show that the Storm Petrel's diet is by no means confined to planktonic organisms and that, like the Fulmar, it is by way of being a scavenger.

Some ornithologists may deplore the manhandling of a defenceless bird in order to find out what it had been eating but in this instance, it seems, there is no other method of getting at the facts; and when all is said and done, parting company with a stomachful of oily waste may be considered a minor indignity compared with the nuisance of having to go pattering over the North Atlantic for the rest of one's life carrying a British Museum ring round one's leg. Observation of Storm Petrels at sea is, in the nature of things, sketchy and inconclusive. Occasionally they may be seen skimming the sides of the waves or flicking restlessly from side to side in the wash of churned up by the propellors, but there is no saying just what it is they get when they dip in the water or pick something from the surface. More rarely they may be observed plunging in head-first, as if trying to catch fish, though it is highly improbable that this is what they are actually doing. The assumption is that planktonic crustaceans are the main source of their food supply. Roberts's study of the life cycle of a closely related species, Wilson's Petrel, in the Antarctic indicates that these minute free-swimming organisms are the staple diet, and Dr. L. H. Matthews's researches show that the glandular secretions of stomach oil are derived from the same source. In addition there are *prima facie* grounds for thinking that the food must be oceanic and not simply marine. It is no accident that all the known breeding stations of the Storm Petrel (with the solitary exception of a pair which bred on the Bass Rock in 1904) face on to the open Atlantic. A glance at any map of their locations at once reveals that they are strung out along the edge of the Continental Shelf. Why this should be so, seeing that there are several breeding stations in the Western Mediterranean, is decidedly puzzling. The inference would seem to be that the species is dependent on forms of zoo-planktonic life which are not found in sufficient quantities in shallow seas. There are vast areas of the North Atlantic where the surface becomes almost soupy and at night phosphorescent with their myriads—a richer harvest than the North Sea ever produces.

But if it is the case that the small Petrels feed mainly on such marine organisms as the copepods and ctenophores (many of which contain droplets of oil) another question arises. These planktonic forms behave photo-sensitively, sinking several fathoms during the daylight and rising to the surface after dark.

That being so, the Storm Petrel might be expected to be a good deal more crepuscular than it normally seems to be in its feeding habits. Can it be that the birds delay their return to the island until nightfall in order to feast themselves to the full when conditions on their sea pasturages are at their best, and not, as is usually supposed, for reasons of secrecy? If so, what are they doing the rest of the day? And why do they not avail themselves of the inshore planktonic population which in spring and summer is swollen by the addition of the "larvae" of many of the larger crustaceans, acorn barnacles and countless others?

Unknowable bird! Peering at it, like Bottom, through a chink in a wall is to be filled with a kind of wondering despair, the recognition that any inkling of its way of life must at best be conjectural. Crouched in its corner it looks so meek, so passive, so devoid of motive and yet by morning, perhaps, it will be a hundred miles or more away careering aimlessly (yet not aimlessly) over a trackless ocean. Where and how far it goes, what prompts it to return, and how it times its arrival—the answers to these questions can only be guessed at.

The domestic life of the Storm Petrel is in keeping with the rest of its character, cryptic. When first the chick is hatched it is treated with the utmost care (loving kindness might be a better word), one or other of the parents brooding it continuously. For the first week of its life the chick is blind and lies quite inert. It is clad in a coarse woolly grey down, naked at the throat, with a curious little bald spot on the crown of the head. When the adult shuffles into a new position or leaves it uncovered even for a moment it sets up a lisping cry, *weet weet weet weet*, until it is comforted. At the time of our landing on Eilean Beag, at the end of July, many of the burrows still contained eggs. When we left, on August 12th, the hatch was practically complete: and even in that short space of time it was possible to detect a distinct change in the treatment of the chick. As soon as its eyes were open and it could raise its head, some eight or ten days after leaving the egg, the solitary mite was often left unattended during the daylight hours, though one or both parents would be present with it after dark. The older chicks, some of them as fat as miniature dodoes, were left to themselves for still longer periods. Already the gradual withdrawal of parental influence had begun, a process which would end only with the more or less complete desertion of all the chicks on the island. Some day in late autumn, after weeks of neglect and near-starvation, they would leave their narrow cells, fluttering out into the wild wind to face the rigours and the chances of life on the high seas.

It would have been instructive, no doubt, to follow the cycle through to the end, but it was enough, for the time being, to have seen one phase of it. Besides, we had a date to keep, and for days the cloud-capped hills of Coll had been beckoning us home. The Glorious Twelfth began with a downpour, only to burst into radiance at noon. Until then there were some anxious moments, but at last the looked-for boat appeared, heading patiently, as all good boats do, across the unsteady sea.

XIX. A Trip to the Craig

GANNET

AT GIRVAN, TO begin with, it seemed doubtful whether the boat could make it, and more than doubtful whether it was wise to try. The old salts along the quayside listened stolidly to those landlubberly souls among us, who urged the need for an early start, and shrugged their shoulders. Patience, it seemed, was a necessary virtue—but who could be patient when the June sun was blazing down from a clear sky and the great dome of the Craig looming up on the horizon, so near that it seemed to be only half an hour's sailing distance from the shore? The old salts could. Maybe the wind would drop with the turn of the tide, they said, maybe not. Nothing for it but to wait and see. Since early morning a stiff nor'wester had flecked the Firth and now, two hours before high water, heavy seas were breaking over the end of the jetty.

Once outside the harbour, the *Lady Ailsa* very soon showed that she was no lady. To say the least of it, her gait was none of the gentlest and to anyone not accustomed to her antics just a little disquieting. Instead of shipping it green in the ordinary way, she fairly stood on her nose as if about to bury herself in the depths like a diving shag and then came up with a gasp and a shiver-my-timbers motion which was distinctly unnerving. Either that or she would rear on her beam ends, bucking at the rollers like a frightened horse, with dozens of circular rainbows lighting the spray that smothered her. Only the skipper wore oilskins and he, lucky fellow, was shut up in his tiny kiosk of a wheelhouse, from which sanctum he looked out on his passengers with a be-it-on-your-own-heads expression, letting it be seen that he had only been prevailed to put out against his better judgment. On our heads it certainly was. One and all were quickly

186

drenched. Flung all of a heap on the kicking deck, the wonder was that none of us was not carried away, for hand-rails were few and far between and there were one or two bad moments when it almost seemed as if the law of centrifugal force had as much to do with our remaining aboard as the determination to hang on. Enough to say that the seven miles crossing took exactly two hours.

Luckily the anchorage was in the lea of the gale and it was possible to moor the boat alongside without much difficulty. A black donkey, evidently resenting the intrusion and taking a poor view of *humanum genus*, greeted the landing party with an outburst of derisive guffaws; and well he might, for never since Trinculo and his fellows were cast ashore did a more bedraggled crowd set foot on an island. All the way up the steep path behind the light-house those belly-laughs followed us, the cliffs ringing with asinine mirth. Still, the sun was hot on the face and the dried salt on our lips tasted of promise.

From the landward side little or nothing can be seen of the gannetry which earns for Ailsa, at least among bird-watchers, the reputation of being one of the seven wonders of Britain. The path to it led up and up over ankle-twisting slopes that were covered with bluebells (now past their best) and white sea-campion. Wrens churred and sang in the bracken—and was it only fancy that lent the notes an unfamiliar ring? Doubtless the rocky background affected the accoustics of the place—even the Blackbird that fluted from a turret of the ruined castle above the lighthouse sounded harsher, more like a Ring Ouzel than a Blackbird—though it seemed feasible to suppose that years of isolation on the island might in fact have produced a distinct local dialect.

Nearing the upper slopes I was challenged by the first of a host of Herring Gulls. Whoof! It drove in with something of the determination of a Skua, banking away with a gruff *heh heh heh*! and diving again before I could screen my eyes against the glare of the sun. Whoof! Here, tucked under a protruding shelf of rock, was its nest with three chipped eggs—and another, and another, until soon they were thick on the ground. All round the turf was brown and worn with the constant treading and picking of hundreds of Gulls, feathers and fish-bone pellets and white-wash everywhere. One bird flew out at my feet, leaving

two newly hatched chicks a-cheeping and a cracked egg. Its
mate, immaculate in grey and white, stood on guard a little way
off and watched me sourly with its pale yellow eye, muttering
remonstrance. Whoof! By this time the whole colony was
roused, the air loud with their cackling and caterwauling.

"The wrinkled sea beneath him crawls." It is a relief to
turn aside for a moment from the confusion and clamour and just
look at the view. From this point, eight hundred feet up, the
Firth looks as smooth as a mirror and the little ships, each carrying
its plume of smoke, all seem to be riding at anchor. To the
the south-west the coasts of Antrim and Rathlin Island show up
as clearly and as green as the Scottish mainland. Looking the
other way, the ragged ridges of Arran, with the humps of Jura
behind, violet in the distance, are enclosed by the long arm of
Kintyre. Due west there is nothing but the glittering perspectives
of the Atlantic. Far below, the floor of the sea is criss-crossed with
countless Gannets sailing in, out and around at all levels, with
soot-brown Guillemots and black Razorbills no bigger than flies
whizzing to and from their ledges, dove-coloured Fulmars tracing
figures-of-eight in the air and midget Puffins spinning along above
the surface. Nearer at hand, (Whoof!) are the Gulls, all wailing
and wheeling; and high overhead, pinned to the blue like a silver
brooch, is a Peregrine Falcon.

At one point it is possible to venture down to the brink—and
this is one of those places where there really is no other word for
it, for, immediately below, the columnar cliff is perfectly vertical—where the matronly Gannets are installed on their pill-box
nests. Some of the attendant birds leave forthwith, shoving off
and spreadeagling themselves on the air as soon as they see me
coming. One, with a get-me-out-of-this-quick expression,
flounders into the midst of a cheek-by-jowl group and gets his
wings so tangled up with his neighbour's that the pair of them roll
headlong over the edge, only separating after they have fallen
fifty feet or more. Most of the broody ones sit tight, however,
and refuse to budge. *Gurruk urruk!* they growl. The nearer ones
stand up, ready to reach out and jab at me: then, thinking better
of it, they spew up chunks of fish, here a whole mackerel (the
tail still fresh, the head more or less digested), there a gobbet that
looks like a herring but turns out to be a composite mass of small

fry. One bird, unable to make up its mind, shuffles off its egg and suddenly casts off with a mournful "*ooer*", between a sigh and a groan. But the upheaval quickly subsides. Provided that I do not move, these nesting Gannets are prepared to let me sit in their midst, content to ignore me and even, if I sit *absolutely* still, to accept me as part of their surroundings. For a time they relapse into a sort of stony calm. At the first hint of a movement, though, they are up in arms again. Up go their heads, and, with their bills wide-open to show their iron-grey gullets, they bark ferociously. *Gurruk urruk urruk!* Like most aggressive displays it is mostly bluff, of course, but effective enough to make one keep one's distance in such a delicate situation as this. Whether or not any of them ever would pluck up courage enough to strike a human being is a question which is better left open when the risk of overbalancing is so great.

At close quarters, the oddities of the adult Gannet's anatomy can be examined in detail. The ridges of the four webbed toes, for example, are lined with lemon yellow—a point which taxidermists and textbook illustrators seem to overlook. A blue ring round the eye and a patch of bare skin in front of it give the face a somewhat skull-like appearance. The eye itself is stony, fixed in a cryptic glare, and the lens is so flattened that it looks exactly like a zinc washer. Looking the bird full in the face one has the impression that it is wearing spectacles! The bill, too, is a curious piece of work. A massive pick, it is designed for strength, the upper mandible being reinforced with a bony plate and tipped with a point of horn. It appears to be cracked a third of the way along its cutting edge and, strangest of all, there are no visible nostrils.

Swan-white, radiant, every feather in place, it goes without saying that each of these sitting birds is in perfect condition. This coign of the cliff is a natural sun-trap and were it not that they kept on the *qui vive* they might doze off in the heat of the afternoon. The pale gold of their heads glistens in the strong light. The air is musty with their ancient and fishlike smell. The ground between the crowded nests is soiled with their excrement as are the eggs, which are stained brown or blackish almost without exception; yet the birds themselves are spotless.

All the time Gannets keep flying alongside, turning their necks to look me straight in the eyes as they sail past. Some of them carry great beakfuls of nesting material (campion or seaweed) which they have grubbed up and intend to present to their mates as tokens of their affection. *Gúrruh gúrruh*, they grunt as they swing past, so loudly that the cliff-face resounds to the crashing of their gears. One trails an extra-large bunch of bladderwrack and lets it fall for another to catch in mid-air, a trick which if it were intentional, would be worthy of a pair of Harriers performing the "pass". Every few moments the composure of the sitting birds is upset by fresh arrivals. Invariably they come in with a rush, throwing up their wings and standing on their tails to land with a thump so violent that it threatens to break every bone in their bodies. To crash-land without offending one or more of their neighbours is virtually impossible and for a few heated moments tempers (and beaks) fly. The greeting of the pairs is apt to be highly extravagant, their love-making violent and unrestrained; and yet, for all its rude excitement, the exchange of affection—if affection it can be called—is strangely unemotional, as cryptic as the coupling of alligators. After overshooting the mark three times in succession the male at last manages to gain a foothold of sorts. He alights, sprawling and spreadeagled as usual, and before he can collect himself the female shoots up her head, growling *urruh urruh urruh*, while every neighbour within striking distance stretches its neck to jab at him viciously. Awkwardly he shuffles forward into position. Face to face, the two of them fence, pointing their bills skywards, wrangling together. Next he taps his bill against hers and they waggle their heads after the style of Great Crested Grebes only rather less decorously. For a moment the excitement subsides and the pair stand staring about them, witless-looking, then, without warning, they are at it again, clattering their spear-points and grunting like pigs. Their neighbours catch the enthusiasm and crane their necks to join in the growing riot, gobbling away for all they are worth, though whether in protest or approbation it is hard to decide. There is a scuffle on the nest as the male seizes the sitter by the scruff of the neck and mounts her in a fluster of wings that threatens to topple the pair of them over the cliff. The sexual act is accomplished with the utmost vigour, over and done with in a moment. After pointing his head at the sky the male makes his obeisance and takes leave of his mistress with that doleful

groan which announces every Gannet's departure. Floundering
to the edge he launches himself into the wind. She, meanwhile,
composes herself and settles down to brooding her egg again.
The crown of her head is blood-stained—the result of a too-hearty
caress—but she is quite unaware of it. The incident, and it is one
which is constantly being repeated, reminds one of Eliot's lines:

"Well now that's done: and I'm glad it's over"
When lovely woman stoops to folly and
Paces about her room again alone,
She smoothes her hair with automatic hand
And puts a record on the gramophone,

—the "record" in this case being a wreath of sea-campion which
has been dropped on one side during the struggle and which she
now proceeds, not very methodically, to work into the edges of
the nest.

Never a dull moment, never a moment of peace. One of the
sitting birds is so upset by an interloper who drops in on her
unexpectedly (surely a cast of mistaken identity), that she coughs
up a silvery mess of fingerlong garfish, dozens of them glued
together so that first sight they look like a herring. The result of
several plunges, obviously involving who knows how many
miles of sea-scouring—and yet she parts with her meal as if it were
of no account. At once the flies are swarming around her.
Another bird, dislodged by this same intruder, remains standing
with one foot clamped firmly on a broken egg. Yet another sits
with her egg uncovered beside her and a half-witless, half-
anxious look in her eyes.

The nearest bird of all (a sedate individual who allows me to
tap her bill with a pencil without getting too worked up about
it) is in charge of a day-old chick. This six-inch piccaninny has a
body the shape of a cigar, naked below with traces of close-set
down already appearing on the back and a woolly top-knot.
Another, left uncovered, is in the act of struggling out of the shell
and keeps up a distressful cheeping. Its neck is folded between one
skinny wing-pit and its legs, a cramped position from which it
seems quite impossible for the mite to extricate itself. Smeared in
green slime, its eyes sealed, the reptilian-looking infant is very
much alive, however, fighting for its place in the world with a

pent-up energy that is heartening to watch. *Chit chit chit* it calls almost incessantly.*

On Ailsa, as on the Bass Rock, the main concentrations of nests are on the most precipitous faces which seem nowadays to be packed to capacity. Competition for places is fierce and it may be that newcomers have no option but to occupy "marginal seats", either on the lowest ledges barely above the splash-zone or near the cliff-top where they are liable to be raided by the Gulls. Both Gannetries have been occupied continuously for several centuries and though they have had their ups and downs the numbers seem to have remained fairly constant over the years, which certainly suggests that these isolated volcanic plugs make ideal breeding stations. But if inaccessibility is the *sine qua non* it is difficult to see why other stretches of the cliffs are not occupied, especially in view of the overcrowding which occurs. The gradual desertion of Lundy and the boom-town growth of the Grassholm population indicate that the geological is not the sole factor which has to be reckoned with; and it is tempting to think that here on Ailsa a southerly aspect has something to do with the choice.

Certainly today, sitting among them for an hour or so, it would be hard to find a pleasanter or more sheltered spot anywhere on the island. Still the stately fly-past continues, above, below and at eye-level, a never-ending stream of Gannets sailing about the walls of their sea-fortress. How many there are in sight at a given moment it is impossible to say, nor does there seem much point in trying. The sober truth is that the colony totals about 6,000 pairs but in the mind's eye their number is legion. It has been estimated that the world population of Gannets is in the region of 170,000, a figure not greatly in excess of the record crowd at Hampden Park, and yet, off hand, anyone would swear that the multitudes here on Ailsa were greater than those which could be packed into the most super-colossal stadium that ever was built. The spectacle is too vast to be taken in as a whole: as well try to cope with the flakes in a snowstorm or keep track of all the moving particles in a cloud chamber. Nevertheless, though the imagination boggles at it, there *is* a pattern just as there is a

* How does it come about, one wonders, that Fisher and Lockley state in their "Sea Birds" that the Gannet chick is voiceless until it is a week old?

Gannet

"The eye is stony, fixed in a cryptic glare, and the lens is so flattened that it looks like a zinc washer"

pattern in the life of a great city. Looking down from this height, the sociologist might be inclined to say that here we had a perfect working model of the collectivist principle, a single community in which all individual identity is lost, composed of lesser groups and having the family as its basic unit.

Musing like this I am jolted back to reality by the blast of a ship's siren somewhere below. In an instant there is a hush as the entire colony takes to the air. The effect of this wholesale uprising is similar to that of a sudden "dread" among Terns or Gulls, only a hundred times more impressive. Before the Gannets can return to their places a burly Great Black-back drops in from nowhere and alights on a pinnacle less than twenty yards away. Evidently he has been hanging about waiting for just such an opportunity and means to take it without dillydallying, only at the last moment he catches sight of me across the gully. In a flash he sizes up the situation: I can see the mean calculating look in his eye as he measures the distance which separates the two of us. We understand each other perfectly. I know what he is after as surely as he knows that I can do nothing to prevent him. So sure of himself is he, indeed, that he does not even bother to hurry over the job. With one insolent eye trained on me all the time, he paces down the slab, cool as you please, and snatches one of the Gannet cheepers from its nest. Before he can gobble it I stand up and clap my hands—all I can do in the circumstances—whereupon the gull takes fright and the chick pitches to destruction down the cliff.

It is for misdeeds of this sort, no doubt, that the Great Black-back has been blacklisted in the latest Protection of Birds Act, most people would say, justifiably. Personally I cannot see it that way. Admittedly the big Gulls take a heavy toll and where their numbers are excessive there is nothing for it but to reduce them if the other sea-birds are to be preserved. But to call the Great Black-back a sneak-thief and a murderer is rather like accusing a Kestrel of cruelty for skewering a mouse. Those who talk so earnestly of a "Charter for the Birds" are often the very ones who refuse to acknowledge that every creature ought to be granted the right to live its own life in its own way. Since the nature of the beast cannot be changed, humanitarian feeling is misapplied when it seeks to persuade us that the avian world would be a better place if this or that species were wiped out altogether. This is no callous judgment, surely. If we are revolted by the sight of a Great Black-back worrying the life out of a helpless chick we may as well take offence at the Gannet every time it crash-dives into a shoal of fish.

So back to the landing-stage and a quieter sea. Before leaving, the *Lady Ailsa* (herself again) chugs round the base of the cliffs and for the first time the full extent of this sea-bird citadel can be seen. Tier upon tier it rises, white with Gannets, like some stupendous open-air theatre packed tight from the pit to the "gods". Guillemots stand shoulder to shoulder on the lower ledges, Kittiwakes on nests that have been glued in situations which can only be described as predicaments. With a mental shudder I recognise the spot where I was sitting half an hour ago: from this angle it looks positively suicidal. A whirling cloud of wings hangs above the cliff, so high that it seems to be revolving in slow motion.

White-faced Puffins race across the bows as the boat heads for the mainland. A Razorbill swims alongside, dangling a fish, and opens its wings as it dives, oaring its way down through the green waters: and as the clamour dies away behind a string of Manx Shearwaters, fancy free, skims by, seven black and silver boomerangs playing their endless game of ducks-and-drakes with the ocean.

XX.   Forth from Auld Reekie

SHORE BIRDS

WHERE ELSE IN the world but in Edinburgh is it possible to
see Long-tailed Ducks from the end of a street or Arctic Skuas
from the top of a bus, I wonder? Having a due regard for its
ancient dignities, Scotland's capital may not care to advertise its
attractions as a seaside resort, yet not least among them for the
bird-watcher is the fact that it has a promenade as long as Black-
pool's. A glance at the map is enough to show that the Forth is
not only the largest of the East Coast estuaries but also that it is
strategically well placed as regards the great migration routes from
Northern Europe. It has its mouth open to the North Sea like a
huge Heligoland trap. As the bird flies the wasp-waist of the
Lowlands is less than fifty miles across, but what an immense
difference there is between the two Firths! On the Clyde there
are the usual waders—Oystercatchers and Redshanks, galore—
innumerable Gulls, a few Ducks (mostly Mergansers, Goldeneye
and Common Scoters) and the fatalism of knowing in advance
that there will be little else of note. On the Forth there is always
the feeling that something out of the way is bound to turn up. It
may be a drove of Waxwings on the roadside at Prestonpans
or a Pectoral Sandpiper on the mudflats of Aberlady Bay or a
Barred Warbler on the May (appropriate name for an islet where
all things are possible) or a party of storm-tossed Little Auks off
North Berwick, according to the time of year. On the East Coast
it is indeed a nipping and an eager air, eager with great expectations.

The extent to which the bird-life of inshore waters depends
upon the state of the tide and on wind conditions needs no
stressing. To an even greater extent, however, it depends on the

nature of the sea floor. The bird-watcher who wishes to understand the comings and goings of waders and wildfowl in an estuary, therefore, must also be something of a marine biologist. This sandy bay here may be good for nothing except as a standing ground for the Gulls. That reef yonder looks to be just the place for Purple Sandpipers and yet there are never any to be seen there, only Turnstones and Oystercatchers. This next bay looks to be no different from the one we have just left behind, but at low water it is crowded with Knots and Bar-tailed Godwits and when it fills up there will be Great Crested and Slavonian Grebes and Heaven knows what else diving in the shallows. Scaup and Seafield, Long-tailed Ducks at Joppa or Gosford, Velvet Scoters at Gullane—each has its favourite feeding grounds.

From Leith Docks to Portobello, where the red stack of the power-station beckons to the incoming shipping, is getting on for two miles. There, in winter, the whole sea front is speckled with thousands of Scaup. In long strings parallel with the shore they ride on the swell, disappearing into the troughs and rising unconcernedly on the crests of the waves for a moment before disappearing again. The black bullet-heads of the drakes flash green as they catch the sun. At low tide they can be seen diving close in, guzzling and slobbering away in the shallows as if their lives depended on it. On hesitates to say it, but a Scaup wallowing in six inches of muddy water, half smothered in filth as it gulps down one sand-worm after another, is not a pretty sight, especially when one remembers that the source of attraction is an outfall of city sewage! There are mussel beds farther east, acres and acres of them, but they never carry anything like the concentrations of Scaup that are to be seen off Leith.

Even at close quarters it is never easy to see just what diving Ducks are getting in the way of food. If the textbooks are to be believed Scaup feed largely on marine bivalves, though how on earth they manage to dispose of mussels more than an inch in length is, to say the least of it, not very obvious. And there is another mystery about these Scaup. Whereas in the Solway they arrive in force in the early autumn, in the Forth they do not appear in any numbers until after Christmas.

The Long-tailed Duck is another comparatively late-comer, one that is well worth waiting for, however, for of all the Ducks none is more elegant. Incidentally, too, the Long-tail is the only Duck which can be said to look much smarter in winter than it does in summer: and no one seems to have explained the significance of its peculiarity in assuming a special breeding plumage. A full-blown Long-tailed drake in all the finery of his snow-ball-white and nigger-brown and black really is a sight to thank God for, to say nothing of his captivating antics. In a flat calm his fantastic tail streamers are carried horizontally, flush with the surface, so that any distance it is difficult to see them. Normally however, they are erected at a rakish angle and in a stiff breeze they often curl up right over the bird's head.

Long-tails fairly revel in a rough sea, diving continuously and half-opening their wings, Auk-wise, as they go under. Merry as schoolboys let loose in a swimming-pool ("beamish" boys at that, for like the slayer of the Jabberwock they chortle in their glee, "Callooh Callay!") they are never still for an instant, always taking short flights to seek fresh company, dropping back into the waves with a splash that is reminiscent of any urchin's belly-flopper. In most cases these companies are composed of equal numbers of adult drakes and ducks and when they break up they are commonly to be seen in pairs. It seems likely, then, that these sportive occasions are not courtship displays in the true sense and that the stimulus is social rather than sexual. Whatever the motive behind it, the Long-tails' behaviour is nothing if not effusive—and what bird could help showing off in so bizarre a rig-out? Harlequinades and quadrilles are the order of the day when Long-tailed Ducks take time off for play. Tail or no tail, the drake has a trick (which he shares with the Common Scoter and performs twice as prettily) of upending in the water like a fisherman's float and tossing his bill in the air.

Unfortunately for bird-watchers in England, the Long-tailed Duck is an uncommon bird south of the Farnes. Odd ones turn up fairly regularly on the London reservoirs, and a few years ago one spent the best part of the winter on the Round Pond of all places, but almost invariably these stragglers lack the elongated tail streamers without which this duck loses its hall-mark of distinction. Whether this thinning out of the adult population is due to the fact that the southern limit of the winter range of *Clangula hyemalis* is located somewhere in the region of the Border or because the nature of the English seaboard is for one reason or another unsuitable is a moot point. The former seems to be the likelier explanation. Long-tails are commoner on the Fife side of the Forth than they are on the Lothian side, and further North they become commoner still wherever there are rocky shores. Judging by its habits, the species is midway between the true "sea" Ducks with which it is classified and the "bay" Ducks as the Americans call them.

By contrast with the spry and restless Long-tails, the Eiders seem to have been built for comfort. Everything about them looks bulbous. Slow and heavy as barges, they like nothing better than to ride at anchor alongside some reef, never stirring very far from one day's end to another and never seeming to exert themselves unduly. Like the seals which lie up on the surfwashed slabs to take their ease after a morning's fishing in the bay, they are sleepy souls. Even their match-making is undemonstrative. In calm weather their gentle crooning, *ah-hóoa ah-hóoa* (neck erect and head stifly depressed), carries far across the water.

Farther out, the sea is lined with flocks of Scoters. At times a solitary Diver shows up in their midst, white-faced and suspicious, only to disappear again with a smooth header which carries it a hundred yards and more at a time. In nine cases out of ten it will almost certainly be a travelling Red-throat, but both the Great Northern and the Black-throat occur quite regularly. Identifying them at a distance is never easy and differences in size are apt to be unreliable; but after a time one learns to distinguish not only between the differences in the *carriage* of three species on the water (the upturned head of the Red-throat with its eternally anxious look, for example) but also between their different facial patterns. So, too, with the Grebes. In late autumn and early winter the numbers of Great-cresteds in the Forth are often quite phenomenal, certainly far in excess of the total breeding population in Scotland. By December most of them have left—which suggests a late passage movement from the Continent, probably from the Baltic. On the other hand it may be that having once taken to salt-water the Grebes simply disperse. As for the Black-necked and the Slavonian, both which occur in small numbers throughout the winter, there is no saying whether they are "natives" or immigrants.

And so to Aberlady Bay, that estuary within an estuary and the Tom Tiddler's ground of Scottish ornithologists from time immemorial. Like Breydon and indeed like most other famous wild-fowl resorts in Britain it has seen better days. Unlike some, however, it has remained tolerably unspoiled—and if it *is* beset with golf-courses at least they have not proved so disastrous as the iron-works and oil-refineries that have gone up elsewhere. The village and its church with the squat steeple still front on to the open saltings where the Wigeon graze and the Shelducks stand bowing to each other. Linnets lilt and Goldfinches prattle on one side of the road: on the other a lithe Heron stands up to its thighs in the creek and a Red-breasted Merganiser is struggling with a flounder that is far too big for it to swallow (only of course, in the end, it succeeds). A wooden foot-bridge leads to the salt marshes, exposed and seemingly featureless save for a clump or two of black sea-buckthorn. Snow Buntings tinkle in the wind.

A visit to Aberlady is in the nature of a lucky-dip: what one gets out of it depends very largely on the turn of the tide. Ideally, the time to arrive is when the bay is already full and the ebb just about to set in. The first strip of mudflat is barely uncovered before the waders are on the move. Hordes of grey Knots come racing in from the coast, a shimmering cloud. Bar-tailed God-wits grunt *kok-kok* as they cross the sand-bar and head towards the land. Grey Plovers whistle sadly. Curlews ripple. Red-shanks yelp distractedly. Oystercatchers hurry in from the fields behind the sea-wall where they have been kept idle these past few hours: and how glad they are to be back! Crowding the edges of the creek, they stand around piping in the greatest excitement, as if this were the very first time in their lives that the tide had turned. So busy are they congratulating themselves on this recurrent miracle, indeed, that they seem to forget what it is they have come for—and for another quarter of an hour their ecstasy of piping, and the communal dance to which it serves as accompaniment, continues.

At such times the place more than lives up to the reputation which it has earned for itself in the past. At others it looks merely empty and uninviting. At low tide on a winter's day there may be only the "regulars" on view—the Dunkin and Redshanks pottering about in the drains, the Wigeon and Shelduck paddling along in the oozy channel, the Gulls far out on the glistening flats. On such occasions the newcomer may be inclined to think that those who sing the praises of Aberlady Bay are living in the past, that nowadays it is no place for wild Geese, grey or black. Since the disappearance of the *zostera* beds the tubby little Brent find little or nothing to attract them here; and as for the Pink-feet, they have long memories and mostly prefer to pass over on their way to and from their grazing grounds "upaland". For several years now, however, the bay has been designated a nature reserve and though they still have to run the gauntlet of the local shore-shooters the Geese are gradually regaining some of their lost confidence. On occasion they drop in in their thousands.

But as often as not there is so little doing that the best plan is to press on and make straight for Gullane Point where the rocky foreshore abuts on to the open sea again. There at least one can count on seeing a Diver or two or some Velvet Scoters, or, if all else fails, the wide-winged Gannets swinging over the grey-blue Firth. On the way, though, it is worth stepping aside to have a look at the buckthorn clumps: sometimes they hold a Long-eared Owl or two. Secretive to the last, they tuck themselves away inside the bushes, their cat-eyes glaring out from the darkness of their hiding-places, and then go flopping out across the marsh. Ringed Plovers run and pipe along the tideline. Rock Pipits dance up squeaking. Then, right in one's path, a Sparrow-like bird darts up with an unfamiliar note, *pyoo*, followed after an interval by a forcible stuttering cry. Pitching among the marrams, the bird dodges about on the ground in a manner which is at once furtive and exasperating for no sooner has one manœuvred into a favourable position than it skips up and away again. It is a providential arrangement which ensures that even the most nondescript species has a voice which is unmistakable, otherwise it is to be feared that few bird-watchers would ever make much or anything of their first Lapland Bunting! In the old days one can well imagine that it was simply written off as a "Sparrow-like bird" with an unfamiliar cry.

At the Point the foreshore ceases to be estuarine and becomes more truly marine. Its rocks, jutting out from the dunes, make a perfect gathering ground for the Turnstones. *Kitter kit kit Kitter kit* they call tersely, flying low across the water, and without more ado begin poking and picking about among the tangles. In winter their bright tortoiseshell breeding plumage is obscured, but even in the poorest light their orange legs show up clearly against the dark background of bladderwrack. As pushing as Starlings in a field (though hardly so aggressive!) they pry into every nook and corner, snapping up a sand-hopper here, tweezering out a tiny periwinkle there, nodding and jerking along all the time with their heads to the ground.

Among them are some smaller, dark-looking waders which keep close to the waterside and rarely stray more than a yard or two away from it: Purple Sandpipers. Of all the birds of the rocky shore these are the most truly typical. No other wader is quite so specialised in its habits or so restricted in its habitat. Oystercatchers, it goes without saying, are to be found on all kinds of shores (and nowhere more plentifully than on the Solway mudflats where their numbers must run into five figures at times), while Turnstones will frequent any beach provided that it is kept well strewn with sea-weed; but Purple Sandpipers *must* have rocks. On stretches of the coast where there are no rocks they are either absent altogether or confined to such man-made substitutes as breakwaters, groynes, or even at a pinch the pleasure piers of seaside resorts. When they are by themselves these dapper little Sandpipers can be very confiding, running about quite happily within five or six yards of the observer, but when they join forces with Turnstones—and as oft as not the two go together—they are by no means so easy to approach, and if there happens to be a Redshank in the party, the chances of stealing up on them are virtually nil.

If it is difficult to see what Scaup are feeding on the problem is worse with Purple Sandpipers, whose diet seems to consist more or less entirely of minute crustaceans. Always intent on their work, always on the trot, they inspect the acorn barnacles in the splash zone, they nimble along the edges of the rock pools, they trip down after each retreating wave to retrieve some invisible trifle or other, flitting up just in time to escape a drenching. Between whiles they twitter softly among themselves, for they are essentially sociable creatures and always keep close together. Twenty is a crowd so far as Purple Sandpipers are concerned, even so, and usually the numbers do not exceed a dozen. Unobtrusive in their smoke-grey dress, they are to the rocky shore what the Tree Creeper is to the woodland.

But the intense activity which follows the ebb is shortlived. For a time the mudflats sizzle and wink with subterranean life. Worm casts appear by the thousand. The mussel-beds sigh on being uncovered and the tangles breathe audibly. As bay and reef alike begin to dry out, however, the waders gradually lose interest. Some stand and preen, some tuck their heads in and snooze, propped on one foot: others take off for more distant stretches of the shore where the feeding is still fresh. Slack water means a slack period in the affairs of the estuarine birds. From now on the Point is deserted save by those which use it as a resting place. Hardly a day passes without one or two Guillemots floundering out on to its ledges, there to trim their oiled breast feathers. Pathetic figures, they look completely out of their element. After a vain attempt to clean up the mess they usually give it up, relapsing into that fatal apathy which sooner or later overtakes all doomed creatures. Even now they get no rest for, sure as fate, there is always a Great Black-backed Gull standing around or prowling overhead on the look-out for any flotsam, dead or alive, left stranded by the latest tide. *How how how!* His surly laughter rings out triumphantly as he circles, ready to swoop down on the derelict. Caught between the devil and the deep blue sea, the Guillemot glances this way and that uneasily, uncertain what to do next, and at last shuffles back into the water again. *How how how!* The great gull sweeps in low, forcing it to dive and keep on diving until one or other of them grows tired of the game. Usually the fugitive will contrive to escape, but there can be no escape from the longing to get back to *terra firma*. Another five minutes and the Guillemot will be close inshore again, looking for a new landing place—and the other will be there waiting for it. Time is on the Black-back's side. He can wait, knowing only too well that there can be only one end to

Purple Sandpiper

Turnstones in
breeding plumage

the affair. It is a wretched business, the more wretched when one considers that it is being repeated twice a day up and down the coastlines of Western Europe. No one can witness it without a sense of bitterness, though it is as well to remember that such indignation is misplaced unless it puts the blame anywhere but upon the civilisation which allows these things to happen.

XXI. American Vagrants

PASSAGE MIGRANTS

A HAWK OWL on the Isle of May, they said. Now there was a news item to tickle the envy of the old hands and start the telephone wires buzzing! None of us had ever seen a Hawk Owl, of course—who *had*? Why, the lighthouse keeper, lucky devil, and from the way we spoke it was clear that the man's stature had gained a full cubit in our eyes as a result. A Hawk Owl! And the maddening part of it was that the bird had already left the island, otherwise not a few of us might have been tempted to take French leave and forthwith charter the first boat out from Pittenweem.

Among the childish things which no bird-watcher ever wants to put away is the thrill of seeing a new species. Without its occasional excitements the game, it seems, would lose some of its attraction. Granted, the addition of a new name to the observer's life-list (or to the British List for that matter) adds nothing to the body of scientific knowledge—the fact that this happens to be the first time he has visited Rothiemurchus and seen a Crested Tit is of no significance—but its importance as a landmark in his personal odyssey is in no way lessened on that account. A new bird is always an event, a triumph of the actual over the improbable, and the thrill it gives is just as great whether the bird is as dingy as a Lapland Bunting or as rich in visual appeal as a Bee-eater. There is, let us face it, a special pleasure in the unusual and the unexpected. If the Lapwing were an irregular passage migrant in Britain instead of being taken for granted as a common resident, it would be sought after as the very nonpareil of waders. No doubt the man who is blessed with the innocent eye will always see his birds that way and no amount of familiarity will breed the least contempt for the common-or-garden species

204

but for the sophisticated a certain craving for novelty makes itself felt sooner or later. If anything, the craving grows with age. The trouble is that the longer one watches the more difficult it becomes to satisfy without going abroad. Whole years may elapse without a single new name being added to one's list. And then, just when one is resigned to the belief that there is nothing new beneath the visiting moon some rarity that one has never dared to dream of seeing presents itself, often in the unlikeliest of places.

Occasionally, however, it may turn out that the longed for moment somehow or other falls short of one's expectations. As a schoolboy I can remember how enchanted I was by Lord Gray's account of seeing a Great Grey Shrike at Fallodon. Time and again I gazed at Seaby's melodramatic portrait of the bird, set against the stormiest of skies, with a goldcrest impaled on a thorn beside it; and I told myself that one day (the end of October it would be, on a wild upland, with a nor'easter blowing and flurries of snow) I, too, would see it like that. The fairytale would come true in the end. Alas for my hopes! Years passed before any Great Grey Shrike came my way—and when it did, lo and behold! it was perched on a railway-siding at Crewe of all places. The compartment was crowded, thick with cigarette smoke. As the train began to move off again after a halt outside the station I rubbed the fogged pane beside me and there it was—like a tiny Magpie—swooping down on to the embankment from a pile of sleepers and back again. The train gathered speed, and to crown my frustration the window jammed at the critical moment so that all I got was the barest of passing glimpses. If ever there was an occasion which justified the pulling of the communication cord this was it; but no, I dared not—as it was, my frantic efforts had caused the raising of several pairs of eyebrows. I gave up and sat back in my corner seat, fuming. To be cheated like that!

It was much the same when, recently, I saw two new species in an afternoon, a feat not likely to be repeated by any serious birdwatcher who is *nel mezzo del cammin di nostra vita*. This time there was no question of the birds being snatched away before the retina could dwell upon them and the mind's-eye realise its good fortune: on the contrary I saw them both splendidly and was able to watch them at my leisure. Rather it was the venue which took the gilt off the gingerbread and made a red-letter day less memorable than it ought to have been. Once again, the place was wrong.

Between the burghs of Motherwell and Hamilton the "smug and silver" Clyde (smug as Trent at any rate if scarcely silver) flows through a green flood-plain. In places the river has burst its banks to form a series of large pools, some of which dry out as water meadows in the summer months while others remain permanent. Surrounded as it is by some of the viler excrescences of industrialism, this stretch of the river nevertheless retains something of the authentic marshland atmosphere, and as an inland resort for wild-fowl of all kinds it has few equals in the United Kingdom. Why worry, then, if it is no beauty spot? At Bothwell Bridge, without leaving the road, there are as many Ducks and Geese on view as will be seen in a whole day on the Broads: a drove of Grey-lags, seven hundred strong, a herd or two of Whooper Swans, Wigeon in their hordes, Goosanders fishing in midstream, Pintails upending and Shovelers puddling around the edges of the lagoons, a white Smew popping up among the Pochards and the Goldeneyes, Herons at stance out in the fields . . .

The most populous pool of all, oddly enough, is beside a municipal rubbish dump. And what a dump! The stagnant water is full of rusty tins, old electric-light bulbs, soiled mattresses, lino, rotten apples, contraceptives and heaven knows what other sordid oddments. Lorries are constantly arriving with fresh loads so that throughout the working week the place never cools, yet the birds take it all quite calmly, unperturbed by the racket and the clatter going on around them. A Coot stands asleep on one leg on the brass knob of a submerged bedstead. A crowd of Mute Swans jampacked at the water's edge jostle for the stale crusts which the workmen keep throwing to them—and usually there will be three or four Whoopers among them, and all so grey with dust as to be almost unrecognisable. In one corner a group of doubtful characters is playing pitch-and-toss while not many yards away the Wigeon are whistling and the Tufted Ducks diving among the floating bottles. A scummy backwater, it offends the eye, and the nose too—yet the wildfowl seem to find it attractive enough. All through the winter there is hardly a day when the pool is not covered with them.

In this displeasing spot I saw my two new species. The first was an American Wigeon, a rufous drake with a snowy forehead and a glint of green on the face, hard to pick out in the crowd of surface feeders. The second, and by far the greater prize, was an immature Snow Goose which had attached itself to the local Grey-lags. Thick-set and sturdy, with a gait rather less rolling than theirs, it looked completely out of place against that background, with the smoke from the burning refuse blowing across the fields . . . But there it was, my first Snow Goose. Beggars cannot be choosers, they say—and the bird-watcher who cannot be grateful for small mercies had better find himself another pursuit. All the same, there was no escaping a slight feeling of disappointment. Yet another illusion had received its quietus once and for all. Next time, supposing there *was* to be a next time, the setting might be different (it could hardly be worse!) but what use would that be? It is the first, fine, careless rapture which counts. A "new" bird is only new once.

The age of the collector may be past but it seems that the selfish desire which once prompted naturalists to horde up stuffed specimens is still at work, albeit in sublimated forms. Mercifully, the camera and the binoculars have replaced the gun: the hunting instinct is more readily satisfied nowadays with trophies of a less tangible kind—a note sent in to one of the journals, perhaps, a photograph, or even a visual memory. At bottom, however, the old acquisitive urge remains the same as ever for all its scientific and pseudo-scientific disguises; and the truth of this is borne out when one considers the pride and the loving-care which goes into the compilation of the "official" British List. Fortunately for all of us new additions to that list are constantly being made, and for those who live in the hope that something extraordinary is bound to turn up there is comfort in the knowledge that hardly a month goes by without some previously unheard of species being reported from some part of the country.

In recent years a high proportion of these "accidentals" have been of Trans-Atlantic origin, and Scotland has had its fair share of them. During the autumn and winter of 1953–54, for example, the tally included the following: Blue Goose, Snow Goose, Harlequin Duck, American Wigeon, Yellow and Black-billed Cuckoos and a Grey-cheeked Thrush. On the face of it, this minor invasion seems to suggest that more birds than ever before are succeeding in getting across from the New World, and many responsible ornithologists are convinced that this is in fact the case. If Mr. Kenneth Williamson is right, "the increasing frequency of American Geese, passerines, Cuckoos and waders in Europe is due to cyclonic drift across the Atlantic and is a corollary of the increased local atmosphere circulation which has resulted in the progressive amelioration of the climate of the north-east Atlantic region." The statement sounds convincing enough, and certainly it is based on a careful examination of the available evidence, though it is easy to see that in order to arrive at this large conclusion Mr. Williamson has not hesitated to make a number of equally large assumptions.

In the first place it is by no means certain that the apparent increase in the number of these oversea vagrants is a genuine increase. To some extent it can be explained as being due to an increase in the number of reliable sight records. Formerly the unusual bird was either overlooked or it was seen by someone who was incapable of identifying it. Today the chances of a White-eyed Vireo or a Stilt Sandpiper being spotted and recognised are infinitely greater than they were fifty, or even twenty, years ago. It is not simply that there are far more observers about than there used to be: the whole *standard* of bird recognition has improved out of all knowledge. At the same time, it has to be confessed that the belief that these chance occurrences *are* a good deal more frequent nowadays is difficult to resist—especially when one happens to have seen an American Wigeon and a Snow Goose within the space of a couple of hours.

Now whereas in the past ornithologists were extremely reluctant to believe that birds were capable of making the 3,000 miles crossing unaided the current view is that this feat is well within the powers of even the smaller passerines. The controversy between those who argue in favour of "assisted passage" and those who support the theory of "wind-drift" still flares up from time to time, but on the whole it is as well to admit that the old school of thought has had the worst of the exchanges. On this issue there has undoubtedly been a marked shift of opinion in recent years. The extent of the change can perhaps best be illustrated by the case of the American Robin which was seen on

Lundy in 1953 and which was duly admitted to the British List. Before this there had been a number of records of the American Robin in this country but each and all of them had been rejected as "escaped from captivity". For the same reason the Mocking Bird, Baltimore Oriole, Meadow Lark, Painted Bunting, American Goldfinch, Red-winged Blackbird and others were refused admission. To some extent this refusal was inevitable in the days when there were no restrictions on the caging of wild birds and when the trade in skins was as profitable as it was unscrupulous. It is too late now to decide which, if any, of these nineteenth-century records were genuine but it is safe to say that many of them would stand a much better chance of being accepted if the same birds were to put in an appearance today. *Autre temps autre moeurs.*

This shift of informed opinion (and let it be said that in our present state of knowledge we are still dealing very largely in opinions), is based on arguments which may be summarised under three headings—meteorological, biological, and distributional. First, it is said that the velocity of the westerly air-stream is enough to explain why a comparatively weak and slow-flying bird can get across within thirty or forty hours. If the aero-dynamics of down-wind drift are correct, the smallest migrant may be carried headlong over the ocean at a speed which is in excess of 100 m.p.h. This, together with the fact that the weather experts are more or less agreed that since the turn of the century there has been a tendency for the North Atlantic depressions to become more frequent and more violent, is one of the main reasons for thinking that more and more American species are reaching this country under their own steam. Second, it is maintained that any bird alighting on a ship very soon dies for want of the right kind of food. To have any chance of surviving it must cross speedily—and the fastest ocean going vessels take several days. Third, it is pointed out that although there are just as many ships going from East to West as *vice versa*, the number of North American species reaching this side of the Atlantic is much greater than the number of Old World species which have travelled in the opposite direction. Not only that, but the countries which have received the lion's share of "accidentals" are the very ones which lie athwart the North Atlantic storm-belt. Thus the total for Great Britain (not counting those that swim) is well over forty, while France can claim only eight and Spain none at all. Iceland, which is far North of the main shipping routes, nevertheless has a considerable list of these vagrants, and no less than seventeen North American Warblers have occurred in Greenland. Yet so far as is known not a single European passerine has ever been recorded from Canada or the United States!

The arguments for the wind-drift theory certainly look to be formidable, so much so that many would say that they are not to be refuted. On closer examination, however, it transpires that they are nothing like so conclusive as they pretend to be.

In the first place there is no proof that the smaller migrants *can* go on flying continuously for thirty or forty hours without breaking down. The great weakness of the wind-drift theory is that it cannot in the nature of things be tested either by direct observation or by controlled experiment, and therefore cannot claim to be anything better than an intelligent guess. Where is the evidence that migrants do, in fact, head straight down-wind once their direction-finding is seriously astray? No one denies the existence of lateral drift, but to assert that at some stage in their flight birds give up the struggle, so to speak, and take on the direction of the air-stream through which they are moving is pure speculation. No one, so far as I am aware, has ever seen a Warbler travelling at speeds in excess of 100 m.p.h. For all we know, the dynamics of down-wind drift may be just as erroneous as those of Gaëtke, who believed that migrants travelled at great heights and were therefore capable of achieving fantastic speeds.

On the other hand it is a fact of common observation that birds frequently *do* alight on ships and occasionally travel very considerable distances on them. Whether or not any of them ever cross the Atlantic from start to finish in this way is another matter —though the case of the Starlings which stayed aboard all the way from England to Venezuela shows that it can be done. There are a number of records of birds of all kinds, including such unlikely species as Shearwaters, Waders and Herons, availing themselves of assisted passage. Hawks and Owls, it is well known, are inveterate stowaways. One of the most amusing stories concerns a Stork which parked itself on a naval vessel in the Carribbean and breakfasted each morning on kippers provided for it by the crew. There are reliable accounts, too, of south-bound Swallows re-

maining on board grain ships off the North African coast, roosting
in the wheel-house at night and hawking flies above the holds by
day. Recently some House Martins took a lift on a destroyer from
Rosyth to Invergordon. Unfortunately for them, it was in the
month of October with the result that the waifs were carried well
over a hundred miles in the wrong direction! In much the same
way a party of Chaffinches made the trip from Portsmouth to
Gibraltar on an aircraft-carrier.

Indeed, anyone who reviews the evidence dispassionately may
be left wondering why ornithologists nowadays are so ready to
dismiss the possibility of "assisted passage" out of hand. There
is a very real danger that in plumping for an alternative theory
which purports to explain everything in terms of one factor—
wind—they may be falling into the commonest errors of pseudo-
science.

Consider the following as a possible test-case. Suppose that
those British Chaffinches left the aircraft-carrier, crossed the
Straits of Gibraltar, and were subsequently caught in the traps of
some bird-observatory on the Moroccan coast. Suppose further
that the person finding them appealed (as he invariable does) to
the relevant weather-charts and found that the signs were
favourable. He would then have no hesitation in fitting this
particular occurrence into the general pattern of his theory. The
methods used in arriving at his conclusion would, to all appearances, be scientific; but, this would not prevent the conclusion
itself from being wholly invalid.

All things considered, we can hardly shut our eyes to the fact
that migrants which are, literally, "all at sea" frequently take
refuge on shipboard. Exhaustion is not the only reason for their
doing so, either. When the mist closes in they will perch on
almost any object which looks like *terra firma*. Even in a slight
haze, a ship's lights shining in the darkness exercise a strong
fascination; and the same is true to some extent of the ship's
smoke-trail during the daylight hours.

But to say that birds are in the habit of alighting on ships is not
the same as to say that having done so they sit tight for several
days. In the vast majority of cases, no doubt, the ship is resorted to
simply as a temporary refuge. As soon as land is within striking
distance (which does not necessarily mean when land is actually

in sight), they usually take off again as soon as conditions are at all favourable. It appears, however, that there are times when the migrant is so far off-beam and faced with conditions so unfavourable that the urge to migrate is in some way inhibited. What then?

In these circumstances, say the proponents of the wind-drift theory, the bird very soon dies of starvation if it settles on a ship. Once again the argument is less convincing than it sounds. After all, if an insectivorous species like the Swallow can subsist for several days on a grain ship there is no reason to suppose that others cannot manage something of the sort. It is true that the diet of many of these migrants is highly specialised, but perhaps we should not attach too much importance to this fact. One of the latest of these trans-Atlantic immigrants, the Myrtle Warbler, has its own ecological niche: at least in its winter quarters in the Eastern United States it is practially confined to those areas where the bayberry is to be found. Yet when the Myrtle Warbler appeared at a bird-table in North Devon what was it feeding on? Bread and marmalade, if you please! Which suggests that even the most highly specialised feeder may be a good deal more adaptable than some of us are apt to think. If the Myrtle Warbler can make do at a pinch with the scraps which it finds on a bird-table surely it could do the same on almost any ship! At any rate who is to say that the feat is impossible?

While it is probably true that there has been an intensification of the Westerly air-stream covering the North Atlantic since 1900 it is also true that both the volume and the speed of ocean-going vessels have increased during the same period; so that when an American Robin turns up on Lundy—bang on the regular Baltimore-Avonmouth run—the doubting Thomases may well be forgiven for feeling just a bit suspicious. We must not underestimate the amount of food (other than offal) which does exist on many ships. On the face of it, the deck of an aircraft-carrier or a "Queen Mary" may be a rather inhospitable place for a hungry bird, though as every passenger knows there are odds and ends to be picked up even there. Still, vessels of this kind cannot be taken as typical. For every passenger steamer there are a score of cargo boats, and the supply of insect and other life carried on some of them is often quite remarkable. There are not so many people moving about as there are on a passenger steamer—the bird has the place to itself so to speak—and the fact that the holds are battened down does not mean that there is nothing to be got by prying about in the hatchways.

As for the distributional evidence, it begins to look less impressive once it is subjected to cross-examination. It can hardly be denied that more birds have crossed the Atlantic from West to East than in the opposite direction. The prevailing winds see to that. Lateral drift, almost certainly, is responsible for the migrant's straying off its "standard-line" in the first instance. In general, it is obvious, therefore, that the danger of a European bird being blown out to sea is nothing like so great as it is for its opposite number in North America. There is all the difference in the world between a Warbler, say, flying down the East coast of Scotland *en route* to North Africa and a Warbler heading for the Gulf Coast alone the eastern seaboard of the U.S.A. Once the latter has been driven so far East off its course as to be unable to re-orientate it may do one of two things. Either it continues to go with the wind until it makes its landfall, or at some stage on the long flight it takes refuge on a ship. The plain truth is that no one can say for certain what happens once the bird is well and truly adrift. Either way, its chances of getting through must be reckoned extremely slim, and it goes without saying that the ones which succeed in doing so are a minority of a minority.

Again, the disparity between the numbers of Nearctic species recorded in Great Britain and those in countries like France and Spain can to some extent at least be accounted for by the fact that we have many more bird-watchers to the square mile than they. As for Greenland and Iceland, they do not afford any fair comparison, being so much nearer to the North American land-mass. In fact, at least forty European birds have reached Greenland, among them the Willow Warbler, House Martin, Swallow, Blackbird, Fieldfare (now breeding), Redwing, Rook, Hooded Crow and Starling. No one, of course, is going to be so foolish as to argue that they were carried there on ships: most of them no doubt, wandered over from Scandinavia, travelling in "easy" stages by way of the Faeroes and Iceland, following the same route pioneered by Leif Ericsson and the long boats. Clearly, a crossing of this kind is neither so strenuous nor so hazardous an undertaking as a non-stop flight from Newfoundland to this country. While it is perfectly true that the number of American birds which have succeeded in crossing the Atlantic is greater than the number of Europeans which have returned the compliment, there is no real justification for the view that what we have to do with is a one-way traffic. Indeed, if wind were the sole factor involved we might expect the exchange of species to be much more one-sided than, in fact, it is. A comparison of the lists of "accidentals" for the two continents reveals some striking anomalies. How does it come about, for instance, that bird-watchers on Long Island can look for the Black-headed Gull and the Little Gull with a fair chance of seeing them when we can expect no comparable *quid pro quo* on our side of the water? Why should the Bar-tailed and Black-tailed Godwits appear from time to time in Massachusetts when neither the Hudsonian nor the Marbled has ever been reported anywhere in Europe? If the answer is that both the Hudsonian and Marbled Godwits are rather rare birds, then why is it that the Ruff is such a frequent visitor to the New England states? And are we to believe that the prevailing winds went into reverse on the fifteen-odd occasions when the Corncrake found its way to the New World?

It appears, then, that whichever side of the argument one favours—"wind-drift" or "assisted passage"—the verdict remains NOT PROVEN. The evidence in favour of drift is considerable, and, on the whole, consistent; the trouble is that it is nearly all circumstantial evidence. A theory which relies more or less exclusively on meteorological data can hardly be called scientific, nor can one which claims a pre-emptive right to ignore the existence of other available data. What little we know of the behaviour of land-birds at sea should be enough to convince us that the picture we have of their seasonal movements may be complicated (possibly "falsified" would be a better word in this context) by the *fact* of assisted passage. The evidence of our own eyes tells us that birds and can do get carried considerable distances on ships, sometimes in a totally wrong direction. That being so, who is to say that ornithologists of the old school were not well advised on placing a questionmark against certain arrivals?

It seems, then, that there is something to be said for both

theories. The two are complementary rather than opposed; and neither one nor the other can afford to be dogmatic on a problem which admits of so many "ifs" and "buts". It may be that in the last instance both are at fault in treating the bird as if it were an inert object, incapable of making decisions which are in any sense its own. To be sure, the migrant cannot perform the impossible; under the stress of heavy weather the limits of its strength are quickly reached and passed. For all that, there is no reason to think that it is ever *entirely* at the mercy of the elements. In our present state of ignorance it may be natural to assert that the bird is simply carried along with the wind behind it of that it accepts the nearest perch which offers itself—and to conclude that there is no other alternative. Until we have a better understanding of the mystery of the bird's mind, to say nothing of its powers of navigation, it might be wiser to suspend judgment, recognising that any hypothesis is at best provisional.

XXII.   Little Bird, Great Man

WILSON'S PHALAROPE

WHENEVER I AM summoned to see a rare bird it happens almost invariably that I arrive on the scene just in time to learn that the visitor has departed. Unlike the fisherman, who never tires of telling you about the ones that got away, the ornithologist usually prefers to keep his private griefs to himself. The Glossy Ibis which he was within an ace of seeing that day in Norfolk ("If only you'd been here *this morning*," they told him), the Woodchat which frequented his neighbour's garden while he was away on holiday, the King Eider which he missed because the telephone was out of order—these and all the other might-have-beens he relegates to the limbo of lost causes.

It was, therefore, with mixed feelings that I received the news that Wilson's Phalarope, a species never previously recorded in Europe, let alone in Britain, had been identified in the Forth area. Was it worth making the trip on the off-chance of this rarity of rarities still being there? It seemed unlikely. More so, perhaps, than other birds of passage, Phalaropes are not in the habit of remaining in the same place for more than a day or two, and the news was already a week old by the time it reached me. On the other hand, there was something to be said for the fact that these lost migrants frequently *did* stay put after making their landfall; and, besides, this was one of those unique chances which was not likely to be repeated in a month of Sundays. I decided to go.

The place was a brackish pool behind the sea-wall of St. Margaret's Hope, almost under the shadow of the famous bridge. As bird-haunts go, this derelict naval-yard was nothing if not typical of twentieth-century Britain. Its character was in keeping with that of the bomb-sites occupied by the Black

216

Redstart in London, the gravel-pits which the Little Ringed Plover has colonised in the Home Countries or the sewage farm which provided a home for the first Stilts ever to breed in this country. Much as we may deplore the exploitation of our countryside the truth seems to be that the more disfigured it is the more attractive it becomes for the outlandish species.

There was no sign of the "gallery" of bird-watchers which I had been told to expect. A bad omen, this: it could only mean one of two things. Either I had been misdirected, or (and this seemed much the likelier explanation) I had come too late as usual.

Crowding the edges of the pool was an assortment of small waders, Redshanks and Dunlins, mostly, with a sleepy Bar-tailed Godwit propped on one leg by itself in the shallows. *Skee skeerek!* A party of five Sandwich Terns came flaunting overhead, their voices strangely harsh in the still air. Like so many ghosts of a forgotten summer, they dipped at the surface in a feckless sort of way and then (apparently deciding, as I had already done, that the place was a dump, unworthy of any closer inspection) they drifted off across the sea-wall towards the open firth.

Screwing up my eyes and at the same time screwing up what little faith I had in the chances of success, I scanned the waterside. In the grey light of an overcast October day the task of finding the proverbial needle seemed relatively easy compared with the difficulty of picking out the Phalarope; and to make matters worse there was one of those sudden, inexplicable "dreads" to which bird-flocks are subject. In a moment all was confusion, Redshanks yelping, Lapwings crying, Dunlins all a-twitter as they raced off. I looked up, expecting a hawk, but there was none to be seen. But wait! As the Redshanks settled again on the far side of the pool, I caught a glimpse of grey wings and a white rump, distinctive and yet unfamiliar. A slender, pearly-coloured wader. Was it ... could it be? Yes, by heavens, it was! A Phalarope of sorts at any rate. There was no mis-taking that dainty, nodding motion as it rode the water, looking for all the world like a toy gull. At first it was too far off to make out the details, though even at a distance it looked to be noticeably bigger than either of the European Phalaropes.

After a time the bird flew back low across the pool and began feeding right in front of me: and what a relief, what a thrill, what a joy it was to have the last shadow of doubt removed from the mind. Maybe the delight of identifying some unheard-of rarity is a sign of vanity but, then, a new species is always an event, and this one was, after all, quite unprecedented.

Its long, needle-thin bill was in constant use, dipping from side to side as it swam, never still for a second. A restless, elegant water sprite! By rights, this little traveller should have been somewhere on the Gulf of Mexico or on the Mississippi fly-way *en route* for its winter quarters in South America so that in all probability it was irretrievably lost, fated to lead a solitary existence for the rest of its days, and yet it seemed to be happy enough in its new surroundings. Among the alien company of Redshanks it moved about quite unconcernedly, picking about on the mud with the same relish as it did when afloat. Unlike other Phalaropes, indeed, it spent most of its time ashore, feeding like the rest of the waders. Unlike them, too, it was quite un-approachable. Once it opened its bill as if in a yawn and uttered a single nasal note, *ork!* On foot it looked rather nondescript: it was only when it waded out beyond its depth and took to swimming that its true qualities were revealed, as if a ballerina had stepped out from the wings and begun some exquisite *pas seul*. Once, twice it pirouetted on its tail and then went nodding along again, light as thistledown, breasting the water so gently as to leave it undimpled.

By now I was no longer alone, and before long a veritable battery of field-glasses and telescopes was trained on the water-side. Their owners came from Edinburgh and Glasgow, from Dunfermline and Dundee, and one by the overnight train all the way from London. Such is the price of fame. How many of them, I wondered as I came away, spared a thought for the great ornithologist after whom this Phalarope was called?

Alexander Wilson was a Paisley man, a contemporary and even a would-be rival of the one and only Robert Burns. By turns weaver, pedlar, schoolmaster and surveyor, his secret ambition was to be a poet. Unfortunately—or fortunately as it turned out in the event—his pen was a shade too biting for the good citizens of Paisley with the result that in 1794 Wilson was sent to prison and ordered to burn his offending lampoons in public. This youthful indiscretion (he was 28 at the time) seems to have been the cause of his leaving the Auld Country and seeking his fortunes in the New World where he was to earn a reputation as a naturalist second only to that of Audubon. That he had long been discontented with his lot and with the conditions of life in Scotland (then suffering from a trade depression brought on by the French Revolution), may be gathered from the titles of some of his early poems: "To the Famishing Bard from a Brother Skeleton", "Groans from the Loom", "The Suicide", "An Expostulatory Address to the Ragged Spectre Poverty", and "The Pedlar Insulted".

> ". . . Nae mair
> My luck I'll try at selling ware;
> I've sworn by a' aboon the air
> To quat the pack
> Or 'deed, I doubt, baith me and gear
> Would gang to wrack",

he wrote, never realising that for the rest of his life he would be fated to go on hawking his wares, not over Scotland, but over half the North American continent. Frustrated and embittered by his failure to win the literary honours which he felt he deserved, Wilson set off on foot for Portpatrick, accompanied by his nephew, William Duncan, a lad of sixteen. Crossing over to Belfast, the two hopefuls took ship on the *Swift*, bound for Newcastle, Delaware, with some 350 emigrants aboard.

"Till the 17th of June we had pretty good weather and only buried an old woman and two children," he wrote home. "On the 15th, we fell in with an amazing number of islands of ice: I counted at one time thirty-four in sight, some of whom that we passed was more than twice as high as our main top gallant mast head, and of great extent. On the 20th we had a storm of wind, rain, thunder and lightning, beyond anything I had ever witnessed. Next day a seaman dropped overboard; and though he swam well and made for the ship, yet the sea running high, and his clothes getting wet, he perished within six yards of a hen coop which we had thrown over to him." At last, after a voyage lasting more than seven weeks, he set foot in the promised land, armed with his fowling-piece and carrying his few worldly possessions on his back. Trekking inland through flat wooded country to Wilmington he shot his first American birds, a Red-headed Woodpecker and a Cardinal. The great adventure story had begun.

There followed a period of unemployment and drifting, during which he tried his hand at this and that without setting his mind to anything permanent. Sad to relate, his young companion, Duncan, went to the bad in a big way, becoming "abandoned to the most shameful and excessive drinking, swearing and wretched company". Wilson himself, it appears, was often in such low spirits that his friends feared for his sanity. Indeed, had it not been for the acquaintance which he struck up with the naturalist William Bartram, who kept a botanic garden on the Schuylkill River near Philadelphia, it is a fair guess that Wilson would never have found his true *métier*. He had always been interested in birds, of course, but only in a vague, haphazard sort of way. With Bartram and others to encourage him the interest suddenly became a ruling passion. As if making up for lost time, he set to work on his *magnum opus*, the "American Ornithology", bringing to it an energy and concentration of purpose that have rarely been equalled. The remaining ten years of his life were devoted unreservedly to collecting, classifying, illustrating and describing the birds of the United States and Canada; a superhuman task for anyone to undertake single-handed. His first major expedition to Niagara, in 1804, in which he covered 1300 miles on foot, was only the forerunner of many such journeys. In 1808 he travelled through the New England states as far as Maine, returning by way of Vermont and calling in at every sizeable town to look for subscribers. (At Princeton, incidentally, he was disgusted to find that the Professor of Natural History a fellow Scot, "scarcely knew a Sparrow from a Woodpecker".) After a few days at home he was off again, this time through the Carolinas and Georgia. In January, 1810, he set out, on foot as as usual and alone, for Pittsburgh (where business was so good that he actually added *nineteen* names to his list of subscribers), thence in an open skiff down the turbulent Ohio to Cincinatti, a distance of 720 miles. On this part of the trip, he tells us, "My stock of provisions consisted of some biscuits and cheese, and a

bottle of cordial presented me by a gentleman of Pittsburgh. My
gun, trunk, and greatcoat occupied one end of the boat. I had a
small tin, occasionally to bail her and to take my beverage from
the Ohio with . . . I rowed twenty odd miles the first spell, and
found I should be able to stand it perfectly well. My hands
suffered the most. . . ." From Cincinatti his way led across
country into the Deep South, to Louisville, Natchez and New
Orleans, from which port he sailed for East Florida, then a
Spanish possession. At the Red River he had one highly sinister
encounter with a mulatto who was reputed to be in the habit of
luring strangers into a cave and murdering them for their money.
It speaks well for Wilson's courage that he accepted the invitation
to be shown into the interior of the cave, though had it not been
for his presence of mind (or possibly because he was next to
penniless) he might have had his throat cut. The going was often
swampy and he suffered terribly from dysentery. In a letter dated
June 1st, 1811, he writes: "I have, since February 1810, slept for
weeks in the wilderness alone in an Indian country with my gun
and pistols in my bosom; have found myself so much reduced by
sickness, as to be scarcely able to stand, when 300 miles from a
white settlement and under the burning latitude of 25 degrees. I
have, by resolution, surmounted all these and other obstacles in
my way to independence." The seventh of the eight volumes of
his "Ornithology" was now in preparation, the end in sight.
Without allowing himself the least respite, however, Wilson set
forth on his travels once more, traversing the Eastern States again,
up the Hudson valley to Lake Champlain (where he found "the
little Coot-footed Tringa or Phalarope"), and so over the
mountains into New Hampshire and home by way of Boston and
Portland. Shortly afterwards he died, worn out by his exertions.

Some day, perhaps, an author in search of a subject will do
for Alexander Wilson what Defoe did for Alexander Selkirk.
He deserves no less of posterity. He was a naturalist of the old
school, and one of the best. "I see new beauties in every bird,
plant or flower I contemplate," he wrote, "and find my ideas of
the incomprehensible First Cause still more exalted the more
minutely I examine his works. I sometimes smile to think that
while others are immersed in deep schemes of speculation and
aggrandisement, in building towns and purchasing plantations, I

am entranced in contemplation over the plumage of a Lark or gazing like a despairing lover on the lineaments of an Owl."

There speaks the artist and the philosopher. True pioneer that he was, Wilson's nature was the very reverse of go-getting. If the recognition which he failed to win in Scotland was not altogether denied him in his country of adoption, his "Ornithology" never achieved the success which attended the publication of Audubon's colourful tome—and for obvious reasons. He was no showman, but rather one of those whose destiny is to go it alone, getting things the hard way. Poor Wilson! sensitive, essentially modest, world-forsaking, obsessed with the desire to prove that his abilities matched his ambitions, he had all the marks of greatness except perhaps the flair that goes with genius. Maybe his writing was like the man—a little pedestrian—yet it has durable qualities, which is more than can be said of the mass of ornithological literature at the present time. His descriptions of the appearance, habits, and songs of American birds are often quite admirable and his prose style, dated as it is, is never without urbanity and charm. How faithfully, for instance, does this passage convey a sound-picture of the Blue Jay's vocabulary:

"He appears to be among his fellow musicians what the trumpeter is in a band, some of his notes having no distant resemblance to the tones of that instrument. These he has the faculty of changing through a great variety of modulations, according to the particular humour he happens to be in. When disposed to ridicule there is scarce a bird whose peculiarities of song he cannot tune his notes to. When engaged in the blandishments of love they resemble the soft chatterings of a duck and, while he nestles among the thick branches of the cedar, are scarce heard at a few paces distance; but he no sooner discovers your approach than he sets up a sudden and vehement outcry, flying off and screaming with all his might, as if he called the whole feathered tribes of the neighbourhood to witness some outrageous usage he had received. When he hops undisturbed among the high branches of the oak and hickory they become soft and musical; and his call of the female a stranger would readily mistake for the repeated screakings of an ungreased wheelbarrow. All these he accompanies with various nods, jerks and other gesticulations."

Though far from being an expert on systematics by modern standards, and writing as he did long before "The Origin of Species", he had some sensible things to say on classification. Dealing with the confusing variations of plumage in the Baltimore and Orchard Orioles, variations which had led some "authorities" to suppose that the two belonged to the same species, he gives his reasons for thinking that they are distinct, adding rather severely: "If all these circumstances, and I could enumerate a great many more, be not sufficient to designate this as a distinct species, by what criterion, I would ask, are we to discriminate between a *variety* and an *original* species, or to assure ourselves that the Great Horned Owl is not, in fact, a bastard Goose, or a Carrion Crow a mere variety of the Humming Bird?" What, indeed?

But perhaps the most revealing insight into the man is contained in a single sentence in one of the letters which he wrote to his friend Lawson before setting out on his last major expedition: "Whether journeying in this world, or journeying to that which is to come, there is something of desolation and despair in the idea of being forever forgotten." It is ironic, and yet fitting, that his eponymous Phalarope should have been the means of reviving the memory of one of Scotland's most adventurous sons. Yet Alexander Wilson need not have despaired. His name is commemorated by one of the leading Ornithological Clubs in the United States; it has been given to several species besides the Phalarope (among others to Wilson's Petrel which is reputed to be the commonest bird in the world). There is even a statue of him in his home town, close by the Abbey. But these are not his only claims to immortality, nor the surest. Though Wilson the man may to all intents be forgotten, the spirit in which he lived lives on wherever and whenever a naturalist looks at a bird and feels, as he did, "exalted in his ideas of the incomprehensible First Cause".

(£1.1/-) ω/x
7/6